ATLA Monograph Series
edited by Dr. Kenneth E. Rowe

1. Ronald L. Grimes. *The Divine Imagination: William Blake's Major Prophetic Visions.* 1972.
2. George D. Kelsey. *Social Ethics among Southern Baptists, 1917-1969.* 1973.
3. Hilda Adam Kring. *The Harmonists: A Folk-Cultural Approach.* 1973.
4. J. Steven O'Malley. *Pilgrimage of Faith: The Legacy of the Otterbeins.* 1973.
5. Charles Edwin Jones. *Perfectionist Persuasion: The Holiness Movement and American Methodism, 1867-1936.* 1974.
6. Donald E. Byrne, Jr. *No Foot of Land: Folklore of American Methodist Itinerants.* 1975.
7. Milton C. Sernett. *Black Religion and American Evangelicalism: White Protestants, Plantation Missions, and the Flowering of Negro Christianity, 1787-1865.* 1975.
8. Eva Fleischner. *Judaism in German Christian Theology Since 1945: Christianity and Israel Considered in Terms of Mission.* 1975.
9. Walter James Lowe. *Mystery & The Unconscious: A Study in the Thought of Paul Ricoeur.* 1977.
10. Norris Magnuson. *Salvation in the Slums: Evangelical Social Work, 1865-1920.* 1977.
11. William Sherman Minor. *Creativity in Henry Nelson Wieman.* 1977.
12. Thomas Virgil Peterson. *Ham and Japheth: The Mythic World of Whites in the Antebellum South.* 1978.
13. Randall K. Burkett. *Garveyism as a Religious Movement: The Institutionalization of a Black Civil Religion.* 1978.
14. Roger G. Betsworth. *The Radical Movement of the 1960's.* 1980.
15. Alice Cowan Cochran. *Miners, Merchants, and Missionaries: The Roles of Missionaries and Pioneer Churches in the Colorado Gold Rush and Its Aftermath, 1858-1870.* 1980.
16. Irene Lawrence. *Linguistics and Theology: The Significance of Noam Chomsky for Theological Construction.* 1980.
17. Richard E. Williams. *Called and Chosen: The Story of Mother Rebecca Jackson and the Philadelphia Shakers.* 1981.
18. Arthur C. Repp, Sr. *Luther's Catechism Comes to America: Theological Effects on the Issues of the Small Catechism Prepared in or for America Prior to 1850.* 1982.
19. Lewis V. Baldwin. *"Invisible" Strands in African Methodism.* 1983.
20. David W. Gill. *The Word of God in the Ethics of Jacques Ellul.* 1984.
21. Robert Booth Fowler. *Religion and Politics in America.* 1985.

22. Page Putnam Miller. *A Claim to New Roles.* 1985.

23. C. Howard Smith. *Scandinavian Hymnody from the Reformation to the Present.* 1987.

24. Bernard T. Adeney. *Just War, Political Realism, and Faith.* 1988.

25. Paul Wesley Chilcote. *John Wesley and the Women Preachers of Early Methodism. 1991.*

26. Samuel J. Rogal. *A General Introduction of Hymnody and Congregationa Song.* 1991.

27. Howard A. Barnes. *Horace Bushnell and the Virtuous Republic.* 1991.

28. Sondra A. O'Neale. *Jupiter Hammon and the Biblical Beginnings of African-American Literature.* 1993.

29. Kathleen P. Deignan. *Christ Spirit: The Eschatology of Shaker Christianity.* 1992.

30. D. Elwood Dunn. *A History of the Episcopal Church in Liberia, 1821-1980.* 1992.

31. Terrance L. Tiessen. *Irenaeus on the Salvation of the Unevangelized.* 1993.

32. James E. McGoldrick. *Baptist Successionism: A Crucial Question in Baptist History.* 1994.

33. Murray A. Rubinstein. *The Origins of the Anglo-American Missionary Enterprise in China, 1807-1840.* 1995.

34. Thomas M. Tanner. *What Ministers Know: A Qualitative Study of Pastors as Information Professionals.* 1994.

35. Jack A. Johnson-Hill. *I-Sight: The World of Rastafari: An Interpretive Sociological Account of Rastafarian Ethics.* 1995.

36. Richard James Severson. *Time, Death, and Eternity: Reflections on Augustine's "Confessions" in Light of Heidegger's "Being and Time."* 1995.

37. Robert F. Scholz. *Press toward the Mark: History of the United Lutheran Synod of New York and New England, 1830-1930.* 1995.

38. Sam Hamstra, Jr. and Arie J. Griffioen. *Reformed Confessionalism in Nineteenth-Century America: Essays on the Thought of John Williamson Nevin.* 1996.

39. Robert A. Hecht. *An Unordinary Man: A Life of Father John LaFarge, S.* 1996.

40. Moses Moore. *Orishatukeh Faduma: Liberal Theology and Evangelical Pan-Africanism, 1857-1946.* 1996.

41. William Lawrence. *Sundays in New York: Pulpit Theology at the Crest of the Protestant Mainstream.* 1996.

Reformed Confessionalism in Nineteenth-Century America

Essays on the Thought of John Williamson Nevin

Edited by
Sam Hamstra, Jr.
and
Arie J. Griffioen

ATLA Monograph Series, No. 38

The American Theological Library Association
and
The Scarecrow Press, Inc.
Lanham, Md., and London

SCARECROW PRESS, INC.

Published in the United States of America
by Scarecrow Press, Inc.
4720 Boston Way
Lanham, Maryland 20706

4 Pleydell Gardens, Folkestone
Kent CT20 2DN, England

Copyright © 1995 by Sam Hamstra, Jr. and Arie J. Griffioen

British Cataloguing-in-Publication Information Available

Library of Congress Cataloging-in-Publication Data

Reformed confessionalism in nineteenth-century America : essays on the thought
of John Williamson Nevin / edited by Sam Hamstra and Arie J. Griffioen.
p. cm. — (ALTA monograph series ; no. 38)
Includes bibliographical references and index.
1. Nevin, John Williamson, 1803-1886. 2. Reformed Church—United
States—Doctrines—History—19th century.
I. Hamstra, Sam. II. Griffioen, Arie J. III. Series
BX9593.N4R44   1995   285.7'092—dc20   [B]   95-32364   CIP

ISBN 0–8108–3058-2 (cloth : alk. paper)

♾™ The paper used in this publication meets the minimum requirements of
American National Standard for Information Sciences—Permanence of
Paper for Printed Library Materials, ANSI Z39.48–1964.
Manufactured in the United States of America.

Dedication

To our mentor and friend, Dr. Patrick W. Carey.

Contents

Foreword

Since 1972 the American Theological Library Association has undertaken responsibility for a modest monograph series in the field of religious studies. Our aim in this series is to publish two studies of quality each year. Titles are selected from studies in a wide range of religious and theological disciplines. We are pleased to publish *Reformed Confessionalism* by Sam Hamstra and Arie Griffioen.

Arie J. Griffioen completed undergraduate studies at Calvin College, took an M.A. at the University of Iowa and a doctorate in theology at Marquette University. He is currently Associate Professor of Religion and Theology at Calvin College, Grand Rapids, Michigan. A specialist in American historical theology, he is the author of articles dealing with the thought of Orestes Brownson and Charles Porterfield Krauth.

Sam Hamstra began his academic work at David Lipscomb College where he completed a B.S. degree, took an M.Div. degree at McCormick Theological Seminary in Chicago, and completed doctoral studies in theology at Marquette University. Dr. Hamstra is currently Vice President for Advancement at Trinity Christian College in Palos Heights, Illinois. An ordained minister in the Reformed Church in America, he served three congregations over a fifteen-year period. His dissertation examined the doctrine of Christian ministry in the thought of Mercersburg theologian John Williamson Nevin.

Kenneth E. Rowe
Series Editor

Contributors

James D. Bratt is professor of history at Calvin College, Grand Rapids, Michigan. His numerous publications include *Dutch Calvinism in Modern America: A History of a Conservative Sub-Culture* (Eerdmans, 1984); and *Gathered at the River: Grand Rapids, Michigan, and Its People of Faith* (Eerdmans, 1993).

Walter Conser, Jr., is professor and chairman of the department of philosophy and religion at the University of North Carolina, Wilmington. His publications include *Church and Confession: Conservative Theologians in Germany, England, and America 1815-1866* (Mercer University Press, 1984); and *God and the Natural World: Religion and Science in Antebellum America* (University of South Carolina Press, 1993).

William DiPuccio is a resident of Cuyanoga Falls, Ohio, and a recent graduate of Marquette University (Ph.D., 1994). His dissertation is "The Dynamic Realism of Mercersburg Theology: The Romantic Pursuit of the Ideal in the Actual."

Stephen Graham is associate professor of American church history at North Park Theological Seminary, Chicago, Illinois. His dissertation is "Cosmos in the Chaos: Philip Schaff's Interpretation of Nineteenth-Century American Religion."

Arie J. Griffioen is associate professor of religion and theology at Calvin College, specializing in American historical theology. He is the author of articles dealing with the thought of Orestes Brownson and Charles Porterfield Krauth.

Sam Hamstra, Jr., is Vice-President for Advancement at Trinity Christian College in Palos Heights, Illinois. His dissertation is "John Williamson Nevin: The Christian Ministry."

Glenn Hewitt is associate professor of religion at Maryville College, Maryville, Tennessee. He is the author of *Regeneration and Morality: A Study of Charles Finney, Charles Hodge, John W. Nevin, and Horace Bushnell* (Carlson Publishing, 1991).

David Wayne Layman is a resident of Elizabethtown, Pennsylvania, and a recent graduate of Temple University (Ph.D., 1994). His dissertation is "Revelation in the Praxis of the Liturgical Community: A Jewish-Christian Dialogue, with Special Reference to the Work of John Williamson Nevin and Franz Rosenzweig."

John B. Payne, author of numerous articles on Nevin, is the Paul and Minnie Diefenderfer Professor of Mercersburg and Ecumenical Theology and professor of church history at Lancaster Theological Seminary, Lancaster, Pennsylvania.

Richard E. Wentz is professor of religious studies at Arizona State University, Tempe, Arizona. He is the author of *Religion in the New World: The Shaping of Religious Traditions in the United States* (Fortress Press, 1990); *Pennsylvania Dutch Folk Spirituality* (Paulist Press, 1993); and *John Williamson Nevin: The American Theologian* (Oxford University Press, forthcoming).

Charles Yrigoyen, Jr., is General Secretary for the General Commission on Archives and History of the United Methodist Church in Madison, New Jersey. He is the co-editor of *Catholic and Reformed: Selected Theological Writings of John Williamson Nevin* (Pickwick Press, 1979).

Biographical Sketch

1803   Born February 20 to John Nevin and Martha McCracken at Herron's Branch, Franklin County, near Shippensburg, PA.

1817   Attends Union College in Schenectady, NY.

1819   Undergoes "conversion" experience at Union during a revival service by Asahel Nettleton.

1823   Attends Princeton Theological Seminary.

1826   Teaches Hebrew at Princeton Theological Seminary for two years.

1828   Returns home to recuperate from poor health. Licensed to preach by the Carlisle Presbytery.

1830   Appointed professor of biblical literature at Western Theological Seminary, Pittsburgh, PA.

183?   Ordained as a minister of the Word by the Presbytery of Ohio while serving Western Theological Seminary.

1833   Editor of *The Friend*, the official publication of the Young Men's Society, Pittsburgh.

1834   Editor and publisher of *Temperance Register*, Pittsburgh.

1835   Marries Martha Jenkins, daughter of Robert and Catherine Jenkins, January 1.

1837   Teaches church history at Western Theological Seminary. Begins study of August Neander.

1840   Resigns from Western Theological Seminary. Awarded the D.D. by Jefferson College.

1840   Received into the classis of Maryland of the German
       Reformed Church (May 16).
       Appointed professor of theology and biblical
       literature, Theological Seminary of the German
       Reformed Church, Mercersburg, PA.

1841   Appointed president and chairman of the board of
       Marshall College, Mercersburg, PA.

1843   Writes *The Anxious Bench*.

1844   Joined by Philip Schaff at the Theological Seminary in
       Mercersburg.

1846   Writes *The Mystical Presence*.

1849   Creates and edits *The Mercersburg Review*.
       Appointed chairman by the Synod of the committee
       to develop a new liturgy for the German Reformed
       Church.

1851   Resigns from Mercersburg Seminary.

1853   Resigns from Marshall College.

1855   Moves to Lancaster, PA.

1861   Appointed to the faculty of Franklin and Marshall
       College in Lancaster, PA as professor of philosophy,
       history and aesthetics.

1866   Appointed president of Franklin and Marshall College.

1867   Writes *A Vindication of the Revised Liturgy*.

1876   Retires.

1886   Dies, June 6.

Introduction

Sam Hamstra, Jr., and Arie J. Griffioen

The past two decades have seen a resurgence of interest in American manifestations of the nineteenth-century high-church movement and the Mercersburg Theology of Philip Schaff and John Williamson Nevin in particular. Often studied as an example of the influence of Romanticism and German Idealism upon antebellum American thought, the Mercersburg Theology has received the attention of many foremost historians and theologians, who have in turn encouraged others to undertake this study.[1]

The formation of the Mercersburg Society has also contributed to the resurgence. Founded in 1983 by the late Howard Hageman, former president of the New Brunswick Theological Seminary, the society has hosted annual convocations featuring presentations on various aspects of Mercersburg Theology, emphasizing especially its contemporary relevance.[2] The society was also a positive force in the development of a chair in the Mercersburg Theology at Lancaster Theological Seminary, currently occupied by John B. Payne, whose essay on Nevin's doctrine of baptism is included in this volume.

Moreover, many Protestant ecumenists and liturgists, especially within the United Church of Christ, have found Nevin's catholicity and critique of sectarianism useful, and have found in his integration of liturgy and theology a model for the development of contemporary forms of worship.[3] Others within the UCC have been attracted to the Mercersburg Theology as a means of recovering their German Reformed confessional heritage as an alternative to contemporary developments within that denomination.

Finally, and most recently, evangelicals and contemporary Reformed confessionalists, among whom the editors of this volume count themselves, have found in Nevin's theology an historical source for articulating continuing concerns with the state of Protestantism in late-twentieth-century America. We believe that entering into historiographic discussion with Nevin's theology will lend itself not only to a better understanding of mid-nineteenth-century American Christianity, but to renewed attention to the fundamental question that has plagued Protestantism in America since its inception: "What is the Church?"

Biographical Survey[4]

Nevin was born in 1803 in Franklin County, Pennsylvania, to John and Martha Nevin, the first of six children born to the Scots-Irish farmers. Baptized in the Presbyterian church in Middle Springs, Nevin received rigorous old school catechetical training under Rev. John Moody, who served the congregation for 50 years. At the age of 14, Nevin attended Union College, Schenectady, where he underwent a conversion experience during a revival service conducted by Asahel Nettleton. Though Nevin later was adamant in his opposition to most forms of revivalism, he acknowledged that this event formed an important step of maturation in his spiritual pilgrimage. But after completing his studies in 1821, Nevin returned home in a state of spiritual, mental, and intellectual exhaustion—a problem that would plague him throughout his career.

In 1823 Nevin began his studies at Princeton Theological Seminary, where he sat under the tutelage of such luminaries as Archibald Alexander, Charles Hodge, and Samuel Miller. Upon completion of his studies in 1826, Nevin's teaching career began as an instructor of Hebrew, substituting for Hodge who was traveling in Europe. While at Princeton, Nevin wrote the first of several books, *A Summary of Biblical Antiquities*. In 1828 Nevin was licensed to preach by the Carlisle Presbytery and in 1830 was called to be professor of biblical literature at the fledgling Western Theological Seminary, Pittsburgh.[5]

While teaching at Western, Nevin edited *The Friend*, a weekly journal dedicated to the defense of Christian virtues, as well as a small paper entitled *Temperance Register*. Ordained by the Presbytery of Ohio, Nevin soon gained an unpopular reputation for his outspoken views on temperance and abolition. Perhaps more importantly, it was at Western that Nevin began an intense study of ecclesiastical history in order to teach church history courses vacated by a retired colleague. During this period, Nevin was attracted to the writings of the German church historian, J. A. W. Neander (1789-1850). Nevin would later single out Neander's romantic and dialectical historiography as the most important intellectual influence of his life.

The congenial relationship and mutual respect that Nevin developed with the ministers and congregations of the German Reformed Church resulted in his recommendation by the Rev. Samuel Fisher for an open position at that denomination's seminary in Mercersburg, PA. Though Nevin was at first reluctant, the General Convention or Synod of the German Reformed Church, meeting in Chambersburg, voted unanimously to extend him the invitation to become professor of theology and biblical literature. In 1840, having resigned from Western Theological Seminary for financial reasons — and perhaps soured on the Presbyterians over the 1837 old school/new school split — Nevin accepted the invitation and by 1841 had gained the additional position of president of Marshall College, located on the same campus.

The first major controversy of Nevin's career as a German Reformed theologian occurred in 1842 when the Mercersburg Village Church invited William Ramsey to preach a trial sermon. Ramsey, a former classmate of Nevin, ended the service with an altar call after the fashion of the well-known revivalist Charles Grandison Finney. Startled by the insertion of such a revivalistic technique into the German Reformed liturgy — and even more startled by the congregation's decision to call Ramsey as its pastor — Nevin adamantly refused to support the call. Ramsey wisely declined. In 1843, Nevin published the first edition of *The Anxious Bench*, a significant work directed against the "new measures" revivalism of Finney and others.

Controversy continued in 1844 when Nevin was joined at Mercersburg by the young German church historian Philip Schaff.[6]   Schaff's inaugural address, "The Principle of Protestantism," stirred vigorous debate by arguing that the Protestant Reformation did not constitute a radical break with ecclesiastical history and a repristination of the early church, but was the product of historical development that could be traced from the early church through the medieval period. Published with Nevin's "Catholic Unity"—in which Nevin argues for the Church as essentially one because it flows from the incarnation in a continual state of growth and organic development—these documents signal the emergence of the Mercersburg Theology.   They soon became the basis of accusations of heresy from fellow clergy as well. Led by the Rev. Joseph Berg of the Race Street Reformed Church in Philadelphia, Nevin and Schaff were accused of "catholicizing" tendencies, but were exonerated by the 1845 Synod meeting in York, PA.

In 1846 Nevin published *The Mystical Presence*. Arguably one of the most significant works of historical theology in the history of American thought, the work reaffirms and re-articulates Calvin's insistence upon a real union with the incarnate and glorified Christ through the sacrament of the Lord's Supper.   In 1849 Nevin helped found and edit *The Mercersburg Review*, a tool for the propagation of the Mercersburg Theology. As chief contributor, Nevin published over 75 articles in its pages throughout his career.

Nevin and Schaff continued as colleagues until 1851 when an exhausted Nevin resigned from the seminary. Two years later he resigned the presidency of Marshall College. Though Nevin remained a high-church Protestant throughout his life, his resignation triggered "five years of dizziness" during which he despaired of Protestantism and is alleged to have considered converting to Roman Catholicism. Such a decision would have been viewed by many friends and foes as the logical extension of his theological convictions. Nichols describes the crisis:

In 1851 came a crisis. John Nevin, the theological leader, was caught up in the current of the more advanced Anglo-Catholics of England. Almost all his theological writing for a year and a half was devoted to the study of the ancient church, toward which he adopted much of the Roman view. His friends and associates watched anxiously as his articles showed increasingly a despair of Protestantism and a loss of confidence in the Mercersburg offices in the German Reformed Church—as professor of theology, chairman of the liturgy committee, chief contributor to *The Mercersburg Review*, president of Marshall College. For months he weighed the question whether to submit to Rome. Having broken down physically and nervously, he felt the choice to be what church he should die in. The validity and continuance of the whole Mercersburg tendency, in the meantime, seemed to hang on the issue of his defection.[7]

Though Nevin overcame the crisis, he continued to defy the typical nineteenth-century American Protestant assumption that the Reformation was historically discontinuous with the medieval period, arguing for it only as a necessary reform of the Church, but not the final one. According to Nevin, the gospel is always in a state of historical development and has taken up into its life the historical reality of Roman Catholicism as well.[8]

Nevin ended his premature retirement in 1861, returning to the classroom as instructor of history at Franklin and Marshall College in Lancaster, where both the seminary and college had moved in 1853. In the years preceding, he was occupied with the development of an official liturgy for the German Reformed Church.[9] He concluded his academic career as president of the college from 1866 to 1876. Until his sight failed him in 1883, Nevin continued his prolific writing, contributing several articles to the *Reformed Quarterly Review*. He died in 1886.

Nevin was known for his "high order of mental endowments, his classical and theological scholarship, his ability in the realm of philosophy, his progressive spirit as exhibited by the assertion and development of a Christological theology, and his educational influence upon the ministry and membership of the Reformed Church."[10] He was also known for his diligence and productivity that periodically left him in a state of exhaustion. But above all, Nevin was a person of

religious conviction and godliness.   As Emanuel Gerhart
eulogized:

> ...for [Nevin] God was first, first in his consciousness,
> first for his will, and in his pursuits. God's existence,
> his presence, his authority, his holiness, his honor were
> for him living and constant realities...He was ever
> looking away from himself to God, the God manifest in
> Christ.[11]

Theological Characteristics

Described by Ahlstrom as a movement of profound
intellectual force,[12] the theological and liturgical contributions
of the Mercersburg Theology flourished well beyond the borders
of the German Reformed Church.[13]   Nevin himself identified
five essential characteristics of the system:[14]   It is a
christocentric system rooted in a theology of the incarnation; it
emphasizes the objective, for it does not rest on private
judgment but upon scripture, the confessions, and tradition; it
is churchly, arguing that grace is mediated by the church and
that the local congregation is endowed with authority to
administer that grace; it is sacramental, for the sacraments are
seals of the actual realities they exhibit; and it is liturgical,
moving worship from an anthropological to a christological
base.

Nevin must be recognized as a confessionalist and
representative of the high-church movement in America.[15]
Embracing such figures as the Lutheran Charles Porterfield
Krauth and the Episcopal Bishop John Henry Hobart,
confessionalism developed in antebellum America as a
distinctive ecclesiastical response to the trans-denominational
and egalitarian character of revivalism.   Proving especially
attractive to recent European immigrants seeking to preserve
their cultural and religious identity in the new world,
confessionalists appealed to historic creeds and confessions of
faith as standards of orthodoxy and interpretive aids for correct
scriptural exegesis.

Antebellum confessionalists drew upon romantic categories in order to propagate a more traditional theology. Reacting to the polarities and deistic tendencies of Enlightenment thought, confessionalists sought to articulate an incarnational and sacramental theology that stressed the unity of the divine and human. This romantic emphasis on unity is evident in the confessionalist assumption that the divine dynamically discloses itself in history. Therefore, continuity, development and progress are emphasized. No longer is history important only for what was common and universal to the past, for each age is believed to possess its own intrinsic significance and characteristic excellence as the flowing and dynamic progression of the divine through the human. Expressed ecclesiologically, confessionalist theology is characterized by its organic sense of tradition.

Moreover, the confessionalist quest for unity is evident in its ecclesiological emphasis upon community — again, conceived as organic. Community is not merely the collectivity of individual wills, but an arena for the activity of the divine. Credal and confessional authority is often emphasized as the means by which the organic unity of the community is held together. As one might expect, confessionalists tended to be social and political conservatives as well, fearful of the excesses of Jacksonian policy, especially as applied to the Church. Consequently, they raised the question of the nature of the Church to the top of their theological agenda, arguing for its endowment with authoritative truth and sacramental power.[16]

Nevin also must be understood as a Calvinist and an evangelical. Reared an old school Presbyterian, he was committed to the authority of scripture and the need for personal transformation, and identified himself as a theologian working in continuity with the Reformed branch of the Reformation. Nevertheless, Nevin labored during the nineteenth century to dismantle the scholastic Calvinist orthodoxy in America. Through his use of romantic impulses and the dialectic of historiographic idealism, Nevin contributed to that dismantling, but always with a view to the recovery and progressive refinement of what he took to be authentic Calvinism. In addition to his opposition to the Arminianism of revivalism and the Second Great Awakening, Nevin rejected the decretal predestinarianism of the Synod of Dordtrecht, as well as the "scholastic" nature of the common-sense realism of the Princeton theologians.

Finally, Nevin was the first American theologian to recover Calvin's eucharistic theology and the reformer's insistence upon real union with Christ,[17] and to recast traditional Calvinist preoccupations in terms of a high ecclesiology. Few American theologians can match the depth of Nevin's thought on the nature and function of the Church. His ecclesiology has been described as "a phase of that extraordinary high church movement which swept Western Christendom in the nineteenth century and, with profound variations, made its presence felt in Roman Catholicism, Lutheranism, Anglicanism—and one small outpost of the Reformed church."[18] The contributions of that "small outpost" continue to be germane to the milieu of Protestantism in late-twentieth-century America.

ENDNOTES

1. See, for example, Sidney Ahlstrom, *A Religious History of the American People* (New Haven: Yale University Press, 1972), 583-632; and Brian Gerrish, *Tradition and the Modern World: Reformed Theology in the Nineteenth Century* (Chicago: The University of Chicago Press, 1978), 49-70. Also see Richard Wentz, *John Williamson Nevin: The American Theologian* (Oxford University Press, forthcoming).

2. R. Howard Paine, "A History of the Mercersburg Society," *The New Mercersburg Review* 13 (Spring 1993):3-17.

3. See Jack Martin Maxwell, *Worship and Reformed Theology: The Liturgical Lessons of Mercersburg* (Pittsburgh: The Pickwick Press, 1976).

4. This material is derived primarily from two sources: James Hasting Nichols, *Romanticism in American Theology: Nevin and Schaff at Mercersburg* (Chicago: The University of Chicago Press, 1961); and Theodore Appel, *The Life and Work of John Williamson Nevin* (Philadelphia: The Reformed Church Publishing House, 1889).

5. Nevin was married in 1835 to Martha Jenkins, the daughter of the Honorable Robert Jenkins, a well-known ironmaster, and his wife, Catherine Carmichael, a Presbyterian pastor's daughter. Together, John and Martha Nevin had eight children, three of whom were sons who died at a young age. See John Weiler, "Notes on Nevin's Family I," *The New Mercersburg Review* 13 (Spring 1993):39-44.

6. In 1847 Schaf changed the spelling of his name to Schaff. See Nichols, *Romanticism in American Theology*, 1.

7. Ibid., 192.

8. Brian A. Gerrish, *Tradition and the Modern World: Reformed Theology in the Nineteenth Century* (Chicago: The University of Chicago Press, 1978), 56.

9. See Maxwell, *Worship and Reformed Theology*, passim.

10. Emanuel V. Gerhart, *Institutes of the Christian Religion* (New York: Funk & Wagnalls, Co., 1894), 51.

11. Ibid., 51-52.

12. See Ahlstrom, *A Religious History*, 615f.

13. A faithful school of supporters kept the Mercersburg Theology alive for at least one generation. Henry Harbaugh (1817-1867) served on the Liturgical Committee, which produced the *Provisional Liturgy* and the *Order of Worship*, and edited the revived version of *The Mercersburg Review*, called the *Reformed Church Review*. Bernard C. Wolff (1794-1870) succeeded Nevin as a professor at Mercersburg Seminary. Elnathan E. Higbee (1830-1889) replaced Schaff at Mercersburg Seminary and became a co-editor of the *Reformed Church Review*. Emanuel Gerhart compiled his massive systematic theology, *Institutes of the Christian Religion* (1891, 1894), and Theodore Appel compiled what remains the most extensive biography of Nevin.

14. John Williamson Nevin, *A Vindication of the Revised Liturgy, Historical and Theological* (Philadelphia, 1867), 28.

15. See Walter H. Conser, Jr, *Church and Confession: Conservative Theologians in Germany, England, and America, 1815-1866* (Macon, GA: Mercer University Press, 1984).

16. Ibid., 258-59.

17. Two recent studies of Calvin's theology continue Nevin's recovery. See Brian Gerrish, *Grace and Gratitude. The Eucharistic Theology of John Calvin* (Minneapolis: Augsburg Fortress Press, 1993); and Dennis E. Tamburello, *Union with Christ. John Calvin and the Mysticism of St. Bernard* (Louisville: Westminster John Knox Press, 1994).

18. Gerrish, *Tradition in the Modern World*, 51.

Nevin and the Antebellum Culture Wars

James D. Bratt

John Nevin's work can give off an otherworldly glow. Sacramental theology, liturgical reform, and patristic studies seem a bit precious, almost effete, in any case far removed from the toil of daily life. Nevin's symbolic mode, his later mystical flights, his fond memories of Princeton Seminary as an "old academical retreat...of pleasantness and peace" breathe a cloistered air. At worst, then, he might be judged escapist, at best another keen but finally unavailing high-churchly critic of the course of modern development.[1]

On the other hand, the biographer who knew him best remembered Nevin as "eminently practical in all his tendencies....With him philosophy and even theology had no interest or value, apart from their actual bearings on the welfare of man and the progress of society." Nevin himself turned the charge of detachment upon his opponents; it was they—new-school revivalists, old-school Princetonians, and Unitarians alike—who were speculative and abstract, while he conjoined God's redemption with the world's real history. Further, Nevin claimed that redemption comprehended all that was earthly. God would save not just a certain number of individual souls for heaven but "the earth in its natural form," "the round and full symmetrical *cosmos* of humanity," and "the moral organization of society." The latter included the family, the state, and the "relations that grow out of them," as well as art, science, business, and trade. "No interest or sphere of this sort then can be allowed to remain on the outside of a system of redemption, which has for its object man as such in his fallen state."[2]

This-worldly or otherworldly? Nevin's mediating spirit would surely have us resolve this dispute. That can be accomplished on the theoretical plane by showing how his theology conceived the "ideal" and "supernatural" working through the "real" and "natural." This procedure alone, however, is too abstract. To take the practical man at his word, we need to locate Nevin's thought in the concrete events of his life. None are more germane than the culture wars of the antebellum era—wars that afflicted both church and state, indeed, that waxed hot just by intertwining the religious and political. These wars drew off ethnic and political loyalties deeply embedded in Nevin's family tradition, involved the same issues that animated his best work, and crested at the same time as the crises in his own career. Nevin, the elite theologian, could not help being a soldier in this strife, although he most wanted to be a peacemaker. The culture war lens discloses in his theology a deeper range of meanings than those usually explored, one that both warrants and raises questions about his claims to practicality and that provides a fair measure of his work's merits and difficulties.

I

Three facts stand out about Nevin's provenance. His family on both sides was Scots-Irish Presbyterian; it was comfortably situated in Pennsylvania's Cumberland Valley, close to the Mason-Dixon line; and it had lively political connections. The first has been well rehearsed, the second duly noted, the third virtually ignored. So it is there we should begin.

Nevin's great-uncle on his father's side was Hugh Williamson, delegate from North Carolina to the Continental Congress and the Constitutional Convention. Williamson signed that document, urged its ratification back home, then returned to Philadelphia for two terms in Congress. Nevin's father (Williamson's nephew), John, Sr., had similar interests but declined to run for Congress out of his diffidence at public speaking. What the father passed by the son obtained in his father-in-law, Robert Jenkins, ironmaster of Lancaster County and two-term (1807-11) Member of Congress.[3] Jenkins' friend and lawyer was James Buchanan whose whole life was politics, from caucuses in Lancaster taverns to a term in the White House.

Nevin knew Buchanan better than just by family connection. The two worked together (Nevin as immediate past-president and Buchanan as chairman of the trustees) to keep Franklin and Marshall College from falling into the hands of Nevin's opponents in 1853. Upon Buchanan's return from the White House to Lancaster, the two were next-door neighbors. Buchanan came frequently to hear Nevin preach in the college chapel, and the two spent long evenings in each other's parlors conversing of providence, history, and metaphysics. Part of the agenda was Nevin's (successful) design to get Buchanan to join the church, but doubtlessly the conversation often turned to the war that had swept up three of Nevin's sons, that in 1862 and 1863 raged uncomfortably close to Lancaster, and that Buchanan's presidential policies had failed to prevent. At his request, Buchanan's funeral service was conducted by the architect of the Mercersburg Theology.[4]

Unquestionably, then, politics was present on Nevin's horizon. What was its substance? Hugh Williamson clearly bore a Federalist profile. While faithful to North Carolina's interests, he distinguished himself by his concerns for education, for the careful disposition of Western lands, and for his own scholarly reputation. The values of stability, order, and cultural progress also marked John Nevin, Sr. As a gentleman farmer he promoted temperance (more a Federalist than a Jeffersonian cause) and bred his children in antislavery. His greatest political moment came on this point at his graduation from Dickinson College (1795). To an audience that included Roger Taney, his classmate and rival, a Democrat, and future author of the Dred Scott decision, Nevin gave a speech on "The Sin of Slavery." The politics of Robert Jenkins are hard to determine from the record but may be surmised from his Buchanan connection. Buchanan was boss of Lancaster County, and until the mid-1820s, his machine faithfully returned the Federalist ticket. When that party was no longer viable, Buchanan shifted his support to the Jacksonians and remained a fervent Democrat thereafter.[5] Nevin's friend, in sum, represented a notable political transition, notable also for its religious connections.

Buchanan's was a Mercersburg politics. That is, his picture of an ideal society always remained this country village where he spent his formative years: a quiet, integrated community that ran its own affairs and sent its best men as representatives to the outside world. The themes of organic connection and natural leadership were Federalist; that of local autonomy, Jeffersonian. The concord among them was broken in the 1820s when anti-Masonic agitation swept down from the Yankee belt of upstate New York into Pennsylvania. Anti-Masonry figured crucially in the birth of the Whig party, for it shattered what was left of the Federalist coalition and brought most of the remnants into the new party. A notable minority went Democratic, however. To Buchanan, a lifelong Mason, the society represented the local natural elite, and Whig fulminations against it amounted to fanatic moralism and outside interference. Accordingly, in 1828 he rejected the upright New Englander John Quincy Adams, for Andrew Jackson, who symbolized toleration and localism.[6]

A similar dynamic worked behind the birth of the Mercersburg Theology. John Nevin grew up in the organic tradition of the Middle Spring Presbyterian Church. Its cemetery held all his grandparents; its practices reproduced "so far as possible...the church life of eighteenth-century Ulster and Scotland." These usages included close family nurture, sober preaching, formal catechesis, and sacramental occasions, altogether, Nevin remembered, making "the Church in her visible character to be the medium of salvation for her baptized children...."[7] But they also included a form of revivalism born in Scotland two centuries before. This was the communion season, a huge, four-day, outdoor gathering that featured intense preaching, personal and often emotional confessions of sin and repentance, and a climactic celebration of the Lord's Supper. The Middle Spring Church had been New Side (i.e., pro-revival) in the mid-eighteenth century Great Awakening, but by that token had honored, not broken with tradition; had pointed personal religious experience toward the objective sacrament; and had wound the individual pilgrimage in rites of communal purification.[8]

By 1830 this union, too, had shattered. A generation before, the communion season had spun off a new form of frontier revivalism that severed the emotional and individual from their counterweights.[9]   Worse for Nevin was the mechanization of the process at the hands of New Englanders: the Nettletonians who were the "miserable obstetricians" of his abortive new birth at Union College; the Finneyite rampage across upstate New York; James Gallaher's version of the same in Pittsburgh in 1835; the crusade among Pennsylvania Germans that triggered his writing of *The Anxious Bench*; and the New Haven theology of Nathaniel W. Taylor that epitomized it all.[10] Again, interlopers with a Yankee accent had disrupted organic unity.

The disturbance came to a head for Nevin in 1837 when the opponents of the New England party ruthlessly excised it from the Presbyterian Church, sundering the body that Nevin owned as "mother."   The old school having become as meddling and "revolutionary" as the new, Nevin sought another home.[11] He found it on native ground but in the German Reformed Church. At Mercersburg he strove to recover the sacramental tradition. He worked at rapprochement with Catholicism exactly at the time when anti-Catholic passions were peaking in American society with profound political consequences. More generally he worked on a mediating theology that would restore unity to the Church. The borderline of slavery that ran a few miles to the south raised the same issue for the nation.

II

Jacksonian politics used to be explained as a conflict over economics and social status.   More recently it has been diagnosed as a conflict of values, as culture war. Doubtless, the two dimensions both deserve notice and, indeed, overlapped, but the latter approach illuminates more about Nevin's case. In the cultural interpretation, the ideological complexes and voting behavior of the age were shaped by religion and ethnicity. Since these were also central in Nevin's career, it is no surprise that a brief sketch of antebellum party alignments should call up so many resonances from his work.[12]

Ethnically, the Whig party had its core in the mainline Yankees of New England and their progeny across upstate New York and the upper Midwest. These were joined by the urban, merchant elite of the Mid-Atlantic states to make the Whigs Anglophilic, oriented to the national whole instead of local parts and fixed upon unity, conformity, and prosperity. The Democrats in the North were a coalition of those left out of this order. In New England they occupied the periphery, whether geographically, economically (subsistence farmers), or denominationally (Baptists and Methodists). In the Mid-Atlantic states they were the ethnics: Scots-Irish, Germans, and Dutch. Before the great party realignment of the 1850s, these all stood united in opposition to Yankee meddling and elite mercantilism, in favor of cultural pluralism and local autonomy.[13]

The two parties also harbored different religious types. The Whigs attracted groups with a "pietist" or "evangelical" disposition; the Democrats, those of a "ritualist," "liturgical" cast. In politics both projected their core theology upon the world at large. The evangelicals, bred in revivalism, pursued fervent activism; they sought "to purge the world of sin, to recreate the world for the greater glory of a personally knowable God."[14] Thus, the Church became a phalanx of voluntary agencies, each attacking an evil of choice to bring in the Kingdom of God on earth. They also bore the heritage of Puritan theocracy, seeing society as an organic whole headed by a positive state which was to enforce moral discipline. The ritualist disposition, on the other hand, saw the Church as an institution formally differentiated from the world, distinguished by its requirements of doctrine, tradition, and liturgical observance. In this view, the Kingdom of God would be fully realized only in eternity; on earth, its closest approximation was the Church. There one should go for peace, security, and grace. In the world sin was finally indelible and particular evils only gradually remediable. Thus, a positive state, especially one not deeply informed by the wisdom of the Church, was suspect as likely to make things worse in its efforts to make them better and as interfering with Church prerogatives besides.

Denominationally, then, the Whig party embraced the offspring of New England Puritanism: Congregationalists,

Unitarians, and the New Schoolers of the Burned-Over District and beyond. The Democrats' core coalition joined Catholics and Southerners (these stamped in revivalism, of course, but as limited to personal, not social, transformation). The Mid-Atlantic ethnics, among whom Nevin spent his entire life, held the balance of power: they were literally in the middle geographically and toward the middle religiously. They were particularly under strain, therefore, as the party system strained beneath the issues of slavery and immigration from the mid-1840s on. Until then, they held with the South in the Democratic party, giving it national hegemony for most of the antebellum period. But as Catholic (especially Irish Catholic) immigration soared and the demands of the South increased, the New England outgroups (Baptists and Methodists) and the middle-state ethnics, first and foremost the Scots-Irish Presbyterians, began to fear Yankee meddling less than Catholic and "slave power" encroachments, and so joined with their former antagonists to create the Republican party.[15]

It is not difficult to locate Nevin in this context. The labels "evangelical" and "liturgical" are tailor-made for his theological polemics. His birth within the Scots-Irish Presbyterianism of the lower North placed him on the crucial edge of the Democratic coalition, and his shift to German confessionalism put him deeper in its culture. Ethnically, his voluntary conversion to things German, his skepticism toward quick assimilation, and his defense of ethnic autonomy gave momentum the same way.[16] On the touchstone of the Mexican War, for instance, Nevin welcomed its fruits, while dismissing the question of its morality, as providing the immense tracts of land needed for personal liberty, small-group autonomy, and national glory—altogether a Democratic statement. And he had no doubt that that glory lay in full and free admission to all immigrants who, moreover, would eventually melt not into Anglo-conformity but into a truly new cosmopolitan nation. In words to chill a New England—and new school—heart, Nevin declared:

> The day for "Nativism," in all its forms, is fast drawing to an end.... the life of Europe is to be poured upon our shores without restraint or stint, till it shall cause the

ancient blood of the land to become in quantity a mere
nothing in comparison.[17]

To round off his Democratic evidence, at the end of the Civil
War Nevin granted the South and Northern dissenters even
more charity than Lincoln would, a pose opposite to that of the
Radical Republicans.[18]

But on other points Nevin did not conform to the profile.
His organic vision of society and of church-state coordination
lay closer to Whiggery than to Democracy. His abhorrence of
individualism comported ill with the Jeffersonian legacy, and his
hopes for the Kingdom of God were not left to eternity as in a
pure ritualist position. Above all, Nevin disliked reckless
partisanship, which in the antebellum years was recognizably
more the property of Democrats than of Whigs. Perhaps these
anomalies reflected the old Federalist strain in his background.
Perhaps they indicated his sense that neither party could master
its own paradoxes, much less solve the nation's problems. For
how could Whigs have it both ways: economic growth and
stable order, individual assertiveness and organic harmony? As
for the Democrats, how long could white and ethnic liberties
live beside black slavery? And what would territorial expansion
do to a simple face-to-face society of local rights?[19]

Nevin's work bears recognition of such confusion of values,
and his career took crucial turns synchronically with the
political conflicts that confusion engendered. His move to
Mercersburg was launched by the Presbyterian schism of 1837,
an event that bore not just sociocultural animus but heavy
political portents. If it was not the first shot of the Civil War,
it, along with the Baptist and Methodist splits that soon
followed, "presaged and to some extent provoked the crisis of
the Union in 1861."[20] Thus, Nevin's attack on "Party Spirit"
in 1839 applied to the Presbyterian battle two years past but
also to the notorious presidential campaign of the year ahead.
Similarly, Nevin's "breakdown" in 1851 and retirement in 1853
anticipated by just a year or two the same developments in the
Whig party and, with them, the collapse of the party system
that had made the Union workable for the previous 25 years.
Both Nevin's inaugural speech at Mercersburg in 1840 and his
farewell address at the opening of Franklin and Marshall College

in 1853 included political prophecy. Nothing would be more important to the nation's future, he said, than what went on in "the mighty mass of mind between the Atlantic and the Alleghenies...."[21]   What he hoped for was the growth of a culture to mediate between Yankee North and slave South. What actually ensued put Pennsylvania in Lincoln's column in 1860, giving the South secession fever.

III

Through all this Nevin worked as a theologian. His new birth in Pittsburgh was triggered by a church historian, and its full consequence was a churchly passion. Nevin turned away from explicit politics in going to Mercersburg, just as he had renounced "political economy" the year before going to Pittsburgh, and for the same reason. Neither was able to "bring any positive aid to Christianity" nor even to solve the secular problem it addressed, and so testified to the need for a "supernatural redemption for society...."[22]   Churchly, sacramental theology, in other words, was politics by transcendent means, the only means adequate to the difficulties at hand. The works for which we remember Nevin thus deserve a re-reading in light of their sociocultural burden and political parallels.

The Anxious Bench is Nevin's most obvious tract of cultural warfare. Just as he used the bench to symbolize the whole new measures system, so that system represented New England's encroachments on Pennsylvania German ground. What Nevin said about new school spirituality applied, by his implication and often in historical fact, to the whole congeries of "ultraism" —perfectionism, reform panaceas, and single-issue politics—it bred. Both were theatrical, mechanical, often shallow, bearing fanaticism and disorder. Both suffered from "quackery," the pretense of a power not actually possessed, requiring ever more extravagance to be believed. Both were rationalistic and individualistic, arising from a piecemeal, legalistic conception of sin and a false estimate of people's ability to change themselves. Exchanging the objective power of God for the subjective state of the soul (and the stage charisma of the leader), reformer and revivalist engaged in self-glorification on the grandest scale. Also of the most aggressive sort, they could not rest until all were made over in their own image.[23]

The anxious bench, Nevin argued, necessarily gave birth to sect and schism, the social manifestation of its self-centered principle. Accordingly, his writings on the sect spirit and system—the "Antichrist"—bore direct political parallels. Nevin characterized "the sect mind" with the same language he applied to "the party spirit" in 1839; both

> run into low cunning, disingenuous trickery and jesuitic policy. Religion [like politics] degenerates with it into a trade, in which men come to terms with God [the nation] on the subject of their own salvation [citizenship and office], and lay away their spiritual acquisitions as a sort of outward property for convenient use.

Nevin's jibes at the sectarians' magic potion of "the Bible alone + private judgment" duplicates the critique made of reformers who placed their own intuitively perceived higher law above custom, Constitution, or common law. Both formulae would tear an intricate, historically woven fabric with the knife of sheer abstraction. Worse yet was the hypocrisy of the process. Such destruction was put forward as progress and private judgment/higher law as grounds of unity. The sects and ultraist cells masked authoritarianism as freedom, their notorious lack of charity as tolerance.[24] The crises of the times they would solve with more of the measures that caused it.

From caustic critique Nevin moved on in *The History and Genius of the Heidelberg Catechism* and *The Mystical Presence* to give more constructive proposals, but here, too, he used politically resonant language. Most striking is the recurrence of "Puritan." Not only did commentators casually tie Yankee traits to their Puritan provenance, but Southerners during the Civil War cast themselves as "Cavaliers" opposing Northern "Roundheads."[25] Nevin's plea for eucharistic orthodoxy could not help but carry political overtones, then, when it scored "the modern Puritan view," "the proper Puritan stand-point," for "falling away from...the old Reformed view" and "for eviscerat[ing] the institution of all objective force."[26] Substitute the Constitution for the Lord's Supper, or Founding Fathers for the Reformers, and the conservative case against immediate abolition emerges.

Indeed, Nevin was often referring to "the Constitution" around 1850, as were the politicians who had to deal with the lands newly taken from Mexico. They debated the intent of Founding Fathers like Hugh Williamson with respect to slavery and came up with the Compromise of 1850. Nevin searched the Church Fathers for the constitution of Christianity and found the creed and sacraments.[27] Both argued that the original frame alone could bind parts into a whole and lead on to destined glory. More specifically, in 1850 Nevin replied to Charles Hodge's review of *The Mystical Presence* with a theological forecast of the party realignment on the horizon. Presbyterian orthodoxy, Nevin declared, had so deeply imbibed of the rationalist heresy on the sacraments that, short of returning to the classic Catholic/Reformed view, it would have to come to rest there in its other tenets as well.[28] In terms of the culture wars, it was precisely anti-Catholicism that moved enough Presbyterians out of the Democratic into the Republican coalition in 1860 to change the shape of the nation.

Nevin usually kept politics implicit, however, because he saw the church question as paramount, absorbing all other problems of the age. All naturally conceived and secularly wrought solutions, he insisted, shared humanity's fateful limitations. Life required a supernatural redemption, which had begun only in the incarnation of Jesus Christ. Here was the objective fact of a new life, a divine and supernatural force present in history, offering power for real change. But that power was available only in the Church, Christ's living body in the world, and there preeminently through the sacrament. As Nevin declared at the Heidelberg Catechism tercentenary in the midst of the carnage of 1862-63:

> What we all need...is not just good doctrine for the understanding, or good direction for the will, or good motives for the heart, but the power rather of a new life, which, proceeding from God and being inserted into our fallen nature, may redeem us from the vanity

of this present evil world, and make us to be in such
sort "partakers of the divine nature."[29]

More colloquially, Nevin was saying to American Christians:
"First things first. If Christ is the sole source of regeneration,
for ourselves and our society, then we had better be sure we
really have him—or better, that he has us. Then we can be a
channel of his power in the world."

For the most part, American Protestants turned a deaf ear
to these words, doubtlessly precipitating Nevin's breakdown
and retirement. But while he still wrote, hard by the Mason-
Dixon line, he contributed by analogy a loving, dolorous
prophecy about the future of the nation as well, a call for
mystical union under the power of the mystical presence.
Nevin's was a border-state theology, as earnest and as
ineffectual as the border-state compromises proposed in the
secession winter of 1860-61. The last of these proposals,
Abraham Lincoln's First Inaugural Address, echoed Nevin's
language remarkably, coming as it did from a similar Romantic,
organicist view of history. With Nevin's new neighbor, James
Buchanan, sitting on the platform, Lincoln closed his plea with
the hope that "the mystic chords of memory, stretching...to
every living heart and hearth stone, all over this broad land, will
yet swell the chorus of the Union...."

IV

Certainly the times were against border states of all kinds.
The lines William Butler Yeats wrote in 1919 applied precisely
to the United States in 1861:

> Things fall apart; the center cannot hold;
> Mere anarchy is loosed upon the world,
> The blood-dimmed tide is loosed, and everywhere
> The ceremony of innocence is drowned;
> The best lack all conviction, while the worst
> Are full of passionate intensity.

Nevin's "failure," then, can be accounted as prophetic "success": the people, not heeding his voice, rushed to their predictable carnage. But his own ceremony of innocence (the eucharist) and core conviction (the Church) were shadowed by his limitations.

First, for one so concerned with the Church, Nevin said little about the means of its mission in the world. Granted the redeemed Church and the sinful but to-be-redeemed world, what are the middle terms of connection and transferral? Nevin said only that redemption works slowly and gradually, like leaven, like the gentle rain instead of the tempest.[30]   That helps some but not much. Partly the problem was that his preoccupation with getting the Church straight left little time for concerns of application. Besides, Nevin was here reflecting the environs of his life: stable, old-fashioned Presbyterianism, quiet Princeton, German Pennsylvania. In ethnic provinces change can proceed much as Nevin describes, by quiet osmosis. In contrast, new school environments tended to be busy and expansive—most obviously, the Burned-Over District, which was bisected by the Erie Canal and animated by the transportation revolution it wrought.[31]   Philosophically, Nevin trusted too much to an innate logic of unification in the historical process, with conservative, sometimes passive, consequences.

Secondly, Nevin's system suffered from a dualism, usually implicit, sometimes explicit. Much as he rejected the sacred-profane dichotomy of his (revivalistic) Union College education, Nevin's language consistently elevated inward over outward, grace over nature, and by extension Church over world. The German idealism that gave him history cost him in ontology. Time and again Nevin played the Kantian triads: body-mind-will, natural-mental-moral, or further elaborated, physical-chemical-biological-mental-moral-religious.[32]   The farther up this scale, the better. Sometimes this promoted escapism, as in the address on "Party Spirit": "Soar in spirit above the region of sense and particular opinion," Nevin counseled his audience, to "the empyrean sphere of absolute and eternal truth." Other times Nevin came close to the idealist identification of Christianity with spiritual culture, only to warn, in the next breath, that "Nature is not Grace. That which is born of the flesh is at last...flesh only, and not Spirit. It can never, in its own order, save the world." Rather,

> We must be children of our country and also children of our age....Only let us try to be so, by the grace of our Lord Jesus Christ, in such sort that we shall be likewise all children of the light and true sons of God, in being at the same time true sons of the Church.[33]

To invoke H. Richard Niebuhr's famous typology, Nevin sometimes intimates Christ against culture, then the Christ of culture, more often Christ and culture in paradox or Christ above culture, without substantiating the option he surely desired, Christ transforming culture.

Niebuhr, of course, made John Calvin an exemplar of the latter strategy. Thus Brian Gerrish's judgment—that, in their exchange on Calvin, Hodge took the decrees and Nevin the sacraments—must be extended further.[34] Together, the two left Calvinism's cultural activism to the New Schoolers. The splintering of American Calvinism did not cause that of the American nation, but it did subvert the tradition's ethical coherence. As Nevin, the critic of all partiality, might agree, predestinarianism, churchliness, and activism are each skewed when removed from the chemistry of the whole. It is no accident that the best political and theological interpretation of the Civil War was Lincoln's Second Inaugural, a homily on Psalm 19, itself a hymn to God's glory in creation and law; and that the speech achieved its power by emphasizing *corporate* sin and the *mystery* of God's decrees—all Calvinistic themes that its antebellum champions missed in one way or another.

Another one-sidedness is all the more striking in light of Nevin's nurture. As prescient as he was about immigration, Nevin upon removing to Mercersburg became silent on slavery. Put more baldly, born and bred as he was to the antislavery cause, sympathetically as he chronicled Theodore Weld's abolitionist debates at Lane Seminary in his own Pittsburgh magazine, Nevin had nothing public to say on the subject after moving to within shouting distance of slave territory.[35] The change cannot be laid to cowardice, for Nevin was brave enough on other occasions. Perhaps he thought, with his collaborator Philip Schaff and with some current historians, that slavery was bound soon to wither away as a labor system.[36] Certainly abolitionism carried much of the "fanaticism" he decried in Yankee culture and so was tainted by association with his ecclesiastical enemies. By that token Nevin's abolition sentiments must be counted another casualty of the culture wars.   Nonetheless, abolitionism cannot be blamed either morally or historically for the Civil War. Southern intransigence and Northern bumbling and preening were more at fault, but Nevin spoke to neither until the war was over.

Speak he finally did, however, in terms that explicitly connected his ecclesiology—indeed, his ontology and historiography—with politics. In all things Nevin yearned for union; just that, he declared at Franklin and Marshall College, the war had accomplished for the American nation. Echoing Lincoln's Second Inaugural, Nevin found the hand of God in the conflict by irony. The war had begun despite human agents' will, endured far beyond their calculations, was prosecuted through their errors, and ended before they could have hoped. It showed courage and good will on both sides; it had also wrought "a terrific dissolution of manners [and] corruption in high places," exposing a "deep-seated rottenness in the social system." But now, with the strife over, the dialectic turned, and Nevin soared into the idiom of redemption and sanctification.   The United States had become the "representative nation" through which "the life of the world at large is mediated.... The crisis is past.... old things have passed away; let us work together now, with united heart and hand, that all things may become new," assured that God, having accomplished so great a task, "will not forsake the work of his own hands."[37]

This flight into civil religion drew something from the occasion: Nevin gave this address on the 4th of July, 1865. Two years later he sounded a different note, with a direct rebuke to the eschatological fantasies of "The Battle Hymn of the Republic":

> ...the march of events (though it may be but John Brown's soul marching on—God knows whither) is trumpeted to the four winds of heaven as the stately

goings of Jehovah Jesus Himself....[But] the millennium
it promises is not the reign of the saints foretold by the
prophets and apostles; and it is only too plain, alas!,
that the agencies and tendencies which are held to be
working towards it, carry in them no sure guaranty
whatsoever of millennial triumph in any form. All the
signs of the times...betoken universal and fundamental
changes. But we have no assurance in these signs that
the change will move on victoriously in the line of
universal righteousness and truth....[38]

To recall Yeats' poem, the rough beast that came slouching
out of the Civil War was a coarse industrialism and far-reaching
materialism that hit close to home. Their corollary in academic
life was the rise of the state university system that posed a
threat to the philosophical curriculum and quiet retreat Nevin
remembered from Princeton and had labored to build at Franklin
and Marshall. At the college's commencement ceremonies in
1867, he crystallized the theme that marked the last phase of
his life:

All we need to protest against...[is] the wild
hallucination...that the great battle and work of life for
man is to be accomplished by physics and mechanics,
by insight simply into the laws of nature and mastery of
its powers...by polytechnic ingenuity and skill applied
in all manner of ways to business and trade. There is
a higher view than all this, in which...the material
meets us everywhere as the sacrament of the spiritual
and divine.[39]

What Nevin would link by sacrament, his descendants split
along the classic divide of Gilded Age culture. Two of Nevin's
sons passed through the Civil War officer corps: Wilberforce
followed the new technology to the Philadelphia *Press* and New
York railroads; Robert pursued the spirit as Episcopal rector of
St. Paul's Within-the-Walls in Rome. Two of Nevin's daughters
were artists and free spirits: Alice working in music and Blanche
in stone, contributing a statue of General John Peter
Muhlenburg to the National Art Gallery in Washington and a

bust of Woodrow Wilson to Princeton. The latter commission probably came via Nevin's third daughter, Martha, who married the new industrialism in the person of Robert H. Sayre, vice-president of the Lehigh Valley Railroad and of Bethlehem Steel. Their son, Francis B. Sayre, married Wilson's daughter Jessie, and the fruit of that union (thus Nevin's great-grandson) was born in the White House.[40]

Wilson's Democratic, Presbyterian presidency Nevin would perhaps have applauded; its turn against his beloved Germany he might have mourned; his great-grandson, as Dean of the National Cathedral in Washington, he would have owned. The Capitol and the Cathedral, Bethlehem Steel and Bethlehem of the Incarnation, symbolize the two poles of his mind. Measured by norms and attention, he vaunted the latter of each pair over the former, but unlike many American Protestants, he would make them neither separate nor identical nor antithetical. What should be their relationship instead was the burden of his life, his children's, and our own.

ENDNOTES

1. The latter is the assessment of Walter H. Conser, Jr., *Church and Confession: Conservative Theologians in Germany, England, and America, 1815-1866* (Macon, GA: Mercer University Press, 1984), 313-29.

2. Quotations from Theodore Appel, *The Life and Work of John Williamson Nevin* (Philadelphia, 1889); and John W. Nevin, "Catholicity," in ibid., 373-79.

3. Louis Potts, "Hugh Williamson: The Poor Man's Franklin and the National Domain," *North Carolina Historical Review* 44:4 (October 1987):371-93;*Dictionary of American Biography*, vol. 20, 298-300; Appel, *Life and Work*, 25-27, 63-64.

4. Philip S. Klein, *President James Buchanan* (University Park, PA, 1962), 27, 29, 210, 424-28; James H. Nichols, *Romanticism in American Theology: Nevin and Schaff at Mercersburg* (Chicago: University of Chicago Press, 1961), 221-23; Appel, *Life and Work*, 432-37, 601-03.

5. Potts, "Hugh Williamson," 376-78, 387-89; Appel, *Life and Work*, 27; Nichols, *Romanticism*, 9; Klein, *Buchanan*, 17-22, 66-67; Shaw Livermore, Jr., *The Twilight of Federalism: The Disintegration of the Federalist Party, 1815-1830* (Princeton, 1962), 157-58, 238, 265.

6. Livermore, *Twilight*, 238-41, 256; Klein, *Buchanan*, 4-5,70-74, 100, 106-08, 427-28.

7. Nichols, *Romanticism*, 5-7, quotation p. 7; Nevin, *My Own Life*, 2-5, quotation p. 3.

8. Leigh Eric Schmidt, *Holy Fairs: Scottish Communions and American Revivals in the Early Modern Period* (Princeton, 1989), and Marilyn Westerkamp, *Triumph of the Laity: Scots-Irish Piety and the Great Awakening, 1625-1760* (New York, 1988), are fine studies of this tradition. On its contact with Nevin, see Nichols, *Romanticism*, 7-8.

9. Schmidt, *Holy Fairs*, 60-68.

10. Nevin, *My Own Life*, 8-11 (quotation p. 10), 125-27; Appel, *Life and Work*, 155-60; Nichols, *Romanticism*, 10-15, 25, 53-63.

11. Nichols, *Romanticism*, 30-34; Nevin, *My Own Life*, 3. The regional-culture dimension of the 1837 split is evident in Earl A. Pope, *New England Calvinism and the Disruption of the Presbyterian Church* (New York, 1987 [1962]); and George M. Marsden, *The Evangelical Mind and the New School Presbyterian Experience* (New Haven, 1970), 7-8.

12. Lee Benson, *The Concept of Jacksonian Democracy: New York as a Test Case* (Princeton, 1961), was the pioneer work of this interpretation. Paul Kleppner, *The Third Electoral System, 1853-1892* (Chapel Hill, 1979), is its most detailed study. Robert L. Kelley, *The Cultural Pattern in American Politics: The First Century* (New York, 1979), is a fine synthesis. Joel H. Silbey, *The Partisan Imperative: The Dynamics of American Politics Before the Civil War* (New York, 1985), treats Nevin's era and answers the method's critics.

13. Kelley, *Cultural Pattern*, 164-75.

14. The labels were first defined in Paul Kleppner, *The Cross of Culture: A Social Analysis of Midwestern Politics, 1850-1900* (New York, 1970); quotation p. 74. For the elaboration below, see Kleppner, *Third Party System*, 143-97; and Kelley, *Cultural Pattern*, 160-74, 268-72.

15. Kelley, *Cultural Pattern*, 164-75, 216-20, 274-81.

16. Appel, *Life and Work*, 129-32. Nevin's key statements on the subject are (all ibid.) "The Christian Ministry" [1840], 112-16; "The German Language" [1842], 178-97; "The Lutheran Confession" [1849], 304-09; and "Pennsylvania, the 'Sleeping Giant'" [1853], 443-54.

17. John W. Nevin, "The Year 1848," *Mercersburg Review* 1:1 (January 1849):10-44; quotation p. 32.

18. John W. Nevin, "The Nation's Second Birth," *Reformed Church Messenger* 30:47 (July 26, 1865):1.

19. On partisanship, see John W. Nevin, "Party Spirit" [1839], in Appel, *Life and Work*, 117-26; and Jean Baker, *Affairs of Party: The Political Culture of Northern Democrats in the Mid-Nineteenth Century* (Ithaca, NY, 1983). On party contradictions, see Kelley, *Cultural Pattern*, 160-63.

20. C. C. Goen, *Broken Churches, Broken Nation: Denominational Schisms and the Coming of the American Civil War* (Mercer, GA, 1985), 13.

21. Nevin, "The Christian Ministry" (quotation p. 114), and "Pennsylvania, the 'Sleeping Giant'."

22. Nevin, *My Own Life*, 31.

23. John W. Nevin, *The Anxious Bench: A Tract for the Times* [1844], in Charles Yrigoyen, Jr., and George H. Bricker, eds., *Catholic and Reformed: Selected Writings of John Williamson Nevin* (Pittsburgh, 1978), 9-126. On the political and social spin-offs of revivalism, see Whitney R. Cross, *The Burned-Over District* (Ithaca, NY, 1950), and Ronald G. Walters, *American Reformers, 1815-1860* (New York, 1980).

24. Nevin, "The Sect System" [1849], in Yrigoyen and Bricker, *Catholic and Reformed*, 130-73, quotation p. 169.

25. William R. Taylor, *Cavalier and Yankee: The Old South and American National Character* (New York, 1961). Kelley, *Cultural Pattern*, 222-23, and Silbey, *Partisan Imperative*, 186-88, cite many examples of the Puritan idiom from the times.

26. Quotations from *The Mystical Presence* excerpt in Sydney E. Ahlstrom, ed., *Theology in America: The Major Protestant Voices from Puritanism to Neo-Orthodoxy* (Indianapolis, 1967), 388,395; see, more generally, 386-400. Other of Nevin's explicit references to Yankee/Puritan traits at the time come in "The Year 1848," 42; and "The Lutheran Confession," passim.

27. Nichols, *Romanticism*, 140-50, 165-67, 182-83, 199-206. Nevin's constitutional language is apparent in, e.g., "Catholicity," 390-95; and "Undying Life in Christ," in Appel, *Life and Work*, 622.

28. John W. Nevin, "Doctrine of the Reformed Church on the Lord's Supper," *Mercersburg Review* 2:5 (September 1850).

29. Nevin, "Undying Life in Christ," 626.

30. Nevin, *The Anxious Bench*, 118; cf. "Catholicity," 383-84.

31. Paul E. Johnson, *A Shopkeeper's Millennium: Society and Revivals in Rochester, 1815-1837* (New York, 1978).

32. Exemplary pieces on this point are "Party Spirit," "Catholicity," "Undying Life in Christ," and "The Wonderful Nature of Man," in Appel, *Life and Work*, 515-28. See also students' notes of Nevin's lectures on history, aesthetics, and ethics in the Evangelical and Reformed Historical Society Archives, Lancaster Theological Seminary.

33. Nevin, "Party Spirit," 125; "Commencement Address" [1867], in Appel, *Life and Work*, 634-54, quotation pp. 648-49.

34. Brian Gerrish, *Tradition and the Mordern World: Reformed Theology in the Nineteenth Century* (Chicago, 1978), 70.

35. For Nevin's antislavery work, see Nichols, *Romanticism*, 20, 27; and Nevin, *My Own Life*, 89-95.

36. Schaff published that view in "Slavery and the Bible," which appeared in no less than the April 1861 number of the *Mercersburg Review* 13:2 (1861):288-317.

37. Nevin, "The Nation's Second Birth," 1.

38. Nevin, "Commencement Address," 647-48.

39. Nevin, "Commencement Address," 653.

40. Appel, *Life and Work*, 64; Eloise L. Johnson, "The Nevin Family," Nevin papers, Evangelical and Reformed Historical Society; "The Late Dr. Nevin," ibid. Robert H. Sayre (1824-1907; profiled in *Dictionary of American Biography*, vol. 16, 405-06) took Martha Finley Nevin as his fourth wife on May 3, 1882; the union produced three children. One of these, Francis Bowes Sayre, married Jessie Wilson in the White House on November 25, 1913; their son, Francis Bowes Sayre, Jr., was born there January 17, 1915. F. B. Sayre, Sr. (1885-1972), spent his life in education, law, and the diplomatic corps; F. B. Sayre, Jr., became dean of the Washington Cathedral in 1951. See August Heckscher, *Woodrow Wilson* (New York, 1991), 322, 343; *Who Was Who in America*, vol. 5, 636; and *Who's Who in America*, 37th ed., vol. 2, 2781.

Nevin and American Nationalism[*]

Richard E. Wentz

It was difficult to be an American citizen during the first half of the nineteenth century and not be caught up in the swelling tides of American mission and Manifest Destiny. Newspaper editorials waxed prophetic as they predicted ever-increasing incidents of revolutions in Europe. Expansionist sentiment suggested the United States assist in the birth of revolutions wherever monarchial reactionaries sought to destroy them. American liberty and republicanism might even be extended to Canada, Cuba, and all the West Indies. "Asia had her day;" said the New York Evening Post, "Europe has had hers; and it remains to be seen whether the diadem must not first be worn by the new world before it reverts again to the old."[1]

Others said we should remain aloof from the actual struggles of Europe, standing aside as "the reserve corps to consummate the triumphs of freedom," ready to serve if liberty called us to arms. In 1848 "the fulfillment of Destiny was delayed by Mexican stubbornness and Whig treason. But why worry?... Europe (had) seen the light, the fire, the polestar, from the depth of her darkness, and (was) successfully shaking off her chains."[2] American expansionism was really a form of "continentalism"—"a vision of future greatness born of expectations bred by a contemplation of a vast continent to be settled and nourished by the millennial hopes of evangelical religion."[3] The people of the earth would be regenerated by the attraction of freedom, Christian piety, and virtue.

[*]This article is republished with permission. It was originally published in the *Journal of the American Academy of Religion* (58:4), 617-32.

The revolutions in Europe were themselves evidence of a stirring of the liberty and equality that America represented. Drawing upon Montesquieu's model of republicanism, Robert Bellah has suggested that the principle of social life for a republic is virtue.[4] Presumably every society is constituted by a set of ideas, values, beliefs, and practices that reflect its perception of reality. As the poet Wallace Stevens expressed it: "We live not so much in a world as a perception of the world." Perception gives expression to those characteristics that constitute a society. The constitution of a republic is nurtured by a perception of the world in which community is internally nourished by virtue, its commitments, and its renewals. During the time of the American Revolution and the revolutionary ferment of the 1840s, the constitution of European and American society was in the process of radical alteration. Perception of the world was changing, and the constitution of society was less concerned with hierarchical and authoritarian values. The way was increasingly open to republican virtue.

Rumblings begun in the sixteenth century had increased in velocity and volume until, in the eighteenth century, the Great Awakening signalled the destruction of an old order and the birth of a new. The American Enlightenment added a touch of confidence to the new order, suggesting that unassisted human reason could sort out the proper constitution of the *novus ordo saeclorum* as self-evident truth.[5] And the Arminian soul that had been in the making found itself comfortable with this Enlightenment posture. There may have been certain theological differences between the two, but the minds of the people were impatient with tedious intellectual hair-splitting.[6]

Of course, not everyone was convinced that a new order or a new constitution was being born. It was easy to see signs of chaos and disorder without corresponding evidence of new birth. Sectarianism, much of it the result of the new revivalism, was very much in evidence. In her study of Mormonism as a new religious tradition, Jan Shipps calls attention to the unsettled character of America during the National Period and into the second third of the nineteenth century. There was a new physical universe, evident in the expanding frontier and in the minds of materialists like Thomas Jefferson:

A new and somewhat uncertain political system existed
and Americans had to operate within it. The bases of
social order were in a state of disarray, and as a result
of the nation's having cut its ties with England and her
history, a clear lack of grounding in the past was
evident. Quite clearly as important in the breakdown of
a once reasonably stable cognitive and normative
edifice of knowledge and understanding of the way
things are was the uncertainty that was the outgrowth
of the development of skepticism, on the one hand, and
direct contention among systems of theology and
doctrine, on the other. That uncertainty placed in
jeopardy the religious dynamic that for centuries—
through formal or informal catechizing—had passed
from one generation to the next a body of unquestioned
information about divinity, humanity, the system of
right relationships that created the social order, and the
nature of experience after death.[7]

"The religious dynamic" to which Shipps refers was a major
contributor to the constitution that had made the new nation
possible. As Henry F. May has expressed it: "The recovery of
American religious history has restored a knowledge of the
mode, even the language, in which most Americans, during
most of American history, did their thinking about human
nature and destiny."[8]   This "mode" and "language"
(constitution) were a "combination of evangelical Protestantism
with American nationalism, with its Enlightenment roots and its
romantic flowering."[9] As some nineteenth-century thinkers,
such as Orestes Brownson, were astute enough to recognize,
it had been the constitution of the colonial enterprise—the
constitution of images, attitudes, ideas, and values—that made
the Constitution a workable document.[10]   And now the
religious dynamic and constitution were experiencing erosion.
The ferment symptomatic of the revolutions of Europe was also
evident in America. Although this was a time of nationalism
and continentalism, as Hudson has shown us, it was also a
time of uncertainty. It was, after all, the period of what Martin
Marty calls "the Modern Schism": "In the middle decades of the
nineteenth century people who had acted in concert to make up

Christendom finally divided into mutually opposing parties; one set devoted itself to religious and ecclesiastical concerns. The other was increasingly preoccupied with the secular."[11] "The years of the Schism," says Marty, "spawned many rivals to Christianity." In America they made little progress; yet a nationalistic spirit had settled in by the Civil War, and clergy, "both evangelical and Catholic, were called upon to give clerical blessing to all the missions and purposes of the nation, on the assumption that the manifest destiny had always been a part of the plan of God."[12]

Of course, not all religious America was satisfied with the simple nationalism, or with the ease with which evangelical Protestantism accepted the signs of the times and moved toward consensual harmony. The early-nineteenth century in America was, in one sense, characterized by the fall-out of the religiosity that was spawned in the religious revolution of the sixteenth century. Sydney Ahlstrom calls attention to "America's religious fecundity" and to the "religious individualism made manifest in America" with the weakening of tradition by Protestant/Puritan principle and geographic distance.[13] In the midst of apparent consensus, many Americans of the early-nineteenth century saw only disarray. Anxiety and despair gave expression to a mood in which there emerged a number of resolutions designed to supply a new religious dynamic appropriate to the times, one that would maintain the constitution essential to national life. First, there were the numerous attempts at repristination, the restoration of a presumably unsullied, pure, and simple original Christianity. To these "Christians," the centuries since the fourth had produced a blighted Christianity.[14] Even the Reformation was suspect as they leaped across the tallest obstacles of history with a single bound.[15] Then, of course, there was Shipps' "new religious tradition"—the Mormonism that represents so radical a restoration that it must be considered an alternative dispensation, a reconstruction of patriarchal Israel in a latter-day promised land.

A third model of response to the religious disorder of the new nation was transcendentalism, a romantic vision of the spirit to be found in the landscape and sinew of the new world, a domestication of the divine and an affirmation of the divinity of the new humanity in a land without a past. "The foregoing generations beheld God and nature face to face," said Emerson, "we through their eyes. Why should not we also enjoy an original relation to the universe?" What was at work was more than Transcendentalism with a capital T; it was a transcendental "submission to the materials of the American experience."[16]

According to thinkers like John Williamson Nevin, the form of religiosity most common to the new nation was what he called a False or Pseudo Protestantism, itself part of the disarray of the times. This, too, was an attempt to provide a new religious dynamic. This fourth and most prevalent model of response to the cultural fatigue was the powerful force of revivalistic evangelicalism that became a kind of American "Protestant" ideology. Nevin frequently referred to this False Protestantism as Puritanism, with little critical attention to the justification of the usage. However that may be, he had little trouble characterizing this False Protestantism as a religion of "Bible and Private Judgement."[17] This was the religion of the democratic mainstream, a tradition with its beginnings in New England Puritanism and its promotion of the evidences of saving faith.[18]

Various schemes of restoration, wrote Nevin, purport to provide a simple principle of unity for all true Christians. That principle is "the unbound use solely of the Bible for the adjustment of Christian faith and practice."[19] In fact, continued Nevin, the principle is a divisive one, leading to sectarian proliferation. This is especially true when we realize that "No creed but the Bible" has a complementary dictum — the idea of private judgment. The supposed supreme authority of the Bible is "conditioned always by the assumption that every(one) is authorized and bound to get at this authority in a direct way for himself, through the medium simply of his single mind."[20] Of course, no sect in existence actually permits the full demands of this dual maxim. Every one of them has a scheme that it claims becomes self-evident in every exercise of Bible and private judgment.[21] The sectarian mind is a utilitarian mind, claiming that maximal private judgment would reward the individual with the assurance of the salvation he sought. "Our national credo," writes Henry May, "has often been described as a combination of simple moral maxims and easy utilitarianism."[22]

The American religious mind became dominated by this spiritual narcissism or utilitarian salvationism, what Nicolas Berdyaev later called transcendental egoism.[23] Of course, there were those for whom the private transformation they sought redirected their lives, turning them in disinterested benevolence to the service of human community through the voluntary societies of the time. But the trend was toward self-interested religiosity. As Nevin stated in his diatribe against Finney's "New Measures":

> The higher force does not strictly and properly take possession of the lower, but is presumed to have been reduced to the possession and service of this last, to be used by it for its own convenience. Religion does not get the sinner, but it is the sinner who "gets religion." Justification is taken to be in fact by **felling**, not by faith; and in this way falls back...into the sphere of self-righteousness....[24]

It is understandable that this tradition should have been fashioned in our society. We were essentially a people who had been divested of their continuity with the past. Large numbers of people were thrown upon their own resources. And, of course, "America, like nineteenth-century Europe, has had its **theoreticians** of dissent, but in far greater abundance has it had its **practitioners**."[25] We were a frontier people, a people on the move.

This was a people "in movement through space—a people exploring the obvious highways and the many unexplored and devious byways of practically unlimited geographical and social space. The quality of their minds and hearts and spirits was formed in that great crucible—and in a very short time."[26] So much space, so little time; time only to gather whatever supplies and energies (material or spiritual) were essential to the trip. Faith and religious resource had to be readily available to the individual in a once-for-all, transforming experience. Fostered by revivalism and the style of the frontier, "the Bible and Private Judgment" became the creed of America. Taking some of the theoretical tradition of Christianity, the new religion fashioned its own morality and ritual system. It found its social expression in the churches as voluntary associations of spiritually endowed individualism. The error of such individualism, according to Nevin, was that it was a false, a pseudo-Protestantism, completely at odds with the Reformation and the truth of its origins. It was a blind new construction, fashioned rationalistically without regard for the roots of the Christian revelation. This false Protestantism, nurtured by the scheme of Bible and Private Judgment, drew the conclusion that the Holy Spirit communicated with individuals, who might then voluntarily associate with each other and form churches. It assumed that the message of the gospel was directed toward a cumulative conversion of **all** the individuals in the world; that, theoretically, when/if that were accomplished, the world would be at one and the claims of the gospel fulfilled. This point of view mistook **allness** for **wholeness**, wrote John Nevin. The whole is always greater than the sum of its parts. Wholeness precedes the response of any single individual or collection thereof. It is also more than the cumulative result of any efforts. Allness, or the collectivity of individuals, is an illusion of the individual seeking the satisfaction of spiritual self-interest. Nevin maintains that it is the **world** that is reconciled-- already reconciled--to God in Christ. Any response to that reconciliation is a response to the **whole**, which is already present, waiting to be recognized.[27]

We have isolated four models of response to the religious fragmentation that was apparent to many in the first half of the nineteenth century: restorationism, alternative (or radical) dispensationalism, transcendentalism, and the dominant tradition of "Bible and Private Judgment" — what may be characterized as revivalistic evangelicalism, what Nevin called false or pseudo-Protestantism. Other models might be added to the list, such as Enlightenment religion[28] or Mead's religion of the Republic.[29] This latter tradition shared many of the same utilitarian interests as the prevailing Protestant ideology. For this

> prevailing Protestant ideology represented a syncretistic
> mingling of the...religion of the denominations, which

was commonly articulated in terms of scholastic
Protestant orthodoxy and almost universally practiced
in terms of the experimental religion of pietistic
revivalism...(and) the religion of the democratic society
and nation.[30]

What the "prevailing Protestant ideology" assumed was the
solution to our religious and cultural dilemma, John Nevin
thought was a further symptom of deterioration.   His own
resolution of the dilemma rejects all four models of religious
reconstruction. To Nevin, America's spiritual predicament was
exemplified by its unhistorical and untheological biases.   All
four models were lacking in theological and historical integrity.
As a matter of fact, theology and history go hand in hand; and
only a sound recognition of this truth could save America from
the ravages of spiritual narcissism.   Restorationism (whether
modest   or   radical,   Campbellite   or   Mormon)   and
transcendentalism were products of the same frame of mind
that institutes revivalistic evangelicalism, with its dual axioms
of the Bible and Private Judgment.[31]

This prevailing American religion tended to view America
through the eyes of a new world nationalism.   From this
perspective America was merely a triumphant version of the
nationalistic impulse rampant in Europe, with the possible
distinction derived from the vision of America as a chosen,
covenant nation. New world nationalism is simply an extension
of the same principle at work in utilitarian individualism; it is a
nationalism   which   is   the   collectivization   of   individual
expectations.   The nation is the contractual and voluntary
association of individuals who will work out their destiny by the
maximization of self-interest. It is to be assumed that individual
claims and expectations are the measure of all goodness; that
the common good, the national good, is magnification of the
individual's pursuit of happiness.

Sacvan Bercovitch has argued that the "myth of America"
emerges out of the need to find sanctions for the hopes and
dreams of the people.   It was assumed by the emergent
Americans that their need to be successful in the building of a
"shining city on a hill" was sanctioned in holy scriptures and
would be made flesh in a new breed of humans.[32]   We may

not agree with Bercovitch about the theory of myth implicit in his argument. Certainly the model of humanity shared by the Puritans was a much more organic concept than the understanding which was to emerge by the nineteenth century when covenant becomes a contractual affair. The Puritan community still shared the mythic heritage of centuries of Catholic Christendom, in which a dialectical tension existed between the orders of creation and the drama of individual selfhood.[33] However, the agenda of Americans nurtured in the independent resourcefulness of the frontier existence readily converted the myth to individualistic utility. The levelling characteristics of the new nation were exceedingly utilitarian and democratic.

The religious spirit generated in this new nation became very contractual and collective. The Bible became a manual for individual spiritual resources or an oracle to be consulted in relation to individual needs naturally considered.

> Consider the alternative claims upon the promise by the self-reliant individual and the self-proclaimed nation of individualism. In that conflict lies a central cultural contradiction: the threat to society inherent in the very ideals of self-interest through which society justifies itself....The rhetoric implies that America's future, and by extension the fate of humanity, hinges on the efforts of the individual representative American.[34]

New world nationalism was in effect utilitarian individualism writ large. It was a spirituality which supported the needs of a people on the move, a nation on the make. Mobility, perfectibility, immediacy, independent resourcefulness, and competition were the agenda of the times. Robert Bellah defines utilitarian individualism as "the maximization of self-interest" with minimal restraints.[35] "Americans have tended to see their freedom and fulfillment," writes Ralph Ketcham, "as proportionate to their lack of public burden and intrusion."[36] Bellah maintains that "utilitarian individualism was never wholly compatible with the biblical tradition."[37] Perhaps not compatible with some essential or normative interpretation of biblical tradition; yet, revivalistic evangelicalism assisted in the transformation of the Bible into a utilitarian resource for individual spiritual expectations. The revivalistic evangelical tradition is very much in harmony with utilitarian individualism. It tends toward the maximization of individual spiritual self-interest. The Church becomes a collectivity of individual spiritual self-interest. And inasmuch as the Church is reduced to utilitarian significance, individuals may project their individual expectations onto a national collectivity as well. Both Church and state have no real covenant or organic reality; they do not represent anything more than collective self-interest, individually considered. Both are mechanical, collective realities.

This critique of American nationalism lies at the heart of John Nevin's understanding of "Catholicism" and his reflections on major public events in the middle of the nineteenth century. Nevin was the theologian of the Mercersburg movement, a nineteenth-century development in American religious thought that asserted itself against the mainstream of American Protestantism, particularly in its revivalistic evangelical forms. He rejected the Americanization of Christianity and affirmed the recovery of the fullness of the Catholic substance. Although historians like James Hastings Nichols have characterized the Mercersburg Theology as the American counterpart of the "traditionalist, 'churchly,' sacramental" romanticism sweeping across Europe "in the second generation of the nineteenth century," they fail to recognize that John Nevin had actually made a revolutionary discovery.[38] Nevin was not merely a spokesperson for the romantic counterbalance to the rationalism that had overtaken the Western world in the eighteenth and early-nineteenth centuries. As Nichols himself acknowledges by giving title to a chapter on "Nevin's 'Dizziness'," Nevin had discovered that the American fascination with individual salvation was a departure from the catholic character of the gospel.[39] The discovery was traumatic, especially as the significance of it descended ever more deeply into his thinking. It was not a discovery that was tenable among the ranks of American Protestants who were nurtured on anti-Catholicism, perfectionism, and utilitarian individualism.

From the beginning of his days at Marshall College and the German Reformed Seminary in Mercersburg, Nevin knew that his "Catholicism" was contrary to revivalistic evangelicalism and that it affected his understanding of American nationalism. "Catholicism" challenged the collective individualism of American religion and culture. It was not in harmony with the maximization of self-interest. For, as we have already seen, Nevin distinguished between **all** and **whole** as two interpretations of the universality implicit in the term "catholic." All, wrote Nevin, is an abstraction; it is merely a collective projection of individuals, "derived from the contemplation or thought of a certain number of separate individual existences, which are brought together in the mind and classified collectively by the notion of their common properties."[40] This kind of generality is limited because it "can never transcend the true bounds of the empirical process out of which it grows."[41] It is a totality existing only in the mind and strictly dependent upon units individually considered.

When **all** is the understanding of "catholic," salvation becomes a gathering, an association, a collective representation of totality. According to this view,

> the work of the gospel is...something comparatively outward to the proper life of man, and so a power exerted on it mechanically from abroad for its salvation, rather than redemption brought to pass in it from the inmost depths of its own nature. According to this view, the great purpose of gospel is to save men from hell, and bring them to heaven; this is accomplished by the machinery of the atonement and justification by faith, carrying along with it a sort of magical supernatural change of state and character by the power of the Holy Spirit, in conformity with the use of certain means for the purpose on the part of men; and so now it is taken to be the great work of the Church to carry forward the process of deliverance, almost exclusively under such mechanical aspect, by urging and helping as many souls as possible **in their separate individual** character to flee from the wrath to come and to secure for themselves through the grace of

conversion a good hope against the day of judgment.[42]

No redemption can be real for humankind individually taken, inasmuch as naked individuality is itself an abstraction. The view of the **all** is faced with the fact that many individuals born and unborn may never encounter Christ or acknowledge their own nature as completed in Him. Yet, according to Nevin, this fact in no way negates the catholic character of the Church. Catholicity is not dependent upon the numerical extent explicit in **all**.

The true meaning of catholic is expressed in the word "whole." Catholicity signifies a whole that is greater than the sum of its parts, an organic unity that radically rejects all partial claims and embraces individuality into itself. "The whole man...is not simply all the elements and powers that enter empirically into his constitution, but this living constitution itself rather as something more general than all such elements and powers, in virtue of which only they come to be thus what they are in fact."[43] Therefore, Christian salvation is catholic to the extent that it covers all constituent interests of human existence. Christianity is catholic in the sense that Christ is our original nature, the fulfillment of all our thoughts, actions, and aspirations. The Catholic Church affirms "that the last idea of this world as brought to its completion in man is made perfectly possible in the form of Christianity...and that this power can never cease to work until it shall have actually taken possession of the world as a whole, and shall thus stand openly and clearly revealed as the true consummation of its nature and history in every other view."[44] Catholicity measures "the entire length and breadth of man's nature." There is no constituent interest that is extrinsic to the catholicity represented by Christianity. Nevin's thought challenges not only the voluntaristic, contractual, and collectivist notion of the Church but the very understanding of salvation itself. Nevin's is a venture in *Heilsgeschichte*, making salvation a mediating and dynamic process. To use one of Nevin's favorite metaphors, it is a constitution of grace that takes the orders of the world into itself. There can be no salvation for the individual which is not at the same time real for humanity in one of many spheres of

moral existence. Salvation is never **mine**, it is **ours** as the
constitution of grace fulfills the partial aspirations of each,
always in relation to a greater whole than is envisioned or
desired by the individual separately considered. "The idea of
the true necessary wholeness of humanity is not helped at all,
by the numerical extent" of salvation among certain collections
of individuals.[45]

This is the point at which Nevin's understanding of
catholicity may be addressed to the role of America in
Heilsgeschichte. The state is not to be considered a "factitious
or accidental institution...continued for the use of man's life
from abroad and brought near to it only in an outward
manner."[46] The state belongs inherently to life. It is an
organic expression of the moral nature, part of the activity of
reason and will that is fundamental to existence. All states
derive their power and significance from this fact. In the
modern world, states tend to convert their roles as agencies in
the moral order into extensions of pride and self-interest
individually but collectively extended. This is nationalism, to
which the American Republic must not fall victim. There are
two essays by Nevin, written approximately 16 years apart,
that demonstrate this dimension of his thinking. Each is a
response to a crisis which Nevin credits with "world-historical"
significance. The first directs the reader's attention to the
revolutionary events of 1848 in Europe and their relation to the
role of America. The second is a discussion of the significance
of the Civil War, written at the end of that American conflict.

In his examination of "The Year 1848," Nevin invests it
with a significance like no other year since the Reformation. It
is an *annus mirabilis*, a time in which the minority of the
American Republic came to an end.[47] As European minds
sought to understand the critical events of 1848, they turned
with increased attention towards the new world across the
Atlantic. The unsettling of Europe took place just after three or
four years of American self-examination related to Texas,
Oregon, and Mexico. During those years, the "vortex of
excitement and agitation into which [America] was so suddenly
drawn" seemed to portend a revolution that would overturn the
new Republic and end in a catastrophe to match the
conflagrations of 1848 in Europe.[48] Instead, says Nevin,

"Texas has taken her place quietly...The Oregon boundary has been peacefully settled. The Mexican War has been conducted through a series of brilliant victories," and we have settled in "on the same political ground we occupied before."[49]

Now, of course, Nevin was writing just at the moment of all this critical circumstance. His view of history was myopic, and he may have been swept along by the spirit of his times. However, he did understand the difference between European revolutions and American upheavals. American success represented not the victory of a nation but the dawn of an epoch. It had to do with "the world-historical epoch [which may be compared]...with the mystic cloud at the Red Sea, which was all darkness, we are told, on one side, and on the other full of light."[50] To Nevin the institutions of the American experiment have demonstrated their "moral sublimity" that vindicated the role of the Republic in the struggle to set the world on its way to an appropriate response to the coaxing of Providence.[51] In Europe the breaking up of old institutions took place "as though this order of life had finished its course" at the same time that an "asylum" and "theater" were to be found for the proper "metempsychosis in the flow of universal history."[52] "We are not so foolish," wrote Nevin, "as to conceive of this under the form of a simple triumph of our national spirit, as it now stands, over the social and political institutions of the old world."[53] He rejected such notions as Manichaean and had no sympathy with the revolutionary actions in Europe as evidence of Providential activity. Those revolutions were "from beneath rather than from above." There is no reason to assume that the ultimate result of the process will be "the American state of society, as it now stands, substituted by universal exchange for every other political order."[54] Ours is not the perfect model of church and state. Here we are merely the theater in which the revolutionary spirit of Europe may view its own developing life.

However, Europe is not a grand failure, its monarchies not inferior modes of evil governance. There is no justification for a narrow American nationalism. That would be to assume that the substance of our life is fixed and under our own control as an individual nation especially "saved" and sharing its narrative of salvation with other nations individually considered. Instead,

Europe still has a role to play in what is happening to the world. For it is "the world itself...wrestling in its own inmost constitution, through the medium of American influence, towards a general and common end, which may be said to enhance the sense of its **whole** history for centuries past."[55] Providence works toward catholic wholeness, not allness. Neither America nor any other nation individually considered is saved; they merely exist in the *Heilsgeschichte*. They will be what they will be **together**. Any greatness for America is comprehended in that fact. We are not a Utica, said Nevin, tempted to make of ourselves the **measure** of the whole world. This may mean, in Nevin's thought, a rejection of the "city upon a hill" in favor of a "theater for the world." The new historical period is not to "proceed from the life of this country, just as it now stands, in an outward mechanical way." We are the theater for the working out of "a properly universal spirit." The wholeness which the world seeks and the catholicity of Christianity represents can counterbalance no "abstract Americanism." It is not a matter of gathering the peoples of the world together in a voluntary association of individuals. That is an abstract allness which can never be achieved. What is at stake is a gathering up of the **inward constitution**, "what is of worth in the mind and heart of all lands," so that what takes place is "an inward reproduction of their true sense under a new organic and universal form."[56] Nevin's understanding of Providence and the working of catholicity provide a comprehension of the nature of the Republic that is quite different from the emergent nationalism of his times.

His rejection of the salvational self-interest present in revivalistic evangelicalism is of a piece with his denial of abstract Americanism. The Bible-and-private judgment sectarianism of the former is the same principle at work in a kind of sectarian nationalism that makes the Republic a voluntary association of individuals maximizing their own self-interest and set apart from the rest of the world in collective pride.

At the close of the Civil War, Nevin lectured on "The Nation's Second Birth." There are nations, he said, which are representative nations, like representative persons. They "take up into themselves and show forth at a given time, beyond others, the central stream of history, regarded as being for the world at large."[57] Such occasions are world-historical; they reveal a course and a resolution quite beyond, often against, "the sense and purpose of the powers that have been employed to bring it to pass."[58] The Civil War, for example, was resolved in a way that defied past experience; the opinion abroad was of our "total and perpetual eclipse." The crisis was too great, too profound, to be handled by any plan of human wisdom. Abraham Lincoln, Nevin reminded his auditors at Franklin and Marshall College, was an astute servant of Providence, who had "a sense of uncertain dependence on the course of events." He committed himself to the circumstances without regard to personal importance. In order that America's deliverance could assume its world-historical role, what God had wrought had to become what humankind elected and sought to understand.[59]

The war was "the nation's second birth." Like the year 1848, the end of the Republic's minority, it was world historical. Perhaps the War occurred because the Republic had failed to take into its "inward constitution" what Providence had been pointing to in the Grand Crisis of 1848. "In Christ," wrote Nevin in a response to Orestes Brownson,

> most literally and truly, the supernatural order came to a living and perpetual marriage with the order of nature; which it could not have done, if the constitution of the one had not been of like sort with that of the other (man made in the image truly of God), **so as to admit and require such union as the last and only perfect expression of the world's life**. It lies then in the nature of the case, that Christ can be no abstraction, no solitary portent, in the midst of the world.[60]

The only real alternative to America's historyless sectarianism was a high doctrine of the Church, which manifests the wholeness for which the world is searching. Nevin's catholicity was radical because it refused to be satisfied with any penultimate or heteronomous claims upon the wholeness that bears within itself the capacity and power to embrace the whole world. The Holy Catholic Church is quite visible in its sacramental reality, but it is an organic whole greater than the sum of its parts. To sectarianism of any kind it says: You are claiming for yourself what can only belong to the whole. The Church has the power to lift the natural life of humanity to a level beyond ordinary knowledge, beyond nature.[61]

Nevin's views of the Christ and of the Church ran contrary to the mainstream of American religion. Nevertheless, they sought to be a contribution to the spiritual dilemma of the American epoch. Prevalent forms of American religion were not equal to the onward movement of the world. Instead, they were symptomatic of its disruptive underside.

ENDNOTES

1. Frederick Merk, *Manifest Destiny and Mission in America* (New York: Vintage Books, 1966), 199.

2. Merk, 201.

3. Winthrop S. Hudson, *Nationalism and Religion in America* (New York: Harper & Row, 1970), 56.

4. Robert Bellah, *The Broken Covenant* (New York: The Seabury Press, 1975), 23.

5. Edwin S. Gaustad, *A Documentary History of Religion in America to the Civil War* (Grand Rapids, MI: Wm. B. Eerdmans, 1982), 5, 37-38.

6. Sidney E. Mead, *The Lively Experiment: The Shaping of Christianity in America* (New York: Harper & Row, 1963), 55-56.

7. Jan Shipps, *Mormonism* (Urbana and Chicago: University of Illinois, 1985), 34.

8. Henry May, *Ideas, Faiths & Feelings. Essays on American Intellectual & Religious History* (New York: Oxford University Press, 1983), 67.

9. May, 171.

10. Orestes Brownson, *Brownson's Quarterly Review* 4 (1847): 473-474.

11. Martin E. Marty, *The Modern Schism* (New York: Harper & Row, 1969), 9.

12. Marty, 134.

13. Sydney Ahlstrom, "From Sinai to the Golden Gate," in *Understanding the New Religions,* ed. Jacob Needleman and George Baker (New York: The Seabury Press, 1978), 10, 11.

14. Edwin S. Gaustad, *Dissent in American Religion* (Chicago: University of Chicago Press, 1973), 315.

15. John Williamson Nevin, "The Sect System," *The Mercersburg Review* 1 (1849): 499.

16. Giles Gunn, *New World Metaphysics* (New York: Oxford University Press, 1981), 171.

17. Nevin, "The Sect System," 495.

18. Edmund Morgan, *Visible Saints* (Ithaca and London: Cornell University Press, 1963), 42-47.

19. Nevin, "The Sect System," 492.

20. Ibid., 493.

21. Ibid., 495.

22. May, 53.

23. Nicholas Berdyaev, *The Destiny of Man* (London: Geoffrey Bles, 1937), 114.

24. John Williamson Nevin, *The Anxious Bench* (Chambersburg, PA: Publication Office of the German Reformed Church, 1844). Reprinted in *Catholic and Reformed: Selected Theological Writings on John Williamson Nevin*, ed. Charles Yrigoyen, Jr. and George H. Bricker (Pittsburgh: The Pickwick Press, 1978), 98-99.

25. Gaustad, *Dissent in American Religion*, 6.

26. Mead, 7.

27. John Williamson Nevin, "Catholicism," *The Mercersburg Review* 3 (1851): 2-3,17,20.

28. May, 149.

29. Mead, 65.

30. Ibid., 135.

31. Nevin, "The Sect System," 503.

32. Sacvan Bercovitch, in *The Bible and American Arts and Letters,* ed. Giles Gunn (Philadelphia: Fortress Press, 1983), 221-29.

33. See Reinhold Niebuhr, *The Self and the Dramas of History* (New York: Charles Scribner's Sons, 1955), passim.

34. Bercovitch, 226.

35. Robert Bellah, *Varieties of Civil Religion* (New York: Harper & Row, 1980), 170.

36. Ralph Ketcham, *Individualism and Public Life* (New York: Basil Blackwell, 1987), viii.

37. Bellah, *Varieties of Civil Religion,* 169.

38. James Hastings Nichols, *Romanticism in American Theology* (Chicago: The University of Chicago Press, 1961), 3.

39. Nichols, 192-217.

40. Nevin, "Catholicism," 2.

41. Ibid., 3.

42. Ibid., 7.

43. Ibid., 3.

44. Ibid., 5.

45. Ibid., 10.

46. Ibid.

47. John Williamson Nevin, "The Year 1848," *The Mercersburg Review* 1 (1849): 21.

48. Ibid., 22.

49. Ibid.

50. Ibid., 23.

51. Ibid., 24.

52. Ibid., 26.

53. Ibid, 28-29.

54. Ibid., 30.

55. Ibid.

56. Ibid., 33.

57. John Williamson Nevin, "The Nation's Second Birth," *Reformed Church Messenger* 30 (July 26, 1865): 1.

58. Nevin, "The Nation's Second Birth," 1.

59. Ibid.

60. John Williamson Nevin, "Brownson's Quarterly Review," *The Mercersburg Review* 2 (1850): 65.

61. Nevin, "Catholicism," 23-26.

Nevin's Idealistic Philosophy

William DiPuccio

It should come as no surprise that for Nevin the incarnation was as paradigmatic for philosophy as it was for theology. The manifestation of God in human flesh was nothing less than the corporification of the spiritual and ideal in time and space. Indeed it is the epitome of what can only be described as a "law of reification" by which the entire sensible order is regarded as the embodiment of a vast spiritual cosmos of powers. The world is a sacrament of the divine.

Nevin viewed the creation as an organism — the product of a single, genetic idea — distinguished by two fundamental orders of being: the ideal (or spiritual) and the spacio-temporal.[1] The spiritual world is the "region of ends and causes from which continually go forth as effects all things belonging to the world of nature."[2] There is, therefore, such an affinity between the spatio-temporal and the ideal that the true significance of the former is realized only as it is assumed by the latter.

This organic union reaches its apex in humanity which is the microcosm of creation.[3] The human body is the acme of sensible nature. The human spirit marks the passage of nature from blind necessity and darkness to will and intelligence. In man, the universal ideal and finite nature are organically united in the power of a common life. The salient point of this life does not rest in the forces of matter, but in the human personality which **externalizes** itself as a body.[4] In assuming a body, therefore, the personality answers the longing of nature for rational and spiritual communion. But this inner necessity can only be consummated when the purpose of humanity itself is realized through a union with the divine. This is the genius of the incarnation.

The implication of this incarnational paradigm is simple but profound: In creation, reality is the synthesis of the ideal and the actual. The former is universal, eternal, and objective; the latter is particular, temporal, and subjective.[5] Hence, the ideal, if it is to be real, must always be mediated through the historical. Conversely, the historical must always be grounded in the universal. "To be **real**," says Nevin in *The Mystical Presence*, "the human as such, and of course the divine also in human form, must ever externalize its inward life." Indeed, the more spiritual a state is, the more it is moved by an inward necessity to actualize itself in this way.[6] Without this union, reality is attenuated into sheer nullity.

As the divine and human natures of Christ are united organically in His person, so the ideal and actual are organically united in the real. The incarnation is the union of two distinct orders, God and creation, accomplished in the assumption of human nature by the divine Logos. By analogy, this union is the archetype for uniting the universal and the particular, the invisible and the visible, and the one and the many. It is an exemplar showing how distinct things, unlike in their natures, are united into an indivisible whole without transmutation or separation, as Chalcedon said.[7]

The actualization of the ideal in space and time is, as we will later show, the philosophical *fons et origo* of the Mercersburg Theology. The incarnation, the Church, the sacraments, the liturgy, and the Word are the reification of Christ's glorified life and His eternal kingdom. Through Christianity "the powers of the world to come" are actually made present in this fallen world.

THE FORMATION OF NEVIN'S PHILOSOPHY

Nevin came to realize the significance of the incarnation only after a long search for truth. His christology came last rather than first in the sequence of his intellectual development. But whatever the chronological order of his discoveries, it is clear that in the order of being (relative to creation) the incarnation was, in his eyes, prior to all else.

The origin of Nevin's philosophy is not easily discernable. He was first and foremost a theologian rather than a philosopher. His quest for truth, therefore, was not so much philosophical as it was pietistic.[8]   He left no corpus of philosophical writings which would enable the historian to readily trace the evolution of his thought. We are left to forage through his theological writings and classroom lectures for insights into his philosophy. The problem is further exacerbated by the sparsity of his early writings (i.e., before 1840). Nevertheless, Nevin's philosophical ideas are so carefully woven into the fabric of his theology that they often declare themselves with unmistakable clarity.

Like the British romantic poet, S. T. Coleridge, Nevin worked out his metaphysics within the broad outline of Kantian idealism and Christian Platonism. This peculiar adaptation of Kant's philosophy by romantics like Nevin and Coleridge highlights the critical disposition of their systems: they acknowledged that the relationship between being and intelligibility was a problem to be reckoned with. Over and against the *tabula rasa* psychology of the Lockean-empirical tradition, they recognized the active contribution made by the subject in the process of knowing.

Nevin's acceptance of the Kantian problem, however, represented more than a desire to align himself with contemporary philosophy. He addressed the epistemological problem theologically as well as philosophically by drawing from the Platonic-Augustinian heritage. In this tradition, knowing entails subjective participation and communion with the object of knowledge, not detachment and passivity as Enlightenment empiricism had imagined. In Nevin's mind, the empiricist view was more than a philosophical error, it was the root of carnal religion. The religion of the carnal mind, he tells us, "is all mechanical, a system of notions and observances artificially grafted on their lives from without. It stands in no organic connection with its own nature, as a development of life from within."[9]

For Nevin, the Kantian problem not only demonstrated the necessity of abandoning the unworkable epistemology of the Enlightenment—an epistemology rooted in Descartes' radical divorce of mind and world—but also pointed the way back to a deeper and more spiritual concept of knowledge. His turn to the subject was not so much a turning to self (Descartes), as a turning to the Logos by whose light the self can be seen. As Augustine sought after God in his memory, so Nevin, Coleridge, and others like them, turned inward to gaze upon the light of Christ in the soul. Yet, unlike the Bishop of Hippo who regarded the world of sense as merely the occasion of knowledge, Nevin viewed truth as substantially incarnate — the ideal in the actual.

The Actual: Nevin's Empiricism

Despite Nevin's later repudiation of empiricism, we should never underestimate the impact that this tradition had on his subsequent philosophy. He was educated at Princeton which had become the guardian of Scottish realism or "Common Sense." This is to say nothing of the fact that the very character of American culture in his day was rooted and shaped by the Enlightenment and the empiricist tradition.

Nevin's empiricist disposition could be seen in his early fascination with history and science. His first major work, *Biblical Antiquities* (1828), was devoted to the geography, natural history, and culture of the Holy Land. In the 1830s he began reading J. A. W. Neander's (1789-1850) *Allgemeine Geschichte der christlichen Religion und Kirche*.[10] As editor of *The Friend* (Pittsburgh) from 1833-1835, he republished a lengthy series on the "Objects, Advantages, and Pleasures of Science" from *The Library of Useful Knowledge*. He also published a series of letters addressed to Louis Merchand, M.D., from his friend and former pupil David Porter, M.D., which attempted to explain "Laws of Nature."[11] Later, at Marshall College, he filled vacancies in the faculty by teaching higher mathematics, mechanics, and astronomy.[12]

Though Nevin's turn toward idealism was a reaction against the rationalism and incipient materialism of the empirical tradition, his early empiricism left a stubborn residue which can be seen in the rich historical and scientific texture of his theology. It was not the empirical itself to which he objected; rather, it was the mistaken notion that only self-evidencing reality lies in the sphere of the senses. Locke and the Common Sense philosophers (i.e., the Baconians) had reduced the ideal to mere actuality by turning ideas into nominal abstractions (i.e., creations of the human intellect based on inductive generalizations of actual phenomena, as opposed to objective, universal, realities).[13] This error of "misplaced concretion" led ineluctably to evidentialism which attempted to demonstrate the veracity of Christianity by appealing to miracles and other sensible phenomena. Nevin, on the other hand, began with the self-authenticating reality of the spiritual which announces itself to the eye of faith. Once this is admitted, the idea of miracles follows naturally as the historical realization of Christ's power and glory.

The Ideal: Puritan Piety and Platonism

The 1830s marked the formative period of Nevin's idealism. The Cartesian dualism (viz., mind/matter) inherent in the empirical tradition, however, clung to him for some time. For the most part, he continued to "disconnect" the ideal from the actual, despite occasional attempts to unite these spheres using the organic model. However, all this would change with Nevin's arrival at Mercersburg where he encountered the German (i.e., Hegelian) idealism of Frederich Augustus Rauch.

Nevin found in Plato fertile ground for his mystical and pietistic inclinations. In his autobiography, he tells us that his evangelical piety was shaped largely by English divines such as Richard Baxter (1615-1691), John Flavel (d. 1691), John Owen (1616-1683), John Howe (1630-1705), Archbishop Robert Leighton (1611-1684), and Henry Scougal (1650-1678), as well as the German mystic, Thomas á Kempis (ca. 1380-1471). Among these he credits Howe, and especially Leighton, with having the greatest influence on him.[14]

The young scholar found both Howe and Leighton congenial to his Platonism. In an early work, after recommending the heavenlyminded Plato, he praises Leighton, saying, "Such influence, as a sacred stream flowing fast by the oracle of God, yet lives in every page of the seraphic, peace-loving Leighton."[15] The writings of the much esteemed John Howe, who was a friend of the Cambridge Platonists (Ralph Cudworth, Henry More, and John Smith) were thoroughly platonic in their approach to Christianity. The "deep Platonizing thoughts" of Howe, says Nevin, "took hold on my mind with great force."[16] As Howe's biographer remarks, "None can peruse his writings, without seeing in almost every page, traces of his ardent admiration of Plato; and it was the admiration of a kindred mind."[17]   Nevin probably read Howe's, *The Living Temple of God, Delighting in God, The Blessedness of the Righteous*, and *The Redeemer's Dominion over the Invisible World*. All these works, as the titles suggest, are permeated with a pietistic sense of God's mystical union with the soul and a conviction of the reality of the spiritual world.

It is clear, therefore, that Nevin's Platonism grew more immediately out of his spirituality rather than his philosophical training.   The latter, however, cannot be wholly discounted since even at an early age Nevin received thorough instruction in Latin and Greek by his father.[18] Such a classical education would have exposed the budding scholar to the Greek philosophers. It is probably not coincidental that while at Union College (1817-1821) he befriended the Platonist Taylor Lewis.[19] In any event, by the time he reached his thirties, Nevin had apparently read Plato in the original language. He cites Karl C. T. Tauchnitz's (1761-1836) Greek edition of Plato's works in one of his early sermons.[20]

What was it about Platonism and the spiritual mystics that held so much fascination for Nevin? He addresses this question in his autobiography: "It had to do with **ideas** at least, which were held to be of objective force, and not merely subjective notions and fancies." Nevin had struggled with the subjective rationalism that evolved out of eighteenth-century pietism. While he was sympathetic to pietism, he rejected its one-sided subjectivity.   In men like Howe and Leighton, he found a corresponding objectivity which brought to life the reality of the spiritual realm and, we may add, the transitoriness of this sensual life. The Platonic contrast between the shadowy world of sense and the brilliant reality of the spiritual was a fixed point in Nevin's writings. His feelings of mortality were stoked, no doubt, by a chronic dyspepsia which clung to him with a "death-like grasp" and seemed to betoken an early death.[21]

Nevin spoke frequently, especially in his early writings (1830's), about the "slavery of matter" and the "dark and narrow sphere of mere sense." "We are never properly **ourselves**," he says, "till we have waked within us the lively consciousness of our relationship to forms of truth and modes of being, of an immeasurably higher order than any with which we become acquainted through the medium of sense." Nevin considered **faith** as the medium by which we commune with these spiritual realities—a concept which he would maintain throughout his life. It is, as he said in 1833, a "deep feeling of the reality of eternal things, overpowering the impressions of sense...."[22]

Like Plato, Nevin was fond of drawing analogies between the reality of the corporeal world and the reality of the spiritual/ideal world. As astronomy consists in "facts," "real phenomena, and things actually taking place in the living world...", so Scripture is the "transcript" of the "truths of religion" not in "abstract form" but "as they are found historically active in the mind of God and the mind of the human sinner." They are "an actual impression taken from the things themselves just as they are." By contrast, he regarded nature as the "shadowy adumbration of spiritual, invisible realities...."[23]

As an antidote to sectarianism, Nevin appealed to the "philosophy of the skies embodied in the mind of Plato." Our connatural home is in "the empyrean sphere of absolute and eternal truth." It is communion with the *ta onta* (ontic) and the *ta agathon* (holy) we seek, not the *ta phainomena* (phenomenal). The medium of the former is "the self evidencing light of the Truth itself" known by the "organ of pure reason." The medium of the latter is sense, which, without this higher vision, is no better than "a sort of drunken delirium."[24] Nevin's speech, as his biographer correctly observed, "shows the indications of a true Christian Platonism, which subsequently expanded and became an underlying element both in his theological and philosophical writings."[25]

Epistemology: Kant, Plato, and Coleridge

The center of Nevin's incarnational philosophy, the ideal in the actual, is also the basis of his epistemology. Reality is the union of the individual mind with nature (i.e., the actual) in order to discern its ideas under a universal form (i.e., the ideal prototype).   Knowledge involves a real conjunction, a communion and participation, of subject and object.[26]   The knowing mind must be organically united to the object of knowledge. Nevin's Presbyterian and Puritanical piety, coupled with his Christian Platonism, formed the ground for his theory of knowledge. His mentors at Princeton, Charles Hodge (1797-1878) and Archibald Alexander (1772-1851), were both deeply spiritual.   The locus of their pietism—Nevin's *unio mystica*—readily lends itself to an epistemology of communion.

However, Nevin's Platonism pressed beyond Reformed and Puritanical piety.   Even in the 1830s, before his arrival at Mercersburg, it was assuming the dimensions of a philosophical system.   The cause of this development was his increasing exposure to Neander (a disciple of Schleiermacher) and romantic exegetes such as Robert Lowth (1711-1787), J. G. von Herder (1744-1803), and Hermann Olshausen (1796-1839).   All of these thinkers emphasized the necessity of forming a sympathetic relation between the interpreter, the author, and the object of a particular work.[27]

Nevin also found a kindred spirit in the Platonic philosophy of S. T. Coleridge (1772-1834).[28] Like Nevin, Coleridge had turned from the English empiricist tradition to Plato and German idealism.   It is not surprising, then, that both men shared a similar philosophy, even though this likeness did not always carry over into their theologies. The influence of Coleridge is not always easy to discern in Nevin's writings.[29] Nevertheless, there existed not only a sympathy between these two men on certain philosophical issues, but in the area of faith and reason at least, we can discern a more definite influence upon Nevin by the British poet.

As a Christian Platonist, Nevin followed Coleridge in attributing to the soul the innate capacity for beholding "the eternal, the necessary, the universal" with the same immediacy as corporeal vision.[30]   He adopted Coleridge's sharp distinction between "Understanding" and "Reason"* which is founded on Plato's analogy of the divided line.[31]

The adaptation of Kantian philosophy by Nevin and Coleridge was fueled, at least in part, by a romantic animosity towards the Enlightenment. In Kant's categories Coleridge found both the antidote to materialism and the speculative boundaries of empiricism. By relegating sensible data to merely phenomenal categories, Kant prevented empiricism from making any metaphysical claims about the noumenal. The knowledge obtained through "Understanding" (which is subject to spatio-temporal categories) can never become the basis of metaphysical speculation or religious knowledge. So far as Coleridge was concerned, therefore, philosophy is beholden always to a higher (i.e., Platonic) "Reason" which enables us to perceive the ideal unity of reality.[32]

Nevin, expressed similar sympathies. In *A Plea for Philosophy*, he concludes with a bitter invective against Locke, Baconianism, and the Common Sense tradition. "The general character of this bastard philosophy is, that it affects to measure all things, both on earth and in heaven, by the categories of the common abstract understanding, as it stands related simply to the world of time and sense." But as Kant has demonstrated, these categories are only the "forms or types" of sensible reality and represent "the conditions merely of existence in space and time..." It was Kant, therefore, who struck the fatal blow against the pretensions of empiricism which aspired to build a metaphysic of the "absolute and infinite upon deductions from the simply relative and finite." As the French Revolution has shown, the whole tendency of empirical philosophy is "towards materialism and infidelity."[33]

Even more than Coleridge, however, Nevin was very cautious in his endorsement of Kant. Though in full agreement with Kant's demolition of systematic empiricism, his metaphysical skepticism was not welcome. Indeed, Nevin's mystical pietism and his Platonic epistemology defied the very spirit of Kant's agnosticism regarding the noumenal. Through

---

*Based on this evidence, it is not unlikely that Nevin had read Coleridge's celebrated works, *The Friend* and *Aids to Reflection*.

the organ of Reason, elevated by faith, we **can** commune with the ontic, the noumenal, and the holy. Therefore, after adapting Kant's contribution to philosophy, Nevin calls for "pressing forward to still higher ground."

The Ideal in the Actual: The Integration of Nevin's Philosophy

Nevin's epistemology was the first step toward an integrated philosophy. By the early 1830s he had come to realize that all knowledge involves the actualization of an ideal or spiritual object in a knowing subject. As early as 1831 there were already indications that he viewed history as the externalization of universal ideas.[34] The same is true of his view of language which, as he said, "embodies" the "mind" of the nation to which it belongs. In order to understand its thoughts we must know the "world of life" from which it sprang, hence, the value of archaeology and history.[35]

This movement toward full integration, though promising, was only the beginning. Nevin had not yet conceived the full implications of these ideas for theology. When he arrived at Western Theological Seminary in 1830, he was still in the grip of dualism. His christology was far from incarnational, his ecclesiology was still mechanistic, predestinarian, and ahistorical.[36] Even by the end of the decade, the dualism, still at work in his thinking, was not difficult to discern. His solution to the problem of "Party Spirit" was thoroughly Platonic: "Soar in spirit above the region of sense and particular opinion, always darkened by the mists, if not agitated by the storms, of passions; and let your home be, mainly at least, in the empyrean sphere of absolute and eternal truth."[37]

The crystallization of Nevin's philosophy was wrought by the work of his one-time friend and Mercersburg colleague Frederick A. Rauch (1806-1841), author of *Psychology; or, a View of the Human Soul*. Nevin arrived in Mercersburg in 1840. Less than a year later, Rauch passed away, leaving the revision of his work unfinished. Nevin completed the editing of the second edition in 1841. A year later, he was already mastering the principles of Rauch's German idealism. In an address on "The German Language," he repeatedly applies Rauch's organic concepts in order to explain the relation between thought and language.[38]

Rauch attempted to unite German idealism and American mental philosophy, as he tells us in the preface to his *Psychology*. His work was the first American exposition of Hegel's philosophy of mind.[39]   Besides the conservative Hegelians, Caurus, Daub, and Rosenkranz, "whose general arrangement he has adopted not without some improvement, however, as he hopes," he also used Locke, Stewart, Reid, and Brown.[40]   According to Nevin (writing in a review of Rauch's work), Rauch is in substantial agreement with Locke in grounding the development of the soul upon the sensuous life; but, he departs from the empiricist tradition by teaching that such experience serves only as the condition for such development. Thus, Rauch's philosophy differs generically from the Scotch-English school in that it is "spiritual more than sensuous. It looks to the real, more than the phenomenal." It does this, however, without falling over into transcendentalism. Nevin commended Rauch for his attempt to unite the German and Scotch philosophies "upon a common ground" and hailed his work "as constituting an **epoch** in the history of philosophy, for this country."[41]   It was, of course, used by Nevin at Marshall College for many years and, according to his biographer, was well adapted to his "idealistic, platonizing tendencies." As Appel correctly observes, "it exerted a potent influence in giving form to his subsequent philosophical thinking and doctrines."[42]

The genius of Rauch's philosophy was his paradigmatic use of the organic idea to unite the ideal and the actual. It was the perfect fusion of Nevin's Platonic yen for ideas, his romantic affinity for organic holism,[43] and his stubborn empiricism. Rauch defines the essence of all life as a "plastic power placed in matter by the divine will." It "materializes, attracts matter, assumes volume, produces fibers...," etc.[44]   Living beings grow "from an invisible power, according to certain unchangeable laws." It is this ideal power "which upholds the species and individuals, and universally produces the same forms according to the same unchangeable laws."[45]   These laws, says Rauch, have an objective existence. General ideas are not merely abstractions, "they truly **exist**...they are the pure being and nature of individual things, their soul, and life." In the sphere of nature, they are the *genus* in the sphere of mind they are the **identity**; and in the sphere of science, they are **generality**.[46]

Nevin's first attempt to apply these principles to theology came in the second edition of the *The Anxious Bench* (1844). He concluded that the priority of the universal ideal was the antidote to individualism, sectarianism, and subjective religion. This solution was not unlike the remedy he proposed five years earlier in his address on "Party Spirit" (see above). There is one important difference however: Whereas before Nevin had viewed the relationship between the ideal and the actual dualistically, now he regarded them organically—i.e., united, one in the other so that the actual is the externalization of the ideal in time and space.

Writing in *The Anxious Bench*, Nevin contended that true religious conversion takes place only as the particular becomes a "tributary to the tendencies and purposes" of the general. In the catechetical system, "the general must go before the particular and support it as its proper ground." Thus, sin is not simply the "offspring of a particular will," but "a general and universal force, which includes and rules the entire existence of the individual man..." Likewise, salvation begins beyond the individual. Fallen humanity is raised in Christ. The individual is saved by a "living union with Christ" through the medium of the Church, not unlike the bond by which he has been joined to Adam. The system of "new measures," on the other hand, is based on a scheme of sin and salvation which is strictly individual.[47]

This, as Nevin would later acknowledge, was the beginning of the Mercersburg Theology.[48] But we should not suppose that Nevin simply reasoned from Rauch's philosophical principles to the incarnation. The process was advanced by his theological studies. Schleiermacher and his disciple Neander played a prominent role in the formation of Nevin's christology. Both understood the incarnation as the historical concretion of the ideal.[49]

THE SIGNIFICANCE OF NEVIN'S PHILOSOPHY
FOR MERCERSBURG THEOLOGY

A whole new world of theology and philosophy opened up for Nevin with the discovery of the incarnational paradigm. The Church, the sacraments, and the scriptures became for him the very embodiment of Christ's glorified humanity in the life of the world. The ideal and the spiritual, thus, are externalized in history.[50]

The Church

The **ideal** Church, says Nevin, is an organic system of life centered upon Christ—a new order of humanity bearing the same constitution as the first humanity under Adam. Since the Church comprehends in itself the "deepest life of humanity," its existence could never be simply inward and invisible. Just as the idea of humanity supposes a body, so the idea of the Church includes visibility as an organic body "in whose presence alone all individual Christianity becomes real."[51]

The **actual** Church is the historical Church which extends from the incarnation to the present. It is the "externalization" of the ideal in space and time. In its ideal aspect it remains unchanged throughout the vicissitudes of history because it is grounded in the power of a single fact, viz., the life of Christ. But as a truly historical constitution, it is in the process of moving toward what it is ideally. Historical development, therefore, is the ongoing actualization of the Church's ideal potential.[52]

Failure to recognize the unity of the ideal and the actual, as Nevin points out, results in a false ecclesiology and even a false christology. Sectarianism, as well as Calvinistic views of the Church which turn on the principle of predestination, so severs the ideal Church from the actual Church that they become two entirely separate orders (i.e., a dualism). The ideal Church becomes a gnostic abstraction. Its order and structure bear little or no resemblance to the empirical Church. The idea of historical development is thus negated. Catholicity and unity are said to be only spiritual and invisible ideals. The actual

Church may be fragmented into a million pieces, but all this is of no account so long as one recognizes its heavenly unity. This is the philosophy of sectarianism against which Schaff, and especially Nevin, expended so much labor.[53]

The organic union of the ideal and the actual, especially as it relates to the Church, is also embraced in one of Nevin's principle comparisons, namely between the **all** and the **whole**. Whereas the **whole** represents a real union between the ideal and the actual, the **all** never transcends the sphere of the actual and empirical. This was the locus of Nevin's critique of American religion and society. It symbolizes the contrast between a voluntary association constituted from the bottom, and an organic community which draws its life from a single center. The former is a product of democracy, empiricism, and individualism. The latter reflects the divine order of being.

The **all**, says Nevin, is merely an abstract collection of individuals grouped according to their common properties. It is strictly a finite quantity—limited by the "empirical aggregation" of individuals which comprise it. The individual, therefore, is primary, universality is secondary. The concept is reached by a process of induction and comparison beginning with single units and ending in generality. The unity in such a case is mechanical and outward. It is an arbitrary product of the mind. The individual components exist separately and independently of the totality. They lack an internal ground or power to unite them together.[54]

The **whole**, by contrast, is an organic concrete reality. "It is wrought," says Nevin, "into the very nature of the things themselves, and they grow forth from it as the necessary and perpetual ground of their own being and life." It is not, then, the product of individuals, but neither can it exist without them. Nevertheless, in the order of being, it is the individual which depends on and subsists in the whole as its "proper original." The parts do not exist independently or apart from the totality (as they might in a machine). Instead, they "draw their being from the universal unity itself in which they are comprehended, while they serve at the same time to bring it into view." This mode of generality, unlike the other, is infinite because it has no empirical limits. It is not "the creature of mere experience." Rather, as an idea it is always more than the actual totality of things in the world of sense and time at a given moment. It includes all potential as well as all actual phenomena.[55]

The application of this organic paradigm to theology was a watershed in Nevin's thinking. It became the basis upon which he distinguished his views of creation, predestination, humanity, Church, and society, from those of the prevailing American culture. The former are organic, objective, holistic, a priori, and deductive; the latter are atomistic, subjective, partial, empirical, and inductive. This position brought him into sharp conflict with a number of American theologians.[56]

The Sacraments

The general principle which underlies Nevin's idea of the sacraments is that they are an externalization of Christ's spiritual kingdom. The ideal becomes actual in space and time—a veritable incarnation of His invisible, theanthropic life. The sacraments, therefore, are the medium by which the hidden powers of the spiritual world are revealed. They are not empty or abstract signs, but "set us in communion with the positive actualities of that world" of grace.[57] What Nevin said about baptism is true of the sacraments generally, viz., "there is a real rending of the heavens—the canopy that separates the world of nature from the world of grace."[58]

Nevin believed that the "sacramental idea" is broader than the two sacraments of the Church. These sacraments do not exhaust the entire presence of the supernatural in the world. "The whole constitution of the world is sacramental, as being not simply the sign of, but the actual form and presence of invisible things." It is for this reason that the Church has not made a clear distinction between "the two regular sacraments" and the secondary sacraments designated by the Church.[59] This sacramental view of reality is also the basis of the liturgy. Like the sacraments, the liturgy is an externalization of the divine economy which grows out of the general life of the Church.[60]

The incarnation is the archetype for the sacraments insofar as it denominates the union of God and creation. Just as the Logos assumes common humanity and ennobles it while yet

preserving the integrity of the created order, so the grace of
God assumes the common elements of the sacraments and
sanctifies them without destroying their integrity.   The
"sacramental union" between the elements and the divine grace
is not, of course, on the same order as the hypostatic union
between Christ's natures.   The relationship is analogous and,
in each case, the union is commensurate with the constitution
of the assumed object.   In both cases the organic synthesis
effects a redemptive union between God and creation which, in
the order of being, fulfills the purpose and inward yearning of
creation for divine participation—a yearning which has been
thwarted by the fall.   A confusion of these natures would
destroy the integrity of creation.   A complete separation would
destroy the potential unity and redemption of creation since its
perfection is predicated on communion with God.

Herein lies the error of transubstantiation and symbolic
memorialism.   The latter destroys the unity and purpose of
creation by severing the sacramental elements from divine
grace.   The former amounts to a deification of creation.   "There
is a palpable contradiction," Nevin says, "in making Christ
identical with matter or symbol.   This is heathenism."[61]   This
principle is applicable to both baptism and the eucharist: "The
spiritual can never be imprisoned, or **banned**, in the bosom of
the mere natural."   Hence, the water of baptism can never be
the efficient cause of regeneration just as the bread and wine
could never themselves be the glorified life of the Lord.[62]

The Word

The Scriptures are the incarnation of the divine life in
human language.   The ideal is thus reified in the medium of
historical speech.   The *unio mystica* forms the link between
sacrament and word in Nevin's theology.   The **life** of Christ is
the "soul"   and animating spirit of both word and the
sacrament.   The external sign, in this case the spoken and
written word, must be united to the Spirit.   The life of the Word
incarnate is the substance of the word written.[63]

This view evolves directly out of Nevin's Christocentric
theology of the divine word and his concept of language.   The

word of God is not a static utterance, but a continuous emanation of the divine life. Creation is not merely a divine fiat taking effect upon the cosmos outwardly and mechanically, but a perpetual stream of life from God Himself filling the universe through His Word. This is how we are to understand the inspiration of the Bible as well. "It is the Word of God, in its ever-living supernal majesty, occupying and possessing the sacred text, not simply as the cause and origin of it at the first, but as its truly informing and actuating spirit through all time. Of the Bible it must be said always in this view, **God is there**."[64] What Jesus said about his words on one occasion is true of the Scriptures generally: They are **spirit** and **life**. His words are not abstractions; rather, "they stream out through all time from the fountain of life in His person." Consequently, they still sustain their original meaning and force as they hold the mystery of His presence.[65]

Nevin believed that the preached word is more powerful than the written word because it is a fuller incarnation of the life of Christ in the world. "Language," he remarks, "is thought itself corporealized and made external, and it must be penetrated of course with the same organic life in all its parts."[66] Words come from living beings and so embody the life from which they emanate. The Word must thus be incarnated both in its origin and in its dissemination. The spoken word, says Nevin, is more efficacious than the written, because the ear is a more inward sense than the eye. Sound reveals the inner constitution of things.[67] "The preaching of the Word," therefore, "implies the actual presence of the life which it represents...It embosoms the mind of the soul from which it proceeds." It is necessary, then, to embody the word in living preachers in order to be effective.[68]

Conclusion

Reality is the organic union of the ideal in the actual. This became the impelling force behind Nevin's philosophy and theology. Out of this one idea came three philosophical principles which Nevin used to construct his own theology and critique of American culture and religion: First, the ideal is an objective and universal reality rather than an abstract creature of the individual mind. Second, in the order of being, the ideal and universal come before the actual and the finite. Third, the ideal and the actual, though distinct, are inseparable and coinhere such that the ideal is always realized in and through the actual. For Nevin, these principles entailed the end of materialism, epistemological skepticism (religious and philosophical), individualism, and dualism.

Nevin constructed an ontology which viewed the spiritual and ideal as the *fundamentum* of the cosmos. His theology, therefore, was characteristically mystical and supernatural, emphasizing the archetypal nature of the divine and heavenly in all spheres of life and existence. Recognizing the limitations of empirical reasoning, Nevin's epistemology transcended Kant's critical limits with Platonic optimism. Yet he was keenly aware of the dynamic role of the subject in the act of knowing. His notion of faith, therefore, is both intuitional and objective. As in the case of natural vision, he believed that there is a innate disposition in the human spirit for the divine light of revelation.   Finally, in response to the individualism of Jacksonian democracy and religious sectarianism, Nevin emphasized the organic nature of Church and society.   The whole (i.e., universal) is prior to the individual.   The life of Christ, which is the Church's foundation, goes before its particular, historical manifestations.

In Nevin's view, the incarnation is prior to all philosophy. It is the paradigm or archetype of reality, the alpha and omega of creation. The philosophy of the ideal in the actual, therefore, is not simply a heuristic device. It reflects the order of being implicit in the constitution of creation, now made explicit by the manifestation of the Son of God.[69]

ENDNOTES

1.   See Nevin, "Election Not Contrary to a Free Gospel,"
     Presbyterian Preacher 2 (1833): 224; William H. Erb, ed. *Dr.
     Nevin's Theology, Based on Manuscript Class Room Lectures*
     (Reading: I. M. Beaver, 1913) 172-73, 187; Nevin, "Lectures on
     Aesthetics" transcribed by George D. Gurley, 1870-71,

AMsS, pp. 4-6, Archives of Franklin and Marshall College, uncatalogued. See also the summary of Nevin's lectures on aesthetics (1866-76), in Theodore Appel, *The Life and Work of John Williamson Nevin* (Philadelphia: The Reformed Church Publishing House, 1889) 668-70. Nevin sometimes used the ideal and the spiritual interchangeably. When referring to ideas, universal laws and powers, and the Divine, they are the same. When distinguishing these from finite spiritual beings (angels, humans), they are different.

2. Nevin, "The Spiritual World," *Reformed Quarterly Review* 23 (1876): 514. See idem, "Brownson's Quarterly Review Again," *Mercersburg Review* 2 (1850): 313-15.

3. On humanity and the order of being see Nevin, *The Mystical Presence, A Vindication of the Reformed or Calvinistic Doctrine of the Holy Eucharist* (Philadelphia: J. B. Lippincott & Co., 1846), 199-204; idem, "The Moral Order of Sex," *Mercersburg Review* 2 (1850): 549-72; idem, "Man's True Destiny," *Mercersburg Review* 5 (1853): 492-520; idem, "Natural and Supernatural," *Mercersburg Review* 11 (1859): 176-210; idem, "The Wonderful Nature of Man," in Appel, *Life and Work*, 515-28 (reprinted from *Mercersburg Review* 11 [1859]: 317-36); idem, "Christianity and Humanity," *Mercersburg Review* 20 (1873): 469-86.

4. John Williamson Nevin, *Human Freedom and a Plea for Philosophy: Two Essays* (Mercersburg: P.A. Rice, 1850) 5-7; idem, *The Mystical Presence*, 156-57, 171-73; F. A. Rauch, *Psychology; or, a View of the Human Soul*, 4th ed., with a notice by John W. Nevin (New York: M.W. Dodd, 1846), 180-85.

5. John Williamson Nevin, *Human Freedom and a Plea for Philosophy*, 3-5. This essay, along with "Christianity and Humanity," *Mercersburg Review* 20 (1873): 469-86, provide the most lucid statements of Nevin's philosophy.

6. John Williamson Nevin, *The Mystical Presence*, 3-4; idem, *The Church* (Chambersburg, PA: German Reformed Church Publishing House, 1847), 10.

7. See Erb, *Dr. Nevin's Theology*, 177.

8. I am grateful to David Layman for his suggestion that Nevin's theology and philosophy developed out of his piety of the mystical union.

9. John Williamson Nevin, *The Seal of the Spirit* (Pittsburgh: William Allinder, 1838), 8.

10. John Williamson Nevin, *My Own Life: The Early Years* (Lancaster: Historical Society of the Reformed Church, 1964), 139-40. Originally published in *The Weekly Messenger of the German Reformed Church*, March-June 1870.

11. *The Friend*, 9 May 1833 - 11 July 1833; 18 December 1834 - 12 March 1835.

12. Appel, *Life and Work of John Williamson Nevin*, 438.

13. To a large degree, Nevin's philosophical struggle with Common Sense turned on the distinction between nominalism and realism. In his classroom lectures, he closed his review of Locke by accusing him of turning "general ideas" into "mere creations of thought" after the manner of medieval nominalism. See John Williamson Nevin, *History of Philosophy Lectures*, transcribed by George B. Russel [1850], AMsS, pp. 11-12, 78, Archives of the United Church of Christ & the Evangelical & Reformed Historical Society, Lancaster.

14. Nevin, *My Own Life*, 122, 127.

15. John Williamson Nevin, *Party Spirit* (Chambersburg, PA: Publication Office of the German Reformed Church, 1840), 28.

16. Nevin, *My Own Life*, 122.

17. Henry Rogers, *The Life and Character of John Howe, M.A.* (London: William Ball, 1836) 22.

18. Nevin, *My Own Life*, 5-6; Appel, *Life and Work of John Williamson Nevin*, 33.

19. See Appel, *Life and Work of John Williamson Nevin*, 36, 253. Lewis later wrote an insightful review on "The Mercersburg School of Theology and Philosophy," *The Literary World* 14 (April 1849).

20. Nevin, *Party Spirit*, 13.

21. Nevin, *My Own Life*, 122, 12.

22. John Williamson Nevin, "The Active Christian," *The Friend*, 22 August 1833; Nevin, "Essay on the Interpretation of the Bible," *The Friend*, 11 July 1833, 6 June 1833.

23. Nevin, "Religion a Life," *The Friend*, 15 Jan 1835.

24. Nevin, *Party Spirit*, 13, 26-27.

25. Appel, *Life and Work of John Williamson Nevin*, 124. See also Theodore Appel, *Recollections of College Life at Marshall College* (Reading: Daniel Miller, 1886), 304, 306, 314.

26. Nevin, "Brownson's Quarterly Review Again," 2 (1850): 318-19. This is also Nevin's view of human freedom (adopted from Rauch). The divine will (ideal) is realized historically in the individual will (actual). The particular will moves spontaneously in the orbit of the universal will, being of the same nature with the law itself. So, in obeying the law it is obeying its own constitution. See Nevin, *Human Freedom*; Rauch, *Psychology*, 154-56, 281, 293-94. This was anticipated by Nevin's earlier concept of freedom; see John Williamson Nevin, "Election," *The Presbyterian Preacher* 2 (1833): 222.

27. See Nevin, *My Own Life*, 41-42, 137-38.

28. For a general essay and bibliography on Coleridge's theology, see Claude Welch, "Samuel Taylor Coleridge," in *Nineteenth Century Religious Thought in the West*, ed. Ninian Smart, John Clayton, Steven Katz, and Patrick Sherry (Cambridge: Cambridge University Press, 1985), 2:1-28.

29. John Williamson Nevin, *Antichrist, or the Spirit of Sect and Schism* (New York: John S. Taylor, 1848), 3-4.

30. Nevin, *Party Spirit*, 13; see also John Williamson Nevin, "The Apostle's Creed," *Mercersburg Review* 1 (1849): 207-8. Cf. Coleridge, *The Friend*, in *The Collected Works of Samuel Taylor Coleridge* 1, ed. Barbara E. Rooke (Princeton: Routledge & Kegan Paul, 1969), 155-56. Like F. H. Jacobi (1743-1819), he defines "Reason" as "an organ bearing the same relation to spiritual objects, the Universal, the Eternal, and the Necessary, as the eye bears to material and contingent phenomena."

31. By 1851 this distinction had become part of his theological prolegomena: "There are two aspects of reason. Understanding is one, which has to do with the finite; and reason in its proper

sense the other, which has to do with the infinite and absolute. It does not depend upon the indications of the senses, but has the power of perceiving divine things in their own light. It includes faith." Erb, *Dr. Nevin's Theology*, 13; see also 66-67.

32. Kant, of course, could not share Coleridge's unbounded optimism regarding the power of Reason. See Coleridge, *The Friend*, 490-91; idem, "Aids to Reflection," in *The Complete Works of Samuel Taylor Coleridge*, ed. W.G.T. Shedd (New York: Harper & Brothers, 1858), 1:251-53.

33. Nevin, *Human Freedom and A Plea for Philosophy*, 42-44. Nevin, like Rauch, did not regard Kant's categories as merely subjective, noetic forms. Reality is both ideal and actual. The actual (i.e., space and time) has existence outside the mind. The *a priori* forms or types of the Understanding correspond to the structures of nature in time and space, while the innate ideas germinal in the Reason correspond to the ideal prototypes immanent in creation. The mind, then, is adapted to its objects just as the eye is to light. See Erb, *Dr. Nevin's Theology*, 77, 98-99; Rauch, *Psychology*, 212-16; Nevin, "Brownson's Quarterly Review Again," 2 (1850): 308-10, 313-15, 317-19; idem, *Lectures on Aesthetics*, 62.

34. John Williamson Nevin, *The Claims of the Bible Urged Upon the Attention of Students of Theology* (Pittsburgh: D. & M. Maclean, 1831), 14.

35. Ibid., 17.

36. See Nevin, *My Own Life*, 39-75; idem, "Election," *The Presbyterian Preacher* 2 (1833): 209-24.

37. Nevin, *Party Spirit*, 26-27. As Nevin's biographer said, Nevin came to Mercersburg with "idealistic, Platonizing tendencies." Indeed, one of his friends was reported to have said at the time that he had a "dash of transcendentalism about him" (Appel, *Life and Work of John Williamson Nevin*, 94; see also 104).

38. See Nevin, *The German Language* (Chambersburg, PA: Publication Office of the German Reformed Church, 1842), 5.

39. See Howard J. B. Ziegler, *Frederick Augustus Rauch: American Hegelian* (Manheim: Sentinel Printing House, 1953). Ziegler certainly overstates his case in trying to prove that Rauch was an ardent Hegelian.

40. Rauch, *Psychology*, v-vi.

41. John Williamson Nevin, "Rauch's Psychology," *Weekly Messenger of the German Reformed Church*, 10 June 1840. The question remains whether Rauch actually achieved a real synthesis between idealism and empiricism. As DeBie points out, there is no immediate evidence in Rauch's work that this synthesis emerges from a struggle with empirical philosophers. Rather, it is an attempt to adapt German idealism to traditional Christian beliefs in the context of American culture. See Linden Jay DeBie, "German Idealism in Protestant Orthodoxy: The Mercersburg Movement, 1840-1860" (Ph.D., diss., McGill University, 1987), 99.

42. Appel, *Life and Work of John Williamson Nevin*, 103, 105.

43. Organic metaphors punctuated Nevin's early writings (1830-1840). E.g., see "Religion a Life," *The Friend*, 25 Dec 1834; idem, *Seal of the Spirit*, 14.

44. Rauch, *Psychology*, 24-25.

45. Ibid., 25, 29.

46. Ibid., 281, 277.

47. Nevin, *The Anxious Bench*, 2nd ed. (Chambersburg, PA: M. Kieffer & Co., 1844; reprint, 1846), 123-30.

48. See his letter to fellow Mercersburg theologian Henry Harbaugh (written sometime between 1860 and 1867) in Charles Yrigoyen, Jr., and George H. Bricker, eds., *Catholic and Reformed: Selected Theological Writings of John Williamson Nevin*, Pittsburgh Original Texts and Translations, ed. Dikran Y. Hadidian, no. 4 (Pittsburgh: The Pickwick Press, 1978), 407.

49. See Friedrich Schleiermacher, *The Christian Faith*, translation of the 2d German ed. (1830), ed. H. R. MaCkintosh and J. S. Stewart (Edinburgh: T. & T. Clark, 1928), 93; Augustus Neander, *Lectures on the History of Christian Dogmas* (London: Henry G. Bohn, 1858), 1:61.

50. Always wary of charges of pantheism, Nevin was careful to preserve the absolute and unrepeatable nature of the incarnation. The union of Christ and His people is not a repetition of the hypostatic union of natures (i.e., the Logos and humanity), but an organic conjunction between Christ's entire

theanthropic person (i.e., His glorified humanity) and believers.
There is, therefore, no "pantheistic dissipation" of Christ's
personality into the "general consciousness of the Church."
See Nevin, *The Mystical Presence*, 173-74, 160-61, 164-65,
167, 169, 196; idem, "Wilberforce on the Incarnation,"
Mercersburg Review 2 (1850): 182-83; idem, "Brownson's
Quarterly Review Again," *Mercersburg Review* 2 (1850): 310;
idem, "The Spiritual World," *Mercersburg Review* 23 (1876):
524; idem, *Antichrist*, 10.

51. Nevin, *The Church*, 10-11; idem, "Catholic Unity," in
    Mercersburg Theology, ed. James H. Nichols (New York:
    Oxford University Press, 1966) 41.

52. Nevin, *The Church*, 10-12; idem, "Catholic Unity," 41-42. This
    became the distinguishing feature of Mercersburg theology and
    its philosophical point of departure from the ahistorical approach
    of New England transcendentalism. See Robert Clemmer's
    striking comparisons, "Historical Transcendentalism in
    Pennsylvania," *Journal of the History of Ideas* 30 (October-
    December 1969): 582, 586-89.

53. Erb, *Dr. Nevin's Theology*, 426-27; John Williamson Nevin,
    "Hodge on the Ephesians," *Mercersburg Review* 9 (1857): 224-
    26; idem, *Mystical Presence*, 148; idem, *Antichrist*, 45-68.

54. John Williamson Nevin, "Catholicism," *Mercersburg Review* 3
    (1851): 2-5; see also Nevin, "History as General or Universal,"
    College Days (Lancaster), April 1873.

55. Ibid., 3-6, 19-20.

56. For a sophisticated critique of the Calvinistic theory of
    predestination based on these distinctions see John Williamson
    Nevin, "Hodge on the Ephesians," *Mercersburg Review* 9
    (1857): 217-21.

57. John Williamson Nevin, "Dorner's History of Protestant
    Theology," *Mercersburg Review* 15 (1868): 597.

58. John Williamson Nevin, "The Old Doctrine of Christian
    Baptism," *Mercersburg Review* 12 (1860): 200.

59. Erb, *Dr. Nevin's Theology*, 373.

60. Nevin, *The Mystical Presence*, 5; Erb, *Dr. Nevin's Theology*,
    415, 418-19.

61. Erb, *Dr. Nevin's Theology*, 394.

62. John Williamson Nevin, "The Bread of Life: A Communion
Sermon," *Mercersburg Review* 26 (1879): 32.

63. Erb, *Dr. Nevin's Theology*, 286-87.

64. John Williamson Nevin, "Christianity and Humanity,"
Mercersburg Review 20 (1873): 476.

65. John Williamson Nevin, "Once for All," *Mercersburg Review* 17
(1870): 108; idem, "Christ and His Spirit," *Mercersburg Review*
19 (1872): 354; idem, "Christ the Inspiration of His Own
Word," *Reformed Quarterly Review* 29 (1882): 38; Erb, *Dr.
Nevin's Theology*, 106.

66. Nevin, *German Language*, 5. Truth is "the externalization of
thought in the form of a word."

67. Cf. Rauch, *Psychology*, 211: "While the eye opens the
universe with its thousands of objects, the ear is their common
echo, and communicates their internal being...The ear excites,
therefore, more deep sympathy than the eye."

68. John Williamson Nevin, "Education," *Mercersburg Review* 18
(1871): 11.

69. The philosophical significance of the incarnation was also
explained by Emanuel V. Gerhart, *An Introduction to the Study
of Philosophy with an Outline Treatise on Logic* (Philadelphia:
Reformed Church Publishing Board, 1857).

Nevin and Schaff at Mercersburg

Stephen Graham

On August 12, 1844, 25-year-old Philip Schaff arrived in Mercersburg, Pennsylvania, to take up his duties as a professor in the German Reformed seminary there. His arrival was a cause for celebration since his professorship would double the size of the faculty. His new colleague, John Nevin, had preceded Schaff to the seminary by four years and was 16 years his senior. Both men must have viewed their future work together with some apprehension, given their significantly different social and educational backgrounds, but they were also hopeful. Little could they imagine the amazing fruitfulness that would result from their work together over the next two decades.

I

Nevin's first permanent appointment as a professor of theology had been at Western Seminary in Allegheny, Pennsylvania. While serving there, he began to read extensively in German theology, and became especially enamored with the church history of Johann Augustus Neander. According to Nevin, the theories of Neander had caused in him an "historical awakening."

My obligations were great to Neander, as a simple teacher of common historical knowledge, as an expositor of ecclesiastical facts and details. But I owed him much more than this. As Kant says somewhere of the influence the philosophical writings of David Hume had upon him, so I may say in all truth of the new views of history set before me by Neander—"they broke up my dogmatic slumbers." They were for me an actual awakening of the soul.

This new historical perspective, he continued, reshaped "my whole theological and religious life."[1]

Schaff likewise spoke of Neander as the most influential of his teachers and very clearly saw himself as an historian in the "school" of the Berlin master.

If any one of the modern divines realized the idea of a church father, equally distinguished for the piety and learning, a giant in knowledge and a child in simplicity of heart, perfectly unconcerned about the things of the visible world, and exclusively devoted to the interests of the spiritual world, living more in the past than in the present, and yet laboring for the rising generation and leading it to the fountain of truth and wisdom, universally revered and beloved as a scholar, a man, and a Christian, it was Neander.[2]

In a journal of reminiscences which he prepared for his children, Schaff spoke of Neander as the "teacher who interested and helped me most."

Berlin never had a better teacher. His character and example were even more impressive than his profound learning and original genius. It was impossible not to revere and love him for his simplicity, purity, humility and unselfish devotion to students. He is one of the greatest and best men I ever knew. He had a most tender and conscientious regard for truth as the supreme object of knowledge.[3]

Both Schaff and Nevin drew from Neander their sense of the importance of the historical element of human existence and both attributed to their German master an understanding of development within the historical process. This key concept would be a major part of the foundation on which they built the Mercersburg Theology.

Nevin had studied church history at Princeton Seminary, but the approach there caused him to discount its value. As his biographer Theodore Appel put it, church history at Princeton appeared to be "the poorest sort of sacred science."[4] Nevin scorned his training in church history at Princeton as neither scientific, nor sacred, nor personally edifying—all qualities he found in abundance in Neander's work.

Both of the Mercersburg theologians attributed this void to Princeton's heritage in the "spirit of Puritanism," which they strangely styled "unhistorical in its very constitution," and which they blamed for much that was wrong in American Christianity. And not only Princeton was affected. In most seminaries, Schaff contended, "history is still regarded and treated as a mere conglomeration of notices, more or less interesting, thrown together in a perfectly outward way." Sorely neglected was what German historians called "the main thing in history, the ideas which rule it and reveal themselves in the process, imparting to it its only true significance and importance." Americans, even those who professed an interest in the Church's heritage missed the main point of the story. Not only did they fail to see the importance of ideas in history, but with their common notion of static truth, they could not recognize "organic development" in the historical process.[5]

The Mercersburg theologians set their theology in opposition to that of the leading Reformed institution in the country, Presbyterian Princeton, by insisting that the church's history could only be understood through the principle of organic development. While Princeton tried faithfully to uphold standards of orthodoxy unchanged since the time of Calvin—prompting statements such as Charles Hodge's boast that no new ideas had originated at Princeton Seminary in 50 years—the Mercersburgers used an organic image of the Church. As a living organism, the Church must change and mature. This principle of the new German historiography became a central theme in the work of Schaff, and Nevin was also convinced of its validity. Without this German idealism and sense of development in history—which both Nevin and Schaff found best illustrated in the writings of Neander—the Mercersburg Theology would never have come to be.

Their studies, with Neander's ideas at the core, led Schaff and Nevin to agree on the most crucial issue of their time, what they called the "Church Question." This problem became so consuming for Nevin that his biographer speculated that the "Church Question" had come to "engage his waking and perhaps his sleeping hours." Nevin's passion for the question was such that "never before, perhaps, did philosopher, scientist or theologian bestow more study or prayerful attention than be to any deep problem that called for solution."[6] Nevin found freedom to wrestle with the issues within the German Reformed Church, and a superb vehicle of expression in the seminary's journal, *The Mercersburg Review*.

Soon after his arrival in America as Nevin's colleague, Schaff had also focused his attention on the "Church Question," with his distinctive historical approach. He agreed that "the great central theme of the Present, around which all religious and theological movements revolve, is the **Church Question**." While Nevin wrestled with theological and philosophical issues, his focus would be on the more purely historical aspects of the question, "Church and History," he argued, "are so closely united, that respect and love towards the first, may be said to be essentially the same with a proper sense of what is comprised in the other."[7]

This remarkably united proposal of the question would produce over the next few years some of the most fruitful reflections on the nature of the Church in American intellectual history. The two scholars agreed that the "question of the age" was the "Church Question," and they agreed that the question was fundamentally historical. Did it make any sense to affirm the creeds which claimed that the Church was one, holy, catholic, and apostolic, when the American church especially was fragmented into literally scores of groups at war with one another, inhabited by all manner of charlatans and crooks, full of members who believed the term catholic was equivalent to antichrist, and plagued by competing groups who claimed to be apostolic, but who knew little of the Church's history beyond the literal text of the Bible? For many American Christians, the Church did not extend beyond their local congregations, or at best, their denomination.

While such close agreement on the central question of the age was noteworthy, even more surprising was the two scholar's unanimity on the answers. Obviously, for both, the Church's character was first of all historical. And the view of the Church's history adopted by both was in the ecumenical spirit of Neander. Every era of Christian history was important, and the hand of God was present even in what appeared to be the most degraded times of Christian history. For example, Schaff's clearly expressed appreciation for the medieval church in his inaugural address as professor at Mercersburg landed him and Nevin, his translator and advocate in the dock, accused of Romanism. Years later, Nevin's love for the early church and the Christian fathers led him to consider conversion to Roman Catholicism. Their work with revision of liturgies in the 1850s and 1860s also revealed an effort to utilize the riches of the whole Christian tradition. As Schaff was fond of saying, "no labor in the Lord can ever be lost."[8]

The Mercersburgers' view of the Church was also highly sacramental. Their views were consciously Reformed, but they understood that designation to refer primarily to Calvin and not Zwingli. Nevin attacked a number of low views of the sacraments in *The Mystical Presence* that appeared in 1846 and presented a powerful argument for Calvin's view of the real, but spiritual presence of Christ in the Eucharist. Episcopalians and those on the high-church end of the spectrum among the Reformed and Lutherans applauded while the majority of American Christians who cared enough to read the book shook their heads in bewilderment or disgust. Schaff himself admitted that the book not only presented the view of Calvin, but also gave a "scientific statement and profound enlargement of the view of the Geneva Reformer" that was directed "not only against the Romish, but also against its opposite rationalist extreme."[9] Further, those who called themselves Calvinist in America were actually more influenced by Zwinglian rationalism and had lost Calvin's conception of real presence. Schaff explained to a German audience in 1854 that Nevin's work provided a necessary corrective to the low church, anti-mystical rationalism of much of American Christianity.

In general, he is entitled to the undisputed merit of having brought the theology of the Reformation period, which is much deeper, more spiritual and churchly than that of modern Puritanism, in a living reproduction, home to the consciousness of the German American Churches.[10]

Sweeping America through the nineteenth century was a new form of Christianity that employed emotionally powerful preaching and stressed personal conversion. Known as revivalism, the movement placed its emphasis on the individual's relationship with God and tended to neglect the historical church with its traditions of catechetical instruction and Christian nurture. Nevin blasted abuses he saw in revivalism with his tract *The Anxious Bench*, published in 1844. He did not shrink from using terms such as heresy, fanaticism, Pelagianism, and error, in his critique of a system that, in his opinion, played more on emotion than substance. He contrasted to the system of revivals the "system of the catechism" through which persons are nurtured through the ordinary means of the Church, its teachings, fellowship, and sacraments to become mature Christians.

Schaff also rejected "new measures" revivalism which he identified with Methodism. His ecumenical sensibilities were offended by those who believed their methods alone could save, and who put forth strenuous efforts to convert other Christians to their groups. In some cases perhaps, the new measures did some good, but for the most part, Schaff insisted, they had led to "most injurious outbreaks of religious fanaticism," and had "nourished a most dangerous distrust of the ordinary means of grace, the calm preaching of the Word, the sacraments, and catechetical instruction."[11] Often, the "new measures," those "quack appliances," affected "the nerves far more than the soul."[12] Not until late in his career when he witnessed first hand the methods of Dwight L. Moody in New York City did Schaff come to affirm revivalism as having an important role to play in American Christian renewal.

A by-product of American democratic freedom that was strengthened by the revivalistic styles was the fragmentation of the American church. Nevin lambasted the "sect system" in an article responding to John Winebrenner's *History of All the Religious Denominations in the United States*. Published in the opening volume of *The Mercersburg Review*, Nevin lamented the "sect plaque" in the United States and insisted that sectarianism had arisen due to an impoverished ecclesiology. The Church, he insisted, is not a human creation and is therefore not to be formed nor dissolved according to human whim. Throughout history the Church has defined itself as one, holy, catholic, and apostolic.   To lose any of those characteristics is to lose its identity as the Church.

> It must lose its true power for faith, if it be conceived as **not** one and universal and historical, not formed for all this, and not demanding it throughout as an indispensable part of its idea. Only where such a sense of the Church prevails, can the danger and guilt of schism be felt at all, or any hindrance be raised at all to the easy multiplication of sects.   In its very constitution, accordingly, the sect spirit is an unchurchly spirit.[13]

Not only is the unity of the Church destroyed and its historical nature ignored by the sect system, but its sacramental character is also denied.

> As thus unchurchly, the sect system tends to destroy all faith in the holy sacraments....The sect mind, therefore, in proportion as it has come to be unchurchly and simply private and individual, is always necessarily to the same extend unsacramental.[14]

Schaff joined his colleague in lament over the American sect system.   His views about sectarian divisions had been shaped by his European training which carried a deep suspicion of American freedoms and the resulting chaos of religious sects.   Schaff feared for the spiritual welfare of his "sect-bewildered countrymen," who had emigrated to the new world and he believed himself called to save them from the poisoned atmosphere of American confusion.   The true danger was for the deceived multitude, [who] having no power to discern spirits, is converted not to Christ and his truth, but the arbitrary fancies and baseless opinions of an individual, who is only of yesterday....What is built is no church, but a chapel, to whose erection Satan himself has made the most liberal contribution.[15]

The root of the problem in America, according to Schaff, was the "puritan" character of religion in America. All Christian groups in the United States had become "more or less puritanized" and suffered from this extreme form of Calvinism "stripped of all its churchly elements," to produce an "extreme, naked Protestantism."[16]

II

Nevin and Schaff were agreed, however, that the Roman Catholic answer of the objective authority of the papal church failed to recognize appropriate developments in Christian history from the Protestant Reformation to the present. Early signals from both Nevin and Schaff, however, must have delighted leaders of the staunchly anti-catholic party within the German Reformed Church. Nevin, for example, had commended Rev. Joseph Berg's *Lectures on Romanism*, in 1840, for exposing "the Romish system" as "the mystery of iniquity, always ready to evolve itself anew from the depths of Satan in the soul of man." Berg was also one of the signers of Schaff's letter of invitation in 1844, who must have been pleased by reports from Germany about Schaff's ordination sermon in which the young scholar had urged the forces of Protestantism to unite against "the [Roman Catholic] enemy, ever waxing stronger," who "is now mustering his legions of war."[17] With colleagues such as these in the seminary, Berg anticipated purging the church of all Romish taint.

As their ecclesiologies developed on remarkably parallel tracks, however, both Nevin and Schaff drastically revised their opinions about Roman Catholicism. Berg and his allies were sorely disappointed by what they viewed as the apostasy of their champions at the Mercersburg seminary. Their sense of betrayal was made manifest in charges of heresy brought against Schaff following his inaugural address on the principle of Protestantism which spoke appreciatively of Catholicism, both medieval and modern.

Despite charges of "popery" and "Romanism" hurled at Schaff following his inaugural address—and by implication also against his defender Nevin—neither had (at that time at least) any intention of abandoning Protestantism. Heresy bloodhounds in the German Reformed Church and beyond sniffed Romish incense coming from Mercersburg and published exposés such as *Antidote to the Poison of Popery in the Publications of Professor Schaff*.[18] Schaff was puzzled by such attacks on ideas that were perfectly acceptable within the Reformed churches in Germany and responded that his objections to the Roman Catholic church were substantial and obvious if only his opponents would take the time to give his writings even a cursory reading. Schaff offered a distinction between Catholicism and Romanism whose subtlety escaped many of his American critics. The catholic substance was sound, he insisted, and necessary for the continued life of the Christian church. This was the deposit of the faith passed down from generation to generation. On the other hand, "Romanism" characterized the numerous papal and ecclesiastical abuses found within Roman Catholicism that should be purged. The anti-catholic party believed their suspicions were confirmed by Nevin's struggles during the early 1850s over whether he could remain a Protestant. Thoroughly frustrated by resistance to the Mercersburg Theology by vocal leaders in the German Reformed Church, and physically and emotionally spent, Nevin sought shelter from the tempest in the safe haven of Rome. He corresponded with the notable convert to Roman Catholicism, Orestes Brownson, and wavered for a number of months. Finally, though, he reaffirmed his commitment to the heritage of the Reformation and returned to his work within the German Reformed fold.

John B. Payne argues that by the time of Nevin's articles "Early Christianity" and "Cyprian" (1851-1852), his views had begun to differ significantly from Schaff's. While Nevin still respected his colleague's view of historical development—a view he had at one time wholeheartedly accepted—he now saw it as one possible theory among others. The most appealing views to Nevin were Schaff's and a perspective that regarded Roman Catholicism as "the principal succession of the proper church life" and Protestantism as "a true outflow, legitimate and necessary," but which must ultimately "fall back into the old Catholic stream in order to fulfill its own mission."[19]

Evidently, Schaff never took the latter alternative seriously. Nevin's own destruction of "Puritan, Presbyterian, and Anglican historical hypotheses" in his articles "Early Christianity" and "Cyprian" left him with no alternative, believed Schaff, than the principle of historical development as he and Nevin had stated it earlier. Nevin had rejected the belief in an unchanging orthodoxy of the Puritans and Presbyterians and the claims of apostolic succession of the Anglicans, and Schaff was sure that his colleague could not finally embrace Roman Catholicism. According to Schaff, as long as Nevin adhered to the "German theory of development...an exodus to Rome will be impossible, as it would be a retrogression, and consequently a nullification of the fundamental law of historical development."[20]

Although at the time he resisted urgings by leaders such as Charles Hodge that he distance himself from Nevin in order to avoid the taint of association with a crypto-catholic—even though Nevin had stood by him in a time of great difficulty—later in his life Schaff was concerned that his differences with Nevin be clearly understood.[21] In a revealing letter written in 1889 to Nevin's biographer Theodore Appel, Schaff responded to Appel's request that he write about his relationship with Nevin and the Mercersburg Theology and called the effort "a very delicate task." Reflecting on their relationship during the 1850s, Schaff described the difference between them as one of perspective.

> We agreed in the developmental theory, but Dr. Nevin looked backward and became Romanizing. I looked forward to new and higher developments. He was inclined to pessimism, I am an optimist or at least an inveterate hoper.[22]

Schaff went on to note that their personal relationship had always been cordial during their Mercersburg years, especially during their first decade together, but he sensed that Nevin's feelings toward him had cooled and noted two possible reasons. The first was Schaff's departure from Mercersburg for New York in 1865. The second is both more likely and more revealing. Perhaps the roots of estrangement came, Schaff speculated, "after [Nevin's] resignation in 1853, when I had to stem the current towards Romanism." This is an attitude that was not expressed publicly at the time, and although Schaff insisted that he "did it as gently and considerately as I could," it certainly indicates a growing divergence of their theological efforts.

Much concerned that Appel's forthcoming biography tell the story fairly—and perhaps not wanting to endure charges of Romanism within his present church home with the Presbyterians, Schaff suggested that Appel allow him to review the section of the manuscript that would deal with Mercersburg.

> In any case I would like to see the chapter on Mercersburg Theology. It really began with my "Principle of Protestantism," but took a wrong and reactionary turn with Nevin's "Anglican Crisis" and articles on Cyprian, etc.[23]

A few months later, Schaff wrote Appel again and agreed to read chapters of the manuscript in which he was mentioned. He was still concerned that differences between the two men be adequately recognized. "I hope you have not identified me too closely with Dr. Nevin's theology. I never was Romanizing and tried to check that tendency without producing a split."[24]

In his early searching and throughout his career, Nevin sought a final objective authority and when he found the Princetonian bedrock of infallible Scripture to be inadequate, he considered the apostolic succession of Rome. In some ways, this step was the logical conclusion to the historiography of Nevin and Schaff. Denying the theory that the Protestant Reformation had made a radical break with the catholic heritage, it was a short step to conclude that the schism should never have taken place. Nevin's continued frustration with American denominational divisions and revivalistic tendency led him to seek what appeared to be the more serene waters of Catholicism. Yet he finally concluded—and Schaff had never seen it any other way—that the Roman church violated the key principle of development in history, and that return to Rome would be a violation of the core of his theology. Schaff spoke of the result as "a providential escape."[25]

As Schaff noted in his letter to Appel, the first collaborative salvo in the Mercersburgers' attack was associated with Schaff's inaugural address as professor at the seminary, "The Principle of Protestantism." Hard on the heels of a classic anti-catholic sermon by Rev. Joseph Berg, the address came in October 1844 and immediately raised a storm of protest for its sympathies with all eras of Christian history, including the medieval. In order to respond to criticisms and to explain himself more completely, Schaff expanded the address and published it as *Das Princip des Protestantismus* later translated into English and introduced by Nevin, who reaffirmed his position as an enemy of Romanism and American sectarianism, and a champion of a high ecclesiology and the theory of organic development in history. The English version also included, at Schaff's request, Nevin's sermon on "Catholic Unity," that had been delivered at a joint convention of the Dutch and German Reformed churches just a few weeks before Schaff's inaugural. Despite the title, Nevin did not call for union with Roman Catholicism. In fact, in the sermon for the last time he referred to the papacy as "Antichrist." Ironically, Nevin's high view of the Eucharist combined with Schaff's emphasis on organic development and the value of the medieval church helped make union between the Germans and the Dutch impossible.[26]

The most important organ for dissemination of the Mercersburg Theology was *The Mercersburg Review*. Nevin and Schaff each contributed dozens of articles, and Schaff served as co-editor with E.V. Gerhart from 1857-1861. With the exception of the years 1861-1867 when the journal halted publication, Nevin published at least one article every year except 1875 until 1883. In each of the early years of the journal, 1849-1853, Nevin never contributed less than the astonishing figure of 269 pages per year.

A final cooperative project was the long-term effort to revise the liturgical resources of the German Reformed Church.

Believing an appropriate liturgical expression of their theological system to be crucial, both Schaff and Nevin worked diligently to bring about reform. Nevin predicted that the liturgy would be the main reason for the survival of the "spirit" of the Mercersburg movement.[27] Schaff agreed that liturgy was vital for bringing theology to the people. "Next to the Word of God," he wrote, "which stands in unapproachable majesty far above all human creeds and confessions, Fathers and Reformers, popes and councils, there are no religious books of greater practical importance and influence than catechisms, hymn-books, and liturgies."[28] Nevin chaired the revision committee of the German Reformed Church from 1849-1852, after which Schaff served as chairman until 1857.

While Schaff was hopeful about the possibilities of the revision throughout his association with the revision committee, Nevin's enthusiasm waxed and waned in relation to his personal struggles over the church. When he resigned the chairmanship in 1852, he defended his action by saying that,

> I had not led the way at all in the movement; my heart was not in it with any special zeal; I was concerned with it only in obedience to the appointment of Synod; other interests appeared to me at the time to be of more serious account; and I had no faith in our being able to bring the work to any ultimate success.[29]

His pessimism and despair with Protestantism was made clear in a letter to Schaff, who had asked Nevin to submit drafts for a number of liturgical services.

> I have no heart, no faith, no proper courage for any such work. A *leitourgia* (communion service) in the old sense demands a sort of faith in the "real presence," which I am afraid goes beyond all that is possible to engraft on Protestantism, even in our German Reformed version of it. And without this, I feel that it is for me at least a species of mockery to pretend to the use of the like words and forms. I cannot bear the sense of unrealness which comes over me when I think of manufacturing on any such plan for public use a form

of worship, into which our faith is not allowed to breathe the same mysterious soul.[30]

However, in this, as in nearly every area of his life and career, Schaff remained optimistic and never gave up his belief that progress could be made in liturgical reform.

The liturgy that the Mercersburgers and their committee advocated raised eyebrows among their opponents because it reached back beyond the sixteenth-century liturgies of the Reformers to include forms and prayers from the early church Fathers. In addition, their dynamic view of historical development allowed them to insist that the liturgy should be not only historical, but at the same time modern and American.[31] The liturgy would be a creative synthesis of old and new. Jack Martin Maxwell highlights Schaff's unique contribution to the process as a synthesizer and compiler of materials:

> Armed with Scripture, a sizable array of historic liturgies, and a sensitive, poetic spirit, Philip Schaff composed his own work, borrowing, adapting, and freely creating fresh forms which would articulate Reformed theology as Mercersburg understood it, yet which would also forge a devotional bond between a small band of nineteenth-century German immigrants in an American Commonwealth and the saints of the ages.[32]

Nevin's contribution to revision, on the other hand, lay in his concern to resist "attempts to tinker with what he believed to be 'theoretically right' in order to make it politically 'expedient'....He did not believe that the church was ready for a liturgy which was 'theoretically right' and in this he was correct."[33]

The committee presented its work in 1857 as a "Provisional Liturgy" which was met with mixed reviews. The opposition demanded additional revisions, but neither Nevin nor Schaff expressed much enthusiasm for continuing their involvement. Nevin tried to resign from the committee, but Synod refused to accept it. Schaff had begun to look elsewhere—eventually he

left Mercersburg and the German Reformed Church for Union
Seminary in New York and the Presbyterian Church — and of the
55 sessions of the revision committee in 1861-1862, he
attended only 17. Not only did the years after 1857 signal a
decline in Nevin's and Schaff's interest in the work of the
revision committee, it also became increasingly clear that the
two colleagues had completed their cooperative work and had
begun to look in other directions.

From the limited evidence that is available, it appears that
Nevin and Schaff enjoyed an unusually cordial relationship
during their time as colleagues at Mercersburg. Their
theological compatibility and the battles they fought side by
side clearly caused them to value each other. Their
personalities and piety also nurtured their friendship and the
harmony between them. Schaff was an extraordinarily
gregarious and irenic person who sought to build friendships
with a huge number and wide variety of people on both sides
of the Atlantic. Nevin was also a warm-hearted and generous
man, as long he was not in the midst of theology conflict. In
addition, both were nurtured by a type of piety that valued
forbearance and forgiveness.

Another common difficulty that thankfully brought the
scholars together rather than producing rivals and tension was
their shared financial struggles due to the precarious economic
condition of Mercersburg Seminary. Relatively new when Nevin
and Schaff came to Mercersburg, the seminary struggled to
make ends meet during their tenures. Finally, the situation got
so bad that Nevin was compelled to submit his resignation in
1850. Intended to shock the church to action, Nevin
complained that

> the church is not prepared, as it seems to me, to carry
> out its present idea of a theological seminary with two
> professors in a truly earnest way; and, if such be the
> case, it is better at once to reduce our views and
> efforts to the measure of this necessity. Let the
> seminary proceed for a time with one professor, and
> whatever of surplus means may be then available for its
> use, let them be applied to pay off its debts, while at

the same time all needful exertions are made to endow
a second professorship.[34]

Ironically, at the same time Schaff was considering a call
from Salem Reformed Church in Philadelphia to become its
pastor. Though not desiring to make the move, he allowed the
call to proceed so that "there might be no financial difficulty in
the way of Dr. Nevin's return to the seminary, where his
presence to him [Schaff] seemed to be a necessity."[35]

Ultimately, Nevin's resignation was accepted—for financial
and other, perhaps more crucial reasons—and Schaff remained
at the seminary.[36] The financial difficulties were by no means
over, however, and Schaff lamented being forced to go on
"begging tours" to bring in necessary funds and library
resources. In his opinion there were simply too many small
theological institutions in the United States competing for
limited resources. His own situation was clearly in mind when
he complained of "institutions where one or two professors
must teach all branches of learning, and spend the vacation in
the humiliating business of collecting their own scanty
salary."[37] Rumors of such conditions must have reached
Schaff prior to his immigration, because as early as his
inaugural address he felt it necessary to point out to his
audience that "a professor of theology and a pack horse are not
exactly the same thing."[38]

That Nevin's resignation in 1850 prompted Schaff to submit
his own resignation in sympathy with this colleague and with
the best interests of the seminary in mind, illustrates the
unusual harmony between the two men. A few years later,
Nevin left the "temporary" presidency of Marshall College, a
position he had held since 1841. The college planned to move
to Lancaster from Mercersburg, and Nevin believed the time
had come for him to resign his position. Even though the board
of trustees "elected" Nevin and urged him to become president
officially, he steadfastly refused. The board then turned to
Schaff—on Nevin's recommendation—but the Synod refused to
release him from his duties in the seminary. In all of the events
surrounding the presidency of Marshall College, there is no
indication that anything except cordiality and mutual respect
characterized the relationship between Nevin and Schaff.

While Nevin and Schaff were nurtured in similar pietistic traditions and retained deep appreciation for their heritages, there are significant differences in their early lives that continued to be reflected in emphases throughout their careers. Nevin's biographer traces the theologian's ancestry to some of the leading Scots-Irish Americans, some of whom were important figures in the American Revolution and Continental Congress.[39] In sharp contrast, Schaff's ancestry is at best unclear and at worst shadowed by scandal. Scholars have speculated that the scanty evidence implies that Schaff was the illegitimate son of a mother of peasant stock and a carpenter father who died when the baby was less than one year old. While Nevin's road to education and career was smoothly paved, Schaff acquired his schooling and pursued his vocation only through the good will of what he could only see as providentially sent benefactors.

While both experienced the warmth of evangelical piety in their early lives, their spirituality had some important differences as well. Schaff recalled the spiritual struggle and anguish of soul that preceded his "conversion" as a teenager at the boys' academy in Kornthal, Württemberg. From that time on, through times of uncertainty and family crises, Schaff retained his confidence in God's providence and an optimism that was never quenched. Nevin, on the other hand, experienced prolonged periods of spiritual struggle and doubt. He spoke of his "spiritual dualism," torn between the "old school" spiritual nurture of his youth which was churchly, sacramental, and based on creeds and catechism, and the "new school" Presbyterianism he discovered as an undergraduate at Union College which stressed personal religious experience. He described the new "Puritan" spirituality as unchurchly and unsacramental and guilty of totally neglecting the objective certainties of the Christian faith, replacing them with the revivalist style of crisis-experience conversion. To this he contrasted the "old proper Presbyterian theory of the seventeenth century," based on the works of Baxter, Owen, and Howe.[40] At the Princeton Seminary many commended the old ways, but Nevin insisted, "the unchurchly scheme, nevertheless, continued to exercise a strong practical force at Princeton."[41] While he never completely rejected the "new" spirituality, Nevin lashed out against abuses in revivalism and came increasingly to approve the old ways. This struggle was a harbinger of the more famous "dizziness" Nevin experienced during the early 1850s.

Throughout his career, Schaff became known for his mediating efforts between European and American theologians and church leaders. Between 1854 and 1890 Schaff traveled to Europe no less than 14 times, often traversing western Europe and Great Britain calling on dozens of friends and acquaintances. Especially after his move to New York and his appointment at Union Seminary, Schaff was thoroughly cosmopolitan in his interests and involvements. In contrast, Nevin rarely left his home state, spending most of his time at home in Mercersburg or Lancaster. His travels took him to synods of the German Reformed Church and visits to local congregations, but only infrequently beyond the boundaries of his home state. Nevin was born, lived, and died in Pennsylvania. Schaff was born in Switzerland, educated in Germany, immigrated to Pennsylvania, toured the United States from coast to coast, and died in New York. The geographical contrast reflects the personality contrast between the introspective, sometimes pessimistic theorist and the gregarious, always optimistic mediator.

Nevin became cosmopolitan in his thinking, but less through travel and contact with leaders of schools of thought than through self-discipline in his study and reading their works. Though it was Charles Hodge who traveled to Germany, leaving Nevin to teach his classes at Princeton, it was Nevin who drank deeply at German wells and allowed the ideas he found at that fount to permeate his thinking. Whereas Nevin responded to the sea of ideas like a sponge, filtering and absorbing new concepts, Hodge was more like a crustacean, whose shell repelled most of the flow.

The calls that brought both men to Mercersburg were also quite different, though both came to the German Reformed Church from the outside. Nevin was a Pennsylvanian who had been raised a Presbyterian, attended the Presbyterian stronghold of Princeton Seminary, and had taught there and at the Presbyterian Western Seminary in Allegheny. He became involved in disputes of his home denomination, wrestling with controversies concerning revivalism and such social issues as temperance. Schaff's early experience was within a German church context of cooperation and union. George Shriver calls Schaff's ordination, "almost prophetic of his later ecumenical activity, a Swiss Reformed candidate was ordained by the Prussian Evangelical Union Church in the Reformed church in Elberfeld according to the Lutheran liturgical form in order to go and serve the German Reformed Church in the United States."[42]

The Synod of the German Reformed Church called Nevin after two other candidates had turned down the position, and Nevin also rejected the offer when initially given. Pursued further, he eventually relented to what he saw as the hand of providence and accepted the call. He called the decision "the crisis of my ministry at least, if not my life."[43] The call came at a turning point in his career and involved leaving the denomination of his birth and training and moving his family into a new and unknown situation. Schaff was not a first choice either. The delegates sent by the Synod to Germany offered the position to the famous preacher Fredrich W. Krummacher. Not wanting to risk his fortunes in the wilds of America, it seems Krummacher did not long ponder the offer. He did, however, give the delegates the name of a young *Privat-docent* of promise. Schaff was astonished by the offer, but the more he thought about it, the more attractive it became. Urged by his professors to accept, he eventually came to see the opportunity as providentially arranged, and he responded to his "Macedonian call."

Responses to the two appointments were similar in a number of ways. A faction within the German Reformed denomination initially saw them as allies in their strident opposition to Roman Catholicism. They sorely disappointed the expectations of that group. Both Nevin and Schaff suffered attacks by the German-American press because of their unguarded comments about the spiritual depravity of the immigrant Germans. Nevin noted that the German immigrants needed "spiritual religion," while Schaff envisioned them teetering over the "threefold abyss" of "Heathensim, Romanism, [and] Sectarianism."[44] Editorials cautioned parents against sending their children to Mercersburg.

Klaus Penzel speaks of the "dominant personality" of Nevin, who undoubtedly exerted a strong influence on Schaff during their first years together at Mercersburg.[45] Particularly in the first few months, Schaff must have been awed by the older and more experienced scholar's brilliance and boldness. Both faced charges of heresy; Nevin led the defense while Schaff wrestled to learn a new culture and language. George Shriver aptly assesses the situation:

> It is a small wonder that Nevin bore the brunt of the attack in later years, for he answered his opponents in kind. Schaff's irenicism and mediational interests forbade him throughout his life from giving public vitriolic answer to criticism. Even in his private diaries he seemed to find it hard to be judgmental on persons and positions.[46]

As James Hastings Nichols wrote, Nevin "entered the German Reformed Church like a cavalry charge," and his entire career can be characterized by the slashing, thundering charge and countercharge of a cavalry battle. Such images, however, simply fail to fit Schaff's career. Even in the midst of controversy and theological conflict, it is impossible to think of Schaff's actions in military terms. Perhaps the closest one can come is to think of a genteel fencing match in which the absolutely untiring Schaff wears his opponents down (politely!) through sheer stamina.

While Nevin struggled all his life with physical infirmity, Schaff was remarkably robust. Except for chronic sea-sickness—on most voyages to Europe, Schaff recounted "making my regular contribution to the Atlantic"—Schaff was in excellent health and able to work exceptionally long hours until the final two years of his life. It is reasonable to assume that physical health or lack of it influenced the temperament of the two men, especially as it was manifest in theological controversy. Nevin was as combative as Schaff was conciliatory. Nevin exhausted his patience and despaired of agreement after a few sharp engagements and seemed to become weary of corroborative work. For example, Nevin's brilliant reply to Charles Hodge's scathing critique of *The*

Mystical Presence devastated Hodge's arguments, but left little room for further conversation. Instead, Nevin, having bested his opponent, was ready to move on to other battles.

In contrast, Schaff's patience seemed limitless. In numerous cooperative ventures, many of them involving dozens of scholars, Schaff's untiring patience allowed him to mediate, conciliate, pacify ruffled feelings, and finally see the project through. His editorial efforts with Lange's biblical commentary and the revision of the Authorized version of the Bible stand as monuments to his indefatigable organizing and mediating skills.[47] As a team, Schaff and Nevin's common vision gave them unity of purpose while their difference of temperament and personality complemented each other in a remarkably productive way.

Though both Nevin and Schaff were strongly ecumenical in their understanding of the Church, neither supported the goals of the Evangelical Alliance, the first fruits of a growing interest in church unity in the 1840s. Ironically, it was because of their ecumenism that the Mercersburgers could not affirm the Alliance; both considered the vision of the Alliance too narrow. The leaders of the Alliance rightly condemned sectarianism, yet they fell prey to sectarian feeling themselves, insisted Schaff, making the new organization a Protestant bulwark against "the encroachments of Popery and Puseyism." In addition, the Alliance represented the unchurchly and unsacramental wing of the church and was too akin to the "puritanism" Schaff and Nevin had taken such pains to oppose. Schaff's views eventually changed, however, and he became an advocate of the later, more open-minded Evangelical Alliance. In fact, it was Schaff who was the main mover and shaker behind the New York Conference of the Evangelical Alliance in 1873, which he called "a feast of Christian union and universal encouragement of faith and hope and Christian work."[48] Attended by delegates from across Europe and North America, the conference provided another example of Schaff's untiring effort to see an idea through and his amazing breadth of friends and acquaintances. Nevin, however, chose not to attend.

Both scholars were amazingly productive, but following their Mercersburg years their efforts took separate directions. Schaff remained primarily a scholar, serving only briefly as

Secretary for the New York Sabbath Committee, while Nevin's energies were increasingly given to administration. Nevin, for example, never produced the complete systematic theology toward which his early writings seemed to point, while Schaff's continuing work as a scholar and professor led to his *magnum opus*, the multi-volume *History of the Christian Church*, and a number of similarly expansive works.[49] As a scholar, Nevin's most productive days came during his Mercersburg association with Schaff, while Schaff brought to full fruition the concepts shaped during the Mercersburg years only after he had left Pennsylvania for New York.

Schaff's assessment of Nevin as "a genuine American" who "looks at everything from a practical point of view" contains the essence of another important difference between the two men. Nevin always recognized and wrestled with the practical consequences of his theological ideas. As Schaff put it, for Nevin, issues such as Protestantism versus Romanism could never be purely academic exercises, but each became also "the most serious life question." For Nevin, Schaff noted that "the Church Question, in its widest extent, is not only the greatest theological problem of the present but, at the same time, one of personal salvation." Nevin, he continued, "reproduced and **lived over again** the entire controversy between Romanism and Protestantism."[50]

Whether Schaff was just more secure in his personal faith or perhaps less rigorously honest about the implication of his ideas, he felt the anguish of soul with which his colleague struggled only through sympathy for his friend. Schaff's own explanation was that the German temperament allowed more separation between the realm of ideas and practical life than that of the utterly practical American.

III

Ultimately, the pilgrimages of Nevin and Schaff, despite their convergence at Mercersburg, drew them in distinctive directions. Nevin, the Presbyterian, discovered German ideas and moved from the faith of his youth through Princeton orthodoxy, to the German Reformed Church and consideration of Roman Catholicism before he settled back into a comfortable position of the high-church end of the German Reformed spectrum.   Schaff, on the other hand, began with a cosmopolitan European pietism that was as much Lutheran as Reformed, moved into and through the German Reformed Church in America, on his way to an open presbyterianism and an ecumenism that would embrace nearly every Christian denomination in the United States. The American had become European in his thinking, but retained some American reflexes in his theology. The European had remained continental in his theology, but had become increasingly "Americanized" in his involvements and his understanding of Christianity.[51]

The story of Nevin and Schaff at Mercersburg is the story of an unlikely combination in the obscure seminary of a tiny immigrant denomination. It is also the story of a remarkably united effort of strikingly dissimilar scholars for a common purpose, and the amazing productivity of two men. They produced a theology that still stimulates and challenges thinkers concerned with theology and the Church.

In later years they drifted apart. Nevin moved to Lancaster and Schaff to New York. They remained in touch, though not regularly, and each continued to express appreciation for their time together.   In 1890, Schaff recorded in his diary his reaction to Appel's biography of Nevin.

> Strange emotions: Principle of Prot[estantism], Synod of York, Mercersb[urg] life.   Strong conviction that Providence used Nevin and myself as agents in stirring up the Germ[an] Ref[ormed] Church to new life and activity.[52]

Sadly, when Nevin died in June 1886, Schaff was in Europe and therefore unable to attend the funeral service or other memorial gatherings. Perhaps that final separation stands as a symbol of their very different origins and tendencies. At the same time, one must recognize that the unity of their scholarship was not something merely geographic or temporal, but an idea that brought them together in a fascinating way and continued to develop beyond their own time. They contributed their own important chapter to the organic development of the

Christian Church. Both would have wanted to be remembered
that way.

ENDNOTES

1. Quoted in Theodore Appel, *The Life and Work of John Williamson Nevin* (Philadelphia: The Reformed Church Publishing House, 1889), 83.

2. Philip Schaff, *Germany, Its Universities, Theology, and Religion* (Philadelphia, Lindsay and Blakiston, 1857), 261-62.

3. Philip Schaff, "Autobiographical Reminiscences of My Youth Till My Arrival in America, for My Children," manuscript copy, Philip Schaff Papers, Evangelical and Reformed Historical Society, Philip Schaff Library, Lancaster Theological Seminary, Lancaster, Pennsylvania, 97a, 98 (hereafter noted as ERHS).

4. Quoted in Appel, *John Williamson Nevin*, 80.

5. Philip Schaff, *What is Church History? A Vindication of the Idea of Historical Development* (Philadelphia: J. B. Lippincott and Co., 1846), 4-5. Included in a collection edited by Charles Yrigoyen, Jr. and George M. Bricker, *Reformed and Catholic: Selected Historical and Theological Writings of Philip Schaff* (Pittsburgh: The Pickwick Press, 1979).

6. Appel, *John Williamson Nevin*, 300. An excellent discussion of the Mercersburgers' wrestling with the church question is John B. Payne, "Schaff and Nevin, Colleagues at Mercersburg: The Church Question," *Church History* 61 (June 1992):169-90.

7. Schaff, *What is Church History?*, 9 (Schaff's emphasis).

8. Philip Schaff, *Theological Propaedeutic: A General Introduction to the Study of Theology* (New York: Charles Scribner's Sons, 1894), 241.

9. Quoted in Appel, *John Williamson Nevin*, 412, from Philip Schaff, *Amerika* (Berlin, 1854), 244. This volume was later translated as *America: A Sketch of the Political, Social, and Religious Character of the United States of North America* (New York: Scribner's, 1855; reprint edition by Perry Miller, Cambridge: Harvard University Press, 1961). Appel's quotation is an abridgement of Schaff's full description in *Amerika*.

10. Schaff, *Amerika*, 245.

11. Schaff, *Amerika*, 138, 143.

12. Philip Schaff, *The Principle of Protestantism as Related to the Present State of the Church*, trans, John W. Nevin (Chambersburg, PA: Publishing Office of the German Reformed Church, 1845); reprint edition (Philadelphia: United Church Press, 1964), 168. Originally published as *Das Princip des Protestantismus* (Chambersburg, PA: Publishing Office of the German Reformed Church, 1845).

13. John Williamson Nevin, "The Sect System," reprinted in Charles Yrigoyen, Jr., and George H. Bricker, eds., *Catholic and Reformed: Selected Theological Writings of John Williamson Nevin* (Pittsburgh: The Pickwick Press, 1978), 147.

14. Ibid., 147-148.

15. Schaff, *Principle of Protestantism*, 149-50.

16. Philip Schaff, "Introduction to the Church History of the United States," *Weekly Messenger of the German Reformed Church* 9 (4 September 1844):1869.

17. Philip Schaff, "Ordination of Professor Schaff," *Weekly Messenger* 9 (4 September 1844), 1869.

18. By Rev. J. J. Janeway, a Dutch Reformed pastor (New Brunswick, NJ: Terhune and Son, 1852).

19. Quoted by Payne, "The Church Question," 182; from John Williamson Nevin, "Early Christianity," *Mercersburg Review* (1851-1852):291, N.3, 292, 294-95, 305.

20. Reprinted in Klaus Penzel, *Philip Schaff: Historian and Ambassador of the Universal Church: Selected Writings* (Macon, GA: Mercer University Press, 1991), 110; from Philip Schaff, "German Theology and the Church Question," *The Mercersburg Review* 5 (January 1855): 124-44.

21. See David S. Schaff, *The Life of Philip Schaff: In Part Autobiographical* (New York: Scribner's, 1897), 200.

22. Letter of Philip Schaff to "Dear Friend," 13 February 1889, ERHS.

23. Ibid.

24. Letter of Philip Schaff to "Dear Dr. Apple [sic]," 18 June 1889, ERHS.

25. Diary entry for "Tuesday, May 13, 1873," Box IV, Philip Schaff Manuscript Collection, The Burke Library, Union Theological Seminary, New York, hereafter cited as UTS.

26. John Williamson Nevin, "Catholic Unity," reprinted in James Hastings Nichols, ed., *Mercersburg Theology* (New York: Oxford Press, 1966), 39, 45.

27. John Williamson Nevin, "The Anglican Crisis," *Mercersburg Review* 3 (1851): 396.

28. Philip Schaff, "The New Liturgy," *Mercersburg Review* 10 (1858): 199.

29. Quoted by Jack Martin Maxwell, *Worship and Reformed Theology: The Liturgical Lessons of Mercersburg* (Pittsburgh: The Pickwick Press, 1976), 141; from John Williamson Nevin, *A Vindication of the Revised Liturgy, Historical and Theological* (Philadelphia, 1867), 15.

30. Quoted by Maxwell, *Worship and Reformed Theology*, 141; from a letter from John Williamson Nevin to Philip Schaff, 3 December 1855, ERHS.

31. See Maxwell, *Worship and Reformed Theology*, 135.

32. Ibid., 236.

33. Ibid., 71.

34. Quote in Appel, *John Williamson Nevin*, 419-20.

35. Ibid., 422.

36. James Hastings Nichols, *Romanticism in American Theology: Nevin and Schaff at Mercersburg* (Chicago: The University of Chicago Press, 1961), 194-95, cites Schaff's opinion that Nevin's resignation came in part "from conscientious doubt whether he was, just now, the man suited...for the service of a Protestant denomination, while the whole Church question was undergoing a radical revision in his mind."

37. Philip Schaff, "Progress of Christianity in the United States," *Princeton Review* 55 (September 1879):232.

38. Philip Schaff, "Conclusion of Dr. Schaff's Address," *Weekly Messenger* 10 (23 April 1845):2.

39. Appel, *John Williamson Nevin*, 25f.

40. Ibid.

41. Ibid.

42. George H. Shriver, *Philip Schaff: Christian Scholar and Ecumenical Prophet* (Macon, GA: Mercer University Press, 1987), 14.

43. Appel, *John Williamson Nevin*, 97.

44. Nevin is quoted by Nichols, *Romanticism*; Schaff's comments are in "Ordination," 1869.

45. Penzel, *Philip Schaff*, lii.

46. Shriver, *Philip Schaff*, 24.

47. See Philip Schaff, ed., *A Commentary on the Holy Scriptures by Peter Lange*, 25 volumes (New York: Scribner's, 1864-1880), and *The Revision of the English Version of the Holy Scriptures by Cooperative Committees of British and American Scholars of Different Denominations* (New York: Harper and Bros., 1877).

48. Schaff, "Autobiographical Reminiscences," 42-43.

49. Philip Schaff, *History of the Christian Church*. 7 volumes. New York: Harper and Bros., 1882-1892.

50. Quoted by Appel, *John Williamson Nevin*, 414-15, emphasis mine.

51. See Stephen R. Graham, "Cosmos in the Chaos: Philip Schaff's Interpretation of Nineteenth-Century American Religion," Ph.D. dissertation, The University of Chicago, 1989; and Henry W. Bowden, "Philip Schaff and Sectarianism: The Americanization of a European Viewpoint," *Journal of Church and State* 8 (Winter 1966):97-106.

52. Diary entry for "Sunday, 11 May 1890," UTS.

Nevin on the Church

Walter H. Conser, Jr.

In 1987 one scholar estimated that there were 1,347 different religious groups in the United States. While the number might be higher and the diversity greater in the twentieth century, the reality of religious multiplicity in North America was already quite apparent during the late-eighteenth and early-nineteenth centuries. In 1849 John Nevin reviewed John Winebrenner's volume, *History of all the Religious Denominations in the United States*, with its portrait of the face of the American religious public. Touting Winebrenner's book as a religious counterpart to "Catlin's Indiana museum," after George Catlin's famous pictorial ethnography of various North American Indian tribes, Nevin's report took measure of the American religious scene and drew several conclusions which were familiar in his religious reflections and emblematic for the Mercersburg Theology.[1]

The invocation of Catlin's book provided a symbolic counter point in Nevin's review. Just as Catlin reported on the imminent extinction of several of the Indian tribes, Nevin, too, noted the short-lived duration and expected dissolution of so many of the religious assemblages. Yet, where Catlin saw poignancy in the passing of the tribes, Nevin discerned a positive and righteous judgment in the demise of these abnormal forms of sectarian Christianity. For over and against this efflorescence of denominational and sectarian religious life, Nevin juxtaposed the Church—one, holy, and catholic—as the essential and true medium of Christianity. Not the Church divided and splintered but the Church unified, emerging out of its necessary organic development, encompassing its historical past, and pressing forward to its future accomplishments, this was Nevin's vision of the true Church.

The doctrine of the Church provides one of the major themes unifying the Mercersburg movement and contains many of its most powerful and influential ideas. This essay shall not attempt to evaluate the entire doctrine of the Church as it is found in Nevin's writings. Instead, it shall focus on several of his essays so as to display his thinking on the issue of the unity of the Christian Church, or, as it is often called, the ecumenical question. Nevin's contribution to this discussion of ecumenism was significant in his own day for it explicitly opposed the prevalent sectarian sentiment and provided an evaluation of the contemporaneous strategies for church union. Beyond that, Nevin spoke to the issue of Protestantism's organic relationship to Roman Catholicism and thus dealt with one of the major issues which has defined twentieth-century ecumenical efforts.

Perhaps because he was less historically inclined than his colleague Philip Schaff, Nevin did not seek to provide answers for why there were so many churches in America nor to assess what were the sources for division among Christian churches in the United States. Nevertheless, a sensitive observer, such as Nevin, certainly could have pointed to theological differences inherited from Europe which separated Catholics and Protestants as well as transplanted or revitalized nationalist antagonisms which further splintered the Protestant traditions into ethnic enclaves. Legal separation of church and state abolished overt political establishment of one denomination and further allowed for the proliferation of religious organizations without hinderance or legal opposition. Finally, during the revivals of the First and Second Great Awakenings, the new validation of individual experience and personal subjective feelings had also enhanced the collapse of earlier more centralized, parish-oriented, and tradition-based patterns of religious authority. Instead, itinerant and charismatic ministers preaching the necessity and possibility of salvation as available through immediate and often emotional conversion experiences articulated divergent theological emphases at the same time that they enjoined believers to come out of churches pastored by supposedly spiritually dead men and to form new spiritually awakened churches.[2]

Strategies for Church Union

These historical circumstances of sectarian multiplicity were the context for Nevin's evaluation of the strategies for church union.   Clearly, sectarian divisions were unacceptable in his view as a proper depiction of what the Church should be. Yet, just as clearly, the Church was presently divided, so how ought it to be reunited?   What ensemble of historical, creedal, liturgical, or ecclesiastical resources were available for reconstruction?   Or was the Church, like Humpty Dumpty, incapable of being put back together again?

While Nevin emphasized the deficiencies and perils of sectarianism, he was aware of the various efforts toward church reunion taking place in early-nineteenth-century America. The Presbyterians and Congregationalists had entered into a common Plan of Union in 1801 in which local congregations could accommodate themselves to either denomination. Skeptics chided this arrangement, claiming it resulted in "Congreterial" and "Presbygational" churches; however, the agreement lasted until 1837 when it was rejected by the old school Presbyterians and until 1852 when it was abrogated by the Congregationalists.   Another example of unitive concerns is William A. Muhlenberg's *Hints on Catholic Union*, published in 1835, which presaged the more famous Muhlenberg memorial to the Episcopal bishops in 1853.[3]

Where the Plan of Union between the Presbyterians and Congregationalists spoke of accommodating the needs of congregations and judicatories, other proposals and suggestions significantly varied the language, envisioning, for example, the absorption of one group by another, or construing the relation as a wedding of equals. In other cases, the recommendations imagined a federation of representatives from individual denominations, modelled in large part on the United States Congress, or as an organic union of parties producing something wholly new.   Again, the language used was significant because it reflected different strategies for reunion and, in turn, reflected different expectations for the future as well as different heritages from the past.

At least four different types of unitive efforts can be identified in America during the first two-thirds of the nineteenth century. The first was an alliance between denominations, represented by the aforementioned Plan of Union between the Presbyterians and Congregationalists. This plan was motivated, above all, by a desire to pursue evangelism in the Trans-Appalachian West, and so reflected the mutual desire to transcend denominational differences in the interest of organized missionary goals. The second type was a federal union and Samuel Schmucker's *Appeal to the American Churches with a Plan for Catholic Union*, published in 1838, is an excellent example. In Schmucker's plan, no denomination would lose control to a centralizing hierarchy, but would rather retain its own ecclesiastical organization, government, discipline, and mode of worship. Invoking a picture of the apostolic Church in which all members were called Christians and geographic distinctions rather than sectarian names were the only emblems of particularity, Schmucker sought doctrinal unity in the affirmation of a confessional statement which he devised and which he believed expressed both the essence of biblical truths and the fundamentals of Protestant doctrine. United in belief and sensitive to expressions of denominational autonomy, Schmucker's plan joined the denominations at the top in a federative union.[4]

The third type of unitive effort can be seen in the formation of the Disciples of Christ under the leadership of Thomas and Alexander Campbell. Lamenting sectarian schisms, the Campbells called for a return to the Bible and to the primitive Church and proclaimed that basis as the framework for Church unity. Claiming to refrain from any practices or beliefs which they felt were not positively enjoined by the New Testament, the Campbells' restorationist and biblicist agenda called on all churches to join together in their movement. Their results, however, were ironic. Conceived as a means to Church unity, the movement eventually crystallized into an independent denomination.[5]

The final type of unitive effort was the popular voluntary associations for reform such as the American Bible Society, American Tract Society, American Sunday School Union, American Temperance Society, and the like. Non-denominational in approach and led by laypersons, these societies grew in number and influence in antebellum America.

Their efforts towards unity were *de facto* in that they brought together various Protestant individuals to cooperate, outside the framework of denominationalism, in assorted activities of charity, reform, and evangelism. That this network grew into a veritable benevolent empire has often been stated. For the present purposes, it needs to be noted that these collaborative associations provided yet another model, and a very popular if non-ecclesiastical one, of unitive efforts during the first two-thirds of the nineteenth century.[6]

The Critique of Sectarianism

Nevin attained his earliest notoriety in 1843 with the publication of *The Anxious Bench*. A repudiation of the psychological assumptions and theological pretensions of popular American revivalism, Nevin took the anxious bench as a symbol of the whole system of new-measures revivalism, including its sectarian tendencies.   Beyond that, Nevin contrasted the "system of the catechism" with the "system of the bench" and excoriated the latter as theologically deficient and ecclesiologically inadequate.   Nevin's denunciation of sectarianism became increasingly emphatic and frank in the succeeding years. In 1844 in "Catholic Unity" he stated that sects "mar the unity" of the Church and were "a vast reproach to the Christian cause."   In 1846 in "The Church" he called them "a most defective abnormal condition of the Body of Christ, an interimistic abomination...which, while it lasts, all good men are bound to deplore."   By 1848 he identified sectarianism as the Antichrist, and one year later he damned sects as "tyrannical...self-constituted ecclesiastical organizations, called forth ordinarily by private judgment and caprice."[7]

Behind such invective lay a forceful analysis of what Nevin considered the short-comings of sectarianism.   First, Nevin sought to make an analytical distinction between a denomination and a sect. A denomination, he suggested, had a confessional basis and thus maintained an organic connection to the universal Church. As such, the Lutheran emphasis on justification by faith alone or the Calvinist stress on divine grace, for example, were necessary counterpoints to medieval Catholic thinking and necessary developments in the progressive growth of the Church. Such denominational episodes should be understood as temporally limited, for the Church would ultimately subsume these groups, reintegrating them back into the one universal Church. Sects, by contrast, held no organic relation to the Church or its historic traditions. They were ruptures from that history and expressions of individual hubris. Although claiming to be complete in themselves, Nevin argued that they were inevitably partial and shallow. The upshot was that for Nevin denominationalism had degenerated into sectarianism, as more and more groups splintered off or proclaimed their own autochthonous existence. Christianity in America, Nevin concluded, suffered from a "sect plague" every bit as noxious as any plague recorded in biblical history.[8]

Second, Nevin castigated the approach to the Bible which he found so characteristic of sectarianism. Sectarianism, Nevin charged, prided itself on its love for the Bible. Neither creeds nor confessional statements held authority, for these were merely the products of human efforts. Instead, the Bible and the Bible alone were enough for the sectarian. The upshot of this position was again a diminution of the authority of the Church and a refusal to accord the faith of Christianity recorded in the life of the Church through all the ages with the same honor and reverence given those testimonies recorded in the Scriptures. Moreover, and this was equally lamentable in Nevin's view, "with all his talk of following the Bible, the sectarian means by it simply, in the end, his own sense of what the Bible teaches." Thus, pride in the Bible became pride in ones own interpretation of the Bible. Not surprisingly, Nevin pointed out that lacking any historical consciousness or confessional guides, recourse to the Bible divided rather than unified believers. It seemed as if one had nearly as many sectarian groups as one had individual interpreters. This ecclesiastical fission reflected the divisive power of an individualistic approach to scriptural interpretation. Nevin's code word for this sort of interpretation was "private judgment" and he denounced it as subjective, solipsistic, ahistorical, and oblivious to the resources of Church and confession.[9]

Proper interpretation of the Bible for Nevin recognized its honor and majesty, yet always coupled that document together with the historical Church, that "actual organic presence of the new creation in Christ Jesus among men, comprising in itself all the supernatural life powers which were introduced into the world by the incarnation." The revelation in the Scriptures, for Nevin then, was intimately related to the revelation of the Incarnation, and beyond that, in the continuing manifestation of the divine in the Church.[10]

An insufficient historical awareness vitiated sectarianism, diminishing its spiritual capacities and enervating its scriptural interpretation. Rather than prizing tradition and creed as resources which could anchor and reunify a splintered and fractious Christianity, the spirit of the sect justified men "to feel themselves for the most part free to act in church matters as they please. To quit a church connection, once viewed even in the Protestant world as a most solemn thing, is now regarded very much as a simple change of residence." Changing the image from rootlessness to social strife, Nevin assailed the sects as

> bent on their own outward prosperity and aggrandizement. They press and rub each other, with constant unpleasant collision, in all their movements. Their activity for God's glory and the salvation of souls takes the form of competition and strife. Even the holy cause of revivals itself, is desecrated to party ends.[11]

The comparison to political parties could still be an invidious one in antebellum America. Reflecting the greater diversity and increased competition of economic and political interests, distinct political parties had become quite visible and increasingly accepted within American society. Yet, Nevin intended here to draw on an older social and political tradition, one which saw in the rise of political parties testimony to the deterioration of social unity and political health. Thus, the sects, just as political parties were alleged to do, pursued their own private goals at the expense of those of the commonwealth. They were contentious and fought with one another, taking satisfaction in the distress and defeat of their opponents rather than seeking harmony and peace. They were individualistic and partial in their perspective, incapable, even if inclined, to rise above the moment and encompass a more comprehensive viewpoint. Thus, just as the body politic was harmed by the presence of the cancer of political parties, so was the well-being of that living, sentient, organic body of the Church threatened by the existence of sects.

Attributes of the Church

In an essay entitled "Catholic Unity" that Nevin wrote in 1844 and later appended to Philip Schaff's *Principle of Protestantism*, he claimed that the Church was holy and catholic. Invoking the precedent of the Apostles' Creed as the warrant for his statement, Nevin insisted that these two attributes were fundamental to any proper understanding of the nature of the Church. Two years later, in his essay "The Church," Nevin expanded upon this initial characterization and added visible, life-bearing, and historical as features which together properly expressed the full meaning of the Church's being.

In stressing the visible character of the Church, Nevin simply sought to repudiate undue emphasis on the Church as an invisible body, as was popular within certain strands of pietism in both America and Europe. In such a view, the Church became "a mere phantom," Nevin wrote, bereft of any real existence, force, or presence in the world. In highlighting that the true Church was life-bearing, Nevin proposed that Christianity "is a perpetual fact that starts in the Incarnation of the Son of God, and reaches forward as a continuous supernatural reality to the end of time." Here then, in a move that would come to demarcate the Mercersburg movement as a whole, consideration of the nature of the Church always led to reflection on the meaning of the Incarnation, on the mystery of the supernatural revelation manifested in Jesus and continued in the Church. For "there is no opposition," Nevin wrote, "between Christ and the Church in the economy of salvation." Finally, Nevin claimed that if the Church was visible and real then it had to be historical. And to say that it was historical was to imply, at the very least, that it had a "connection with its own life in all previous ages." This insistence on the historical nature of the Church was to become another characteristic feature of the Mercersburg theological enterprise and one to which Nevin repeatedly returned. Beyond that, as Nichols has suggested, the very development of modern ecumenical thinking depended in no small measure on the emergence of just such a historical awareness with reference to the Church together with a recognition of its implications for individual denominations. Holy and catholic, bearing the life of Christianity, and universal in its extent and measure, these were the attributes of the one true Christian Church for Nevin.[12]

Every era has its particular marks, its images, metaphors, and signs that capture its standpoint and express its own message. The organic metaphor was one of the central images for the romantic movement which played such a significant role in nineteenth-century arts, letters, and science. Protestant theology was no exception to this influence, and Nevin's writings are suffused with biological allusions, organic metaphors, and developmental images. Nevin also used these linguistic conventions to express more formal theological points.

As early as 1844, for example, he insisted that the Church was an organic entity, "not a mere aggregation or collection of different individuals, drawn together by similarity of interests and wants." In the first place Nevin was protesting against the view which would construe the Church as a voluntary association comprised simply of like-minded individuals. To Nevin it was a fundamental mistake to confuse the Church with any of the voluntary moral or political reform associations which had emerged in such great numbers in America during the first 40 years of the nineteenth century. No matter how noble their purposes, "a Bible society, a temperance union, a benevolent association of any kind," was no Church. This was the case, in Nevin's view, because such organizations were always partial in their perspectives, oriented toward specific purposes which never could encompass the fullness of the spiritual dynamism of the Church. Beyond that, the Church was simply not a voluntary association, on the model of some contractual society formed through the free volition of individuals, albeit regenerate ones, for their own common purposes. Rather, Nevin insisted that the Church was an *anstalt*, a divine institution which existed prior to the formation of any given congregation or parish. For Nevin maintained that the Church was an organic institution founded by God, not a collection of individuals, which existed and grew through the mechanical addition of individuals.[13]

Nevin's emphasis on the Church as an *anstalt* not only represented a reaction to developments in America, such as the rise of benevolent associations, it also reflected his thorough familiarity with contemporary German controversies over the church question. Of equal importance, it provided Nevin with a context to showcase his organic view of the Church. While organic metaphors could be found in his writings as late as the 1850s, one finds in his essay "Catholic Unity" the assertion that the Church as one unified organism contains within it the active presence of its origins which vitalize and direct the growth taking place in the present. "The whole is older and deeper than the parts, and these last spring forth perpetually from the active presence of the first," Nevin wrote, "the oak of a hundred years, and the acorn from which it has sprung, are the same life."[14]

The Church, then, was an entelechy, a growing, maturing entity with deep roots in the past. As such, Nevin reiterated that the Church was a historical entity which could not be cut off from its historical roots without causing fundamental damage. More specifically, Nevin insisted, that the present-day Protestant church derived in important ways from the Roman Catholic tradition stretching back to the Church's very origin. Nevin conceded that the Roman church had been corrupt in certain periods, however, he urged that to believe the Church "might take an entirely new start, under such visible organic character, in the fourth century, or the sixteenth, or at any other time, springing directly from the Bible or from heaven," would repudiate its historical character and reduce the true Church to an evanescent phantom.[15]

Nevin's message cut several ways at once. Clearly, it distanced him from those Protestants who celebrated Pentecost and then went on to ignore the intervening centuries of church life until the Protestant Reformation and the birth of their own denominations. Nevin and Schaff often found themselves assailed by the forces of popular Protestantism in America for their affirmation of the historical continuity of the Church. Such an affirmation, however, provided a basis for ecumenical inquiries, not only between Protestant groups who often shared strikingly similar liturgies, theologies, as well as histories, but also between Protestants and Roman Catholics, whose pasts might be more attenuated, but, nevertheless in Nevin's view did share many commonalities.

Finally, Nevin's developmental and historical consciousness provided him with the context for his assertion of the Church as ideal and actual. In one sense these categories allowed Nevin to protest that the familiar dichotomy of the Church as invisible and visible was defective in two ways. First, visible and invisible were static categories which did not do justice to the dynamic, growing nature of the Church. Second, assertions of the invisible nature of the Church, again, undermined proper acknowledgment of the presence of the Church in the world as a real, external form. In a more positive light, Nevin emphasized that the categories of ideal and actual were interrelated dynamically to one another rather than standing in stationary opposition to each other. Beyond that, the actual Church was one always in process, always guided and judged by the ideal, and never completed or fulfilled until that day when it and the ideal Church were joined together in the millennial Church Triumphant. Thus, for Nevin, ultimately, the historical Church was always the true Church, comprehending in itself its past and pressing forward to its future. As actual it fell short in all historic eras of the ideal, however, Nevin maintained, it did remain the depository of all the resources needed for the full redemption of humanity. Here, then, in this comprehensive, dynamic conception of the Church as ideal and actual, Nevin brought together the various strands of his views on the nature of the Church. Imbued with a deep historical sense, his conception both reflected many of the theological currents of the day and also applied them in the American context in distinctive ways.[16]

In 1844 in his essay "Catholic Unity" Nevin insisted that a "no-sect party in the Church" would be a futile response, probably an even more mischievous one than the malady it sought to correct. The reunion of the Church could not be achieved by force, he stated, but must emerge out of the necessary development of the institution itself. Here again, the negative allusion to party politics was clear, as was the organic imagery of a developmentalism which bided its time until the process of growth had matured by itself to the appropriate moment.[17]

By 1848, in his tract *Antichrist and the Spirit of Sect and Schism*, Nevin's tone had sharpened and he identified three approaches to church unity, each of which he believed was deficient. The first alternative crusaded against sects and called for unity by abolishing all differences in a return to the Bible pure and simple and a restoration of apostolic Christianity in ecclesiastical practice. This was the alternative proposed by the Campbells and, as previously suggested, it fell apart in Nevin's view on two grounds. First, rather than uniting believers, such a method had only led to a new sect. Second, the appeal to the Bible as the authority for belief and practice was naive and symptomatic of the sect consciousness. Here again, pride in the authority of the Bible became pride in ones own interpretation of that message, and the individualism and subjectivism which Nevin damned as "private judgment" reemerged on the scene. The second view proposed to form a union based on indifference to confessional traditions and substituting philanthropy for religion. This was the alternative of the voluntary associations, and Nevin found it quite unsatisfactory. The Church was more than a voluntary association, and the truths of religion were greater than the platitudes of moral reformers. Purposes counted for more than intentions and the purposes of Christianity, as revealed by the mystery of the incarnation and continued through the Church, Nevin believed to be qualitatively different and more profound than those of a reform society no matter how well intentioned its members might be. Finally, there was the alternative of a compact among the denominations themselves to form a common church organization. Here was Schmucker's plan, and Nevin conceded that such a federal union might be the best that one might expect in the way of unitive efforts. However, in the end, such federations amounted to merely outward forms of union in Nevin's view and thus they, too, were not satisfactory.[18]

The upshot for Nevin was that the only satisfactory church union would be an organic one, an inner determination which grew out of its historical past and developed toward its future goals. His language invoked the familiar attributes of the Church as one, holy, and catholic and saw the resuscitation of faith in such a Church as the only real remedy to the present dolorous conditions. Such a faith, a "faith in the mystery of one universal historical Church," stood against the subjectivism of the "sect plague." It represented a distinctive stage in the progressive development of the Church. It was a vision which was, indeed, catholic and universal, one which anticipated not only the gathering together of the assorted Protestant denominations, but also the reunion of the Protestant, Roman, and Eastern Orthodox branches of Christianity. It was a vision which reflected deep roots in its own era, yet still remained relevant well into the twentieth century. For as Nevin concluded, with deep conviction, such a vision represented the "one catholic Church of the Future."

ENDNOTES

1. J. Gordon Melton, *The Encyclopedia of American Religions*, 2 vols., (2nd. ed., Detroit, 1987) 1: xiii-xiv; John W. Nevin, "The Sect System," originally published in *The Mercersburg Review*, now reprinted in *Catholic and Reformed: Selected Writings of John Williamson Nevin*, ed., Charles Yrigoyen, Jr., and George H. Bricker (Pittsburgh, 1978): 133.

2. Winebrenner himself neatly illustrates this dynamic. Originally he had been a minister within the German Reformed Church and had charge of four congregations in the Harrisburg, Pennsylvania area. A revival in which he played a prominent role began in his congregation in 1820. The revival split the congregations and Winebrenner and his followers left the German Reformed Church in 1825. In 1829 these independent congregations formed the Church of God under Winebrenner's leadership and pledged themselves to no creed but the Bible and to governance by no body but that chosen by a majority of

the members of each congregation. See H. K. Carroll,
"Winebrennerians," *Schaff-Herzog Encyclopedia of Religious
Knowledge*, 4 vols., (3rd ed., New York, 1894), 4: 2538-39.

3. On the various union efforts see Sydney E. Ahlstrom, *A
Religious History of the American People* (New Haven, 1972),
456-58; Don H. Yoder, "Christian Unity in Nineteenth-Century
America," *A History of the Ecumenical Movement, 1517-1948*,
eds. Ruth Rouse and Stephen Charles Neill, (2nd ed.,
Philadelphia, 1967), 233-34; E. R. Hardy, Jr., "Evangelical
Catholicism: W. A. Muhlenberg and the Memorial Movement,"
Historical Magazine of the Protestant Episcopal Church, 13
(1944): 155-92.

4. Samuel Schmucker, *An Appeal to the American Churches With
a Plan for Catholic Union* (New York, 1838).

5. On the Campbellite efforts see Yoder, "Christian Unity," 236-
41; Nathan O. Hatch, *The Democratization of American
Christianity* (New Haven, 1989).

6. See Charles Cole, *The Social Ideas of the Northern Evangelists,
1826-1860*, (New York, 1954); Charles I. Foster, *An Errand of
Mercy*, (Chapel Hill, 1960).

7. John W. Nevin, *The Anxious Bench*, reprinted in *Selected
Writings of Nevin*, eds. Yrigoyen and Bricker, 9-126; "Catholic
Unity," 44; "The Church," 70; *Antichrist or the Spirit of Sect
and Schism* (New York, 1848); "The Sect System," 158.

8. Nevin, *Antichrist or the Spirit of Sect and Schism*, 69, 71.

9. Nevin, *Antichrist*, 57-59; "Sect System," 138-139.

10. Nevin, "The Church," 74.

11. Nevin, *Antichrist*, 80, 84.

12. John W. Nevin, "The Church," reprinted in *Mercersburg
Theology*, ed. James H. Nichols (New York, 1966): 66-71.
Nichols' comment is quoted from page 18 of that volume. The
Mercersburg emphasis on the Church as a visible, life-bearing
and historical entity stood in clear contrast to those who
privileged primitive Christianity as the model which was
retrievable and ought to be restored and emulated. See Richard
T. Hughes, *Illusions of Innocence: Protestant Primitivism in
America, 1630-1875* (Chicago, 1988).

13. Nevin, "Catholic Unity," reprinted in *Mercersburg Theology*, ed. Nichols, 40, 54: Nevin, "The Church," 68.

14. Nevin, "Catholic Unity," 40. On the German discussion of the church question, see Walter H. Conser, Jr., *Church and Confession: Conservative Theologians in Germany, England and America, 1815-1866*, 13-54.

15. Nevin, "The Church," 70-71.

16. Nevin, "The Church," 59-64.

17. Nevin, "Catholic Unity," 46-47.

18. Nevin, *Antichrist*, 81-83.

Nevin on the Lord's Supper

Arie J. Griffioen

The confessionalism of the Mercersburg Theology represents one of two major philosophical and theological adaptations of romantic impulses to antebellum American theology. In distinction from the revelatory immediacy and intuitionism of such well-known transcendentalists as Ralph Waldo Emerson and Theodore Parker, the Mercersburg Theology embodies a high-church confessionalism that attempts to define religious identity and theology by stressing the necessity of traditional and normative means of sacramental mediation.

Both transcendentalism and confessionalism represent romantic attempts to reconcile the deistic polarities of Enlightenment thought and therefore are characterized by an idealistic, metaphysical stress on the unity and harmony of such dualities as infinite/finite or divine/human. For example, the supernatural is not understood to be extrinsic to nature and history as Enlightenment thought would presuppose, but as dynamically unfolding itself within nature and history. Translated theologically, both transcendentalism and confessionalism are marked by a preoccupation with the question of the relationship of the divine and human, often articulated as the dynamic disclosure of the infinite within the finite.

But in contrast to the immediate intuitionism of transcendentalism, confessionalism attempts to articulate this relationship in traditional theological categories by appealing to historical creeds and confessions of faith as normative.[1] Developed largely in opposition to the trans-denominational and doctrinally relativizing tendencies of revivalism, antebellum confessionalism represents a distinct ecclesiastical response that appealed to the waves of recent European immigrants seeking to preserve their cultural and religious identity, as well as presenting an ecclesiastically and liturgically traditional alternative to the many who had tired of the excesses of "new measures."[2]

In contrast to transcendentalism's attempt to articulate a radically new and uniquely American ethos on the basis of a naturalistic intuitionism, confessionalism in America served to link Lutherans and Calvinists with their European religious heritage by utilizing the historical consciousness and communitarian impulses of romanticism, often expressed in organic metaphors.[3] For the transcendentalists the primary mode of disclosure of the infinite or divine is nature; for confessionalists like Nevin, it is history and community, or tradition and Church. History takes on significance as the arena within which the divine discloses itself dynamically through the human. Therefore, growth, development, and organic continuity with tradition are emphasized.[4] Likewise, the quest for the unity of the divine and human manifests itself in community, not merely as the collectivity of individual wills, but as an arena for the activity of the infinite.

Accordingly, antebellum confessionalist theology is decidedly oriented toward the sacramental expression of the means whereby the person and benefits of the incarnate Christ are constituted and conveyed by the Church as an historical organism. The use of communal and organic metaphors, and the allowance for the dynamic and unfolding presence of mystery within history and community, tradition and Church, facilitates the historiographic retrieval of reformational sources and the elaboration of confessionalist theology. The result is a uniquely nineteenth-century romantic retrieval and rearticulation of reformational theology and high-church concerns expressed within the milieu of American antebellum religious liberty, egalitarianism, and revivalism.

The 1846 publication of Nevin's *The Mystical Presence* signals the emergence of the Mercersburg Theology as an intellectual force in antebellum America. Arguing that Reformed churches in America had abandoned Calvin's sacramentology in favor of, at highest, a Zwinglian memorialism, Nevin argued for a real and substantial participation in the glorified life of

Christ.[5] In so doing, Nevin exposed the essential components of the Mercersburg Theology while presenting to American audiences what remains one of the most penetrating analyses of Calvin's sacramentology.

According to Nevin, the doctrine of the Lord's Supper is central to Christian theology because it concerns the very union of the believer with the person of Christ, and therefore the very nature of Christianity and the Church. Appealing continuously to Calvin, Nevin argues that the doctrine properly understood teaches that this union is neither merely moral nor legal, that is, neither a mere inward devotion or pledge of consecration, nor an external representation or imputation. Rather, union with Christ is **"real, substantial, and essential"**;[6] it is a real union with the person of Christ from which follow the merits and benefits of his sacrifice. Moreover, this union is not merely with Christ's divine nature separately considered, or with the Holy Spirit as Christ's representative in the world, it is with the Word incarnate, with Christ's divinity and humanity inseparably united in his glorified person.[7]

However, Nevin continues, real union with the person of Christ through the sacrament does not entail a local, corporeal presence as entailed by the Roman Catholic doctrine of transubstantiation or the Lutheran doctrine of con- substantiation. The significance of the sixteenth-century Calvinist doctrine lies in its ability to assert a real union with the person of Christ without necessitating the literal local presence of Christ's body in the elements to be orally received by the believer. The believer is united with the glorified person of Christ through the work of the Holy Spirit; participation in Christ's body and blood is spiritual, not corporeal.[8]

Recognizing that the sixteenth century use of the term **real** implied a local, corporeal presence, Nevin distinguishes the Calvinist position by referring to the "spiritual real presence" of Christ in the Lord's Supper. It is spiritual in that Christ's body is held to be in heaven and the believer's on earth, and the communion is not material; but it is real in that Christ's body is truly made present to the believer in the sacrament through the work of the Holy Spirit. The believer spiritually communes with the glorified person of Christ, inseparably divine and human, whose life, or "vivific virtue" flows into the communicant.[9]

This "old Reformed view" has been abandoned in America, either through a failure to recognize that it was ever believed, or through the assumption that the Reformation had not succeeded in completely overcoming the "Popish superstition"[10] of the real presence of Christ in the sacrament. At stake, Nevin contends, is the very nature of Christian salvation itself, that is, the relation and real union of the believer to Christ. Consequently, he continues his exposition by contrasting the "old Reformed view" with the "modern Puritan view" on five crucial points.[11]

First, according to the old Reformed view, the union of the believer with Christ accomplished through the Supper is specific to the nature of the sacrament and differs from anything else that takes place in Christian worship. This "specific peculiar virtue" of the Supper is not recognized by the modern Puritan view because it assumes that the Supper consists merely of outward signs that confirm the already present subjective state of the communicant. Second, according to the old Reformed view, the union of Christ and the partaking believer, the "sacramental transaction," is a supernatural mystery. The modern Puritan view, though perhaps respecting the Supper, relegates it completely to material or natural ends.

Third, the old Reformed view assumes that the "objective force" of the Supper belongs to its institution as sacrament and is not owing to the faith of the communicant. There is a sacramental union of the sign and the thing signified that is owing to the nature of the ordinance itself. This assumption does not allege that grace is conveyed in a purely mechanical way, in the manner of the Roman Catholic *opus operatum*, for the efficacy of the sacrament for the communicant remains dependent upon the condition of faith. But the sacramental transaction—but not the elements—objectively communicates the life of Christ, sealing to the believer "the grace it carries in its constitution."

Modern Puritan theology also assumes that the sacraments seal and exhibit the grace they represent, but something quite different than the objective validity of the Supper is intended. The seal simply ratifies a covenant between Christ and his people in which the two parties pledge to be faithful to each other. The sacrament thus exhibits the benefits of an existing and mutual contract, but not the thing signified. The Supper does not truly present and exhibit grace, but is only a pledge that the blessings accrued by Christ's merit are applicable to the believer "in a general way, apart from this particular engagement."

Moreover, the modern Puritan view is guilty of confusing the condition of faith with the objective virtue or principle of the sacrament and in so doing assuming that an insistence upon the condition of faith precludes the real presence of Christ. Employing romantic imagery, Nevin responds:

>...the difference between **condition** and **principle** is one that meets us on all sides, in every sphere of life. The plant cannot vegetate and grow without the presence of certain conditions, earth, moisture, heat, light, &c., required for its development. Are these conditions then in any sense the principle or ground of its life as such? Shall we say of the seed that it has no life in itself till it is thus called out in an actual way? On the contrary, we affirm the life to be in the seed objectively, even though it should never have an opportunity to make its appearance. And so we say, the sacrament of the Lord's Supper—not the **elements**, of course, as such, but the **transaction**, the sacramental mystery as a whole—includes, or makes present objectively, the true life of Christ.[12]

By implication, the same life is exhibited to the unbeliever, but he eats and drinks judgment to himself by not accepting it in faith.

Fourth, the invisible grace conveyed by the sacrament is the person of the Savior himself. The substantial life of Christ is made present to the believer, which is itself salvation. Christ communicates himself, not merely the privilege to partake of his benefits. Through the mystery of the Lord's Supper, the believer truly is joined with and participates in the person of the glorified Christ and as such receives all his benefits. "Christ first, and **then** his benefits. Calvin will hear of no other order but this."[13] The modern Puritan view teaches that union with Christ is moral only, or perhaps entails an incorporation with his

Spirit. Consequently, the believer is assumed to profit from all the mediatorial work of Christ, but does not participate in the substantial life of Christ himself.

Fifth, the old Reformed view teaches that the believer communes not merely with Christ's divine nature or with the Holy Spirit as Christ's representative on earth, but with the Word made **flesh**, with Christ's divinity **and** humanity inseparably united in his glorified person. The modern Puritan view repudiates this as "semi-popish mysticism," limiting whatever is admitted of Christ's presence to his divinity or the energy of the Spirit. What is stated in the Supper concerning Christ's body and blood is merely a figurative means of recalling his benefits. No communion with the incarnate Christ, who was once on earth and is now in heaven, is possible except as a remembrance.[14]

These five distinctions between the "old Reformed view" and the "modern Puritan view" do not constitute the end of the matter, for Nevin. As truth dynamically develops and unfolds in history, so Calvin's sixteenth-century articulations stand in need of reiteration and correction. This is particularly true with respect to three Christological matters that call into question the **extra-Calvinisticum** and have immediate sacramental implications.[15]

Reflecting the influence of romantic impulses, Nevin claims that Calvin failed to distinguish between the "organic law" that forms the proper identity of a human body, and the materiality that the human body exhibits to the senses. The identity of the body, which is constant, is not bound to its continuously changing materiality. Consequently, the communion between the body of Christ and the bodies of believers involves no literal transference of his flesh into their persons, a notion that Calvin rejected as well. Nevertheless, Calvin's confusion makes too much of the necessity of a local presence of Christ at the right hand of God in heaven, requiring an "awkward and violent" attempt to overcome a "vast separation in space" between Christ and the believer, albeit through the miraculous work of the Holy Spirit. Such an attempt cannot "sustain a strict continuity of existence" between Christ and the believer.

Second, Calvin failed to satisfactorily emphasize the absolute unity of Christ's **person**. By over emphasizing the virtue of Christ's flesh, his "single indivisible life," including his soul and divinity, is compromised. The acts of the incarnate Word, Nevin argues, constitute one life and belong to Christ's person as a whole. So his life is received by believers who are themselves a unity of body and soul.

Third, Calvin failed to distinguish between the individual personal life of Christ and his generic or general life as head of the new creation. As Adam was both an individual man, yet generically involved in the whole of humanity, so Christ lives in his people as he continues his personal incarnate existence:

> In one view of the Savior is a man, Jesus of Nazareth, partaking of the same flesh and blood with other men, though joined at the same time in mysterious union with the everlasting Word. But in another view he is again the man; in a higher sense than this could be said of Adam; emphatically the Son of Man, in whose person stood revealed the true idea of humanity, under its ultimate and most comprehensive form. Without any loss or change of character in the first view, his life is carried over in this last view continually into the persons of his people. He lives in himself, and yet lives in them really and truly at the same time.[16]

Hence, Nevin argues for a real supernatural communication of Christ's incarnate life to his people without a local mixture with his person.

Here, then, is the key to Nevin's sacramentology. Through the organic metaphors of romantic thought, he articulates a synthetic soteriology that forms a *via media* between the conflicting poles of the Protestantism of his day. On the one hand, Nevin rejects the naturalism—the position he calls "Socinian" or "Rationalism without disguise"—that cannot assert any real union with God because it regards Christianity as of the same natural order as other religions, only more highly evolved; on the other hand, he rejects the supernaturalism that allows only for the communication of Christ's benefits through the work of the Holy Spirit. This position, which he terms "Pelagian," receives the more elaborate critique, for it admits the central tenets of Christianity into its system.

The Pelagian position teaches that the truths of Christian faith are unfolded to the believer through the influence of the Spirit, not through an immediate effect upon the soul itself, but as mediated through God's word. The Spirit is said to infuse light and power into the truth of God's word in such a way as to favorably present that truth to the mind. This truth, Nevin acknowledges, includes the supernatural facts of the gospel, "the outward apparatus in full...of the Christian redemption" accompanied by the moral suasion of the Holy Spirit. But this amounts to no more than a persuasive presentation of facts to the human mind. The mediatorial life of Christ is then only something to be grasped and admired, but is in no way joined to the believer who is "left to starve and perish spiritually in the midst of a merely moral and rationalistic redemption."[17]

The doctrine of imputation, Nevin continues, is often introduced at this point in order to overcome the assumption that the work of Christ is merely displayed to the believer for moral effect.[18] As the fall of Adam was attributed to all his posterity, so the righteousness of Christ and the benefits of his work are forensically attributed by God to all who believe. Sinners are regarded by God as righteous, though they are not so in fact. But this will not do, Nevin contends:

> How can that be imputed or reckoned to any man on the part of God, which does not belong to him in reality?...A simple external imputation here, the pleasure and purpose of God to place to the account of one what has been done by another, will not answer.[19]

The Bible knows nothing of such an external and legal imputation with respect to either Adam or Christ that does not presuppose life in fact. Humanity participates in the actual unrighteousness of Adam's life; likewise, righteousness in Christ is not merely a legal or forensic declaration, but a communication of the very mediatorial life of Christ itself in the believer:

> The legal union, to be of any force for the imputation that is here required, must be a life union. In the very

act of our justification, by which the righteousness of
Christ is accounted to be ours, it becomes ours in fact
by our actual insertion into Christ himself. He is joined
to us mystically by the power of the Holy Ghost, and
becomes in this way the principle of a new creation
within us, which from the very start includes in itself
potentially, all that belongs to it already in his person.
The life thus set over into the believer, by the creative
fiat of his justification itself, is the bearer of all the new
relations in which he is thus brought to stand, as well
as of all the other **benefits** he is made to receive on
Christ's account.[20]

The relationship between Christ and the believer is neither
merely moral nor legal, but the sharing of a common life.

This common life, Nevin contends, is more than a sharing
of the same Spirit. Orthodoxy often assumes that the mystical
union between Christ and the believer consists of the work of
the Spirit in the life of the believer, causing the believer to
become increasingly of the mind of Christ. The Spirit is said to
have a supernatural influence, but only insofar as the Spirit
presents to the believer the power of the truths of Christianity.

But the presence of Christ in the life of the believer is
greater than the divine moral suasion of the Spirit. The Spirit
conveys a new life; the Spirit is the medium of the presence of
Christ in the Church and the believer. Though Christ does not
dwell in the believer physically, Nevin repeats, he does dwell in
the believer supernaturally, or mystically, through the Spirit, not
merely by way of representation. The imputation of Christ's
merits presupposes that his life, "the only real bearer of these
merits," should be conveyed to the believer. This is the work
of the Spirit:

Christ does dwell in us by his Spirit; but only as his
Spirit constitutes the very form and power of his own
presence as the **incarnate** and everlasting Word. The
Spirit (which is thus truly the Spirit of Christ) does form
us by a new divine creation into his glorious image; but
the life, thus wrought in our souls by his agency, is not
a production out of nothing, but the very life of Jesus

himself, organically continued in this way over into our persons.[21]

The work of the Spirit in the life of the believer is not a new creation out of nothing, but a new creation out of the actual life of Christ as it already exists and is extended to the believer. And again, union with the mediatorial life of Christ is not union merely with Christ's divinity—often itself confused by the orthodox with the Spirit—but with the incarnate Christ.[22]

Nevin's doctrine of the Lord's Supper is clearly indicative of his understanding of the whole of Christianity and the Church as the continuing presence of Christ in the world. Through the use of romantic categories, Nevin recovers the heart of Calvin's theology, so often wrongly conceived as predestination, by articulating the real union of Christ and the believer.[23] In so doing, Nevin's Protestant sacramentology represents a unique alternative not only to the theologies of his day, but to the contemporary American religious situation.

ENDNOTES

1. See Walter H. Conser, *Church and Confession: Conservative Theologians in Germany, England, and America, 1815-1866* (Macon, GA: Mercer University Press, 1984).

2. "New measures" included protracted revival meetings featuring cooperative participation by clergy of several denominations; fiery, animated preaching; evangelistic techniques designed to exert direct and public pressure upon individuals, often named, to decide immediately for conversion; sustained prayer and hymn singing designed toward that end; and the use of the "anxious (or mourners) bench"—usually an area of pews located directly in front of the pulpit and reserved for those who felt the need of special prayer and injunction to "see them through" to conversion.

    Confessionalism developed not so much in direct opposition to the use of "new measures" on the frontier, but to their systematic incorporation into the traditional liturgies of established churches. This form of revivalism was a more sedate, trans-denominational variety that had undergone a process of systematization and formalization through the work of such figures as Charles Grandison Finney and Benjamin Kurtz.

3. On Lutheran confessionalism, see Arie J. Griffioen, "Charles Porterfield Krauth and the Synod of Maryland," *Lutheran Quarterly* VII, 3 (Autumn 1993): 277-91.

4. For a description of romanticism as it comes to expression in American antebellum theology, see Arie J. Griffioen, "Orestes Brownson's Synthetic Theology of Revelation (1826-1844)" (Ph.D. dissertation, Marquette University, 1988), 105-106. For European roots, see Bernard M. G. Reardon, *Religion in the Age of Romanticism* (Cambridge University Press, 1985).

5. For Nevin's place as a nineteenth-century Reformed theologian, see B. A. Gerrish, *Tradition and the Modern World: Reformed Theology in the Nineteenth Century* (Chicago: University of Chicago Press, 1978), 49-70. This study remains one of the best available treatments of Nevin's sacramentology and I acknowledge my debt to it.

6. John Williamson Nevin, *The Mystical Presence: A Vindication of the Reformed or Calvinistic Doctrine of the Holy Eucharist* (Philadelphia: J. B. Lippincott & Co., 1846), 58.

7. Ibid., 54-58.

8. Ibid., 58-60.

9. Ibid., 61 — "vivific virtue" is Calvin's phrase.

10. Ibid., 109.

11. Ibid., 118-21.

12. Ibid., 120.

13. Ibid., 122.

14. Ibid., 125.

15. Ibid., 156-60.

16. Ibid., 161. Also see James Hastings Nichols, *Romanticism in American Theology: Nevin and Schaff at Mercersburg* (Chicago: The University of Chicago Press, 1961), 104.

17. Nevin, *The Mystical Presence*, 188.

18. See John Williamson Nevin, "Dr. Hodge on the 'Mystical Presence'," *Weekly Messenger of the German Reformed Church* 13 (24 May - 9 August 1848); and "Doctrine of the Reformed Church on the Lord's Supper," *Mercersburg Review* 2 (September 1850): 421-528.

19. Nevin, *The Mystical Presence*, 189.

20. Ibid., 191-92.

21. Ibid., 197.

22. Ibid., 197-98.

23. See Brian Gerrish, *Grace and Gratitude: The Eucharistic Theology of John Calvin* (Minneapolis: Fortress Press, 1993).

Nevin on Baptism

John B. Payne

In mid-nineteenth century American Protestantism, there raged a great debate concerning baptism between advocates of infant and proponents of believer's baptism. The champions of believer's baptism, the Baptists and that new breed of baptistic persuasion, the Campbellites, were on the march. The defenders of infant baptism were in retreat. In his *Mystical Presence* Nevin deplored the fact that not only had the Baptists become the most numerous denomination in the country but the baptistic principle had come to prevail, namely that the ordinance had no sacramental value.[1]

In the *Biblical Repertory and Princeton Review*, Charles Hodge lamented the "Neglect of Infant Baptism" in Presbyterian churches.[2] He published statistics that showed a steady decline in the ratio of infants baptized to the total number of members over the previous 50 years not only in the Presbyterian Church but also in the Dutch Reformed and Congregational Churches. Hodge pointed out that in 1811 among Presbyterians there were about 200 children baptized for every thousand communicants; in 1856 there were only 50. He reported for the Dutch Reformed Church that in 1856 sixty-eight children were baptized per 1,000 members, but the statistics for 1856 revealed a still greater neglect on the part of New England Congregationalists—only 16 children baptized per one thousand members. Hodge commented: "in the Congregational churches in New England, infant baptism is, beyond doubt, dying out."[3]

Hodge set forth what he considered to be the reasons for such extensive neglect of infant baptism. He named first the growth of anti-pedobaptist bodies, such as the movement of Alexander Campbell, and the influence of Congregational,

Arminian and semi-Pelagian elements in Presbyterianism. But the disease was blamed not only on germs from without, but also upon germs from within, namely, the neglect of pastors to give full instruction concerning baptism, the improper administration of the ordinance, dispensing it to children of parents with whom the minister is scarcely acquainted, the failure of the Church to recognize baptized children as members after baptism, and the decline in family worship.[4] Hodge thus pointed to certain practical reasons for the neglect of infant baptism.

To Nevin the causes of the depreciation of infant baptism lay deeper. They were not just practical but theoretical. They had to do with the conception of the Church and the sacrament, and between these two there is the closest connection. In *The Mystical Presence* he argued already that:

> In proportion as the sect character prevails, it will be found that baptism and the Lord's Supper are looked upon as mere outward signs, in the case of which all proper efficacy is supposed to be previously at hand in the inward state of the subject by whom they are received. It is this feeling which leads so generally to the rejection of infant baptism, on the part of those who affect to improve our Christianity in the way of new schisms.[5]

But he went on to assert that the "baptistic principle" which negates the objective sacramental value of baptism rules not alone among Baptists but also among good Reformed Protestants. What he called the modern Puritan view with its sectarian spirit and subjective, anti-sacramental tendency he thought was responsible for the disposition to reject infant baptism.

> If the sacraments are regarded as in themselves outward rites only, that can have no value or force except as the grace they represent is made to be present by the subjective exercise of the worshipper...it is hard to see on what grounds infants, who are still without knowledge or faith, should be admitted to any

privilege of the sort. If there be no objective reality in the life of the church, as something deeper and more comprehensive than the life of the individual believer separately taken, infant baptism becomes necessarily an unmeaning contradiction.[6]

To some extent Nevin and Hodge agreed as to the causes of the depreciation of infant baptism, what Hodge called "the influence of Congregational, Arminian, and semi-Pelagian elements" and what Nevin named as the Modern Puritan or the sectarian spirit. Both had in mind revivalism and the theology of revivalism which put the emphasis upon the human decision in the process of salvation and for entrance into the Church and upon the work of the Spirit directly in the hearts of believers without need of external sacraments. The roots of this anti-sacramental piety of revivalism go back to the Great Awakening when already Calvinistic sacramental doctrine was waning among New England Congregational clergy and laity. Concomitant with its demise was the departure of many Congregationalists from the fold to become Baptists.[7] But, as Brooks Holifield points out, Nevin, with the label "Modern Puritan," must have been aware that the nineteenth-century "Puritans" were not necessarily to be identified with their seventeenth-century counterparts. Indeed Holifield demonstrates that, though seventeenth-century Puritans were by no means of the same mind, there was a strong Calvinistic sacramental doctrine and piety among them.[8] Of course, Hodge and Nevin differed as to what in revivalism and its theology was primarily responsible for the neglect of infant baptism; for Hodge it was the false theory of salvation, Arminian and semi-Pelagian, with the emphasis upon the human will rather than upon divine grace, whereas for Nevin, though this consideration played a role, he excoriated far more a false doctrine of the Church and of the sacrament.

Although Nevin touched on baptism already in *The Mystical Presence*, his first substantial treatment occurred in a long review article of Horace Bushnell's famous work *Discourses on Christian Nurture* which entitled him to be known as the forerunner of modern religious education. His review extended over four issues of *The Weekly Messenger* in the summer of

1847.[9]   Nevin showed a deep appreciation for this work of Bushnell. It was especially welcome to him as emanating from the home of Puritanism which he usually castigated as embodying the subjectivistic, individualistic, anti-churchly, and anti-sacramental tendencies of much of American Protestantism.   Nevin commented: "The tract is at bottom contrary to the whole Puritan theory of religion; and yet, strange to say, the author is himself a Puritan and fails at last to make any real and full escape from the power of his own system."[10]   But before launching into a critique of Bushnell's ideas, he set them forth fully and fairly and pointed out the value in them.   He agreed with Bushnell's criticism of the then dominant scheme of Christian nurture, revivalism, which assumed that the child grew up a sinner until experiencing a sudden, dramatic conversion.   In contrast, Bushnell set forth in his tract the now familiar proposition: "That the child is to grow up as a Christian."   Already in a well-known treatise, Nevin had pitted the "system of the catechism" against the "system of the anxious bench," a system which stressed the gradual spiritual growth of the child under the working of divine grace and proper religious training over against a system which emphasized spasmodic conversions.[11]

Nevin agreed also with Bushnell in his attack upon the rampant individualism in the religious life of nineteenth-century America with the concomitant failure to recognize the law of organic connection in life.   He quoted with favor Bushnell's statement: "A pure separate, individual man, living wholly within, and from himself is a mere fiction."[12]   Nevin was fully persuaded that "the whole constitution of the world contradicts that atom theory of religion," that humanity is not a sum of discrete particulars but an organic whole.   Individuals are shaped and bound by the social context in which they find themselves—family, race, nation.   The Pelagian individualistic notion goes counter both to experience and Scripture, for also in Scripture there is expressed the view that there is an organic connection between Adam and the whole human race, and Nevin was pleased that Bushnell acknowledged "an important truth underlying the old doctrine of federal headship and original or imputed sin."[13]

Nevin welcomed Bushnell's insight that infant baptism is consonant only with an organic understanding of religion which underlay his concept of Christian education. While Bushnell noted the neglect of infant baptism on the part of parents, he urged the rite upon them not because of what it operates, namely, any actual regeneration of infants, but because of what it signifies, namely that "the faith and character of the parent will be reproduced in the child," and that "God promises...to dispense that spiritual grace which is necessary to the fulfillment of its import."[14]

But for all the praise that Nevin lavished upon Bushnell's treatise as an excellent antidote to the "rampant, fanatical individualism" of Protestant Christianity in mid-nineteenth-century America, he found fault with it. His major criticism was that Bushnell seemed to have based his theory of Christian nurture on the constitution of human nature rather than "upon the constitution of grace, as a strictly supernatural system." "In other words," Nevin wrote, "the argument is rationalistic." In spite of Bushnell's seeming acceptance of the doctrine of original sin, Nevin did not think that the Hartford minister took that doctrine with sufficient seriousness, for he asked: "If our nature is radically corrupt, how can it be expected to unfold itself by simple religious culture into a truly Christian form? The case would seem to require at least a supernatural change to begin with...."[15] Nevin goes on to criticize Bushnell's doctrine of original sin as defective, for it understood that doctrine not in the traditional sense as signifying a radical debilitation of human nature but rather in a Hegelian sense as "a necessary accident," which, rather than precluding our Christian development, is "the occasion or medium by which it takes place." Correspondingly, Bushnell's doctrine of regeneration appeared to Nevin as resting primarily upon the "capabilities of human nature" assisted, to be sure, by God's spirit, rather than upon a new supernatural act, the implantation of a new divine seed to do battle with the old germ which has produced the disease.

The deficiency of Bushnell's view becomes clear, according to Nevin, in his conception of Christian baptism. He complimented Bushnell's recognition that the practice of infant baptism presupposes an organic theory of Christianity which flies in the face of the individualistic religion advocated and carried on not only by the Baptists but even by denominations who traditionally favor infant baptism, such as Bushnell's own Congregationalists. But Bushnell's theory of infant baptism, which understood baptism as a sign and seal of faith not actual but "presumed," because it is presumed that the child will grow up in the faith and character of the Christian parent, was faulty. In Nevin's view what was missing from Bushnell's account was any notion of baptism as truly a divine sacrament conveying supernatural grace.

According to Nevin, Christian nurture rests not just upon the organic connection between Christian parent and child but upon the organic connection between Christ and His Church, "which is the continuation of Christ's life in the world and denominated for this very reason his body..." The Church is thus of a supernatural constitution, yet at the same time it exists "in harmony with the laws of this life." In the Church, as the bearer of Christ's life, humanity finds its fulfillment. We become incorporated into this new humanity through baptism, which is not simply a rite sealing faith, but a holy sacrament with objective, supernatural force. Not by mere natural birth, not by the faith and character of the parents only, but by grace mediated through the sacrament of baptism do infants become "children of God: and cease to be 'children of wrath'."[16]

In his *Argument for Discourses on Christian Nurture* written in reply to criticisms of his treatise, Bushnell responded at length to Nevin's critique. His response was as cordial and agreeable toward Nevin's review as Nevin's review was toward his *Discourses*. He rejoiced that Nevin appreciated the organic as opposed to the atomic theory of religion. But Bushnell rejected Nevin's charge that his view was at base naturalistic and rationalistic. He admitted that he adopted a naturalistic rather than a supernaturalistic language, not intending to deny the supernatural element, but in order to prevent confusion with the kind of "fantastic" supernaturalism opposed by them both, which assumed the supernatural influence as entering the world only in an abrupt, external manner without an inner, organic union. When he affirmed that the child's faith and character are rooted in the character and treatment of the parent, he had in mind that this character and treatment are themselves the result of divine grace.[17]

Bushnell did not really deal with Nevin's criticism of his doctrine of baptism except to suggest that Nevin's views on "the sacramental grace" of baptism and "the Church" were doubtful. How far removed he was from Nevin on this subject is clear from the following statement:

> But if we take this view, so ably set forth in the extract here given [in which Nevin put forward his teaching of "the supernatural in human natural form"] it follows, of course, that the Christian family and its organic laws are penetrated by the supernatural element; and as the family is closer about the child, and touches him in points more numerous, and ways more sovereign over character, "the Church that is in the house" has a great deal more to do with him, in the first years of his life, than the Church universal or any public sacrament.[18]

It is no wonder that Bushnell's defense did not wholly satisfy Nevin who reviewed it in the *Weekly Messenger*. Nevin seemed to retreat from his charge of a naturalistic rationalism, but he still accused the Hartford minister of a rationalism in the refined sense, characteristic, in his opinion, of New England theology in general, what he chose now to call "rationalistic supernaturalism,"[19] which he did not really define but by which he seemed to mean the anti-churchly and anti-sacramental tendencies of Puritanism.

Charles Hodge, the eminent old school Presbyterian Divine of Princeton, made this debate a three-cornered affair with his review of Bushnell's two tracts in the October 1847 issue of *The Biblical Repertory and Princeton Review*. He declared his agreement with Bushnell on two major points: "the intimate religious connection between parents and children," and "the primary importance of Christian nurture as the means of building up the Church."[20] Like Nevin, Hodge welcomed Bushnell's critique of revivalistic religion with its emphasis on abrupt conversion as the means of the edification of the Church. However, also like Nevin, he was critical of a perceived naturalistic explanation of the connection between parent and child. For Hodge, the basis for the religious link between parents and children was the covenant promise. "It is," he wrote, "a scriptural truth that the children of God, as being within his covenant with their parents, he promises to them His Spirit, he has established a connection between faithful parental training and the salvation of children...."[21] Just as circumcision in the Old Testament, so baptism in the New Testament testifies that children of Christian parents belong to the covenant and they are signs and seals of the same, and here Hodge used a favorite Reformed argument for infant baptism that goes all the way back to Zwingli. For both Hodge and Bushnell, baptism is not the means of incorporation into the Church. It is not a channel of grace. For Bushnell it is simply the sign of the organic connection between the parent's faith and character and the child's; for Hodge it is the sign of the divine promise which already before baptism includes the children of Christian parents in the covenant. Such a conception Nevin criticized in his review of Bushnell even before Hodge wrote his own:

> What do good men mean, when they tell us that the children of professing parents are Christians likewise, members of the Church and heirs of all its grace, by their mere **natural birth**?...Our birth relation to pious parents may give us a right to be taken into the Church, but it can never of itself make us to be in the Church as our born privilege, authorizing our parents to bring us up as Christians from the womb.[22]

For Nevin the basis for our belonging to the Church and for this authorization is rather the sacrament of holy baptism.

To Hodge such a view as Nevin's smacked of ritualism and magic. Without naming him, Hodge, at the end of his review of Bushnell's treatise, characterized Nevin's understanding of the sacraments, Church, and redemption as un-Protestant and false, namely, that the sacraments have an efficacy apart from the faith of the believer, that the external Church rather than the community of believers is the body of Christ and is the one medium of approach to Christ, that redemption involves the partaking of the human nature of Christ rather than the indwelling of the life of God in the soul by the Holy Spirit. "The whole doctrine," he writes, "is nothing but a form of the physical theory of religion."[23]   In other words, Hodge suggested that the Mercersburg Theology was guilty of a medieval Catholic theory of the Church with a crude *ex opere operato* understanding of the sacraments.

To Nevin, on the other hand, the standpoint of his great teacher, Hodge, was unsacramental, spiritualistic, and unchurchly just like so much of the New Light Protestantism that Hodge otherwise denounced. In the very next spring and summer, 1848, Nevin and Hodge would engage in a famous quarrel over these same matters when the focus of their discussion would be the Lord's Supper rather than baptism.

Just after the series of review articles on Bushnell's *Discourses on Christian Nurture*, an inquiry concerning "baptismal grace" directed to Nevin was penned for the August 11, 1847, issue of the *Weekly Messenger*. Nevin's response provides us with some understanding as to how he would reply to Hodge's accusation of sacramental magic in his doctrine. The inquirer asked whether Nevin viewed "baptismal grace" as equivalent with "baptismal regeneration." "Does he believe that baptism, when rightly administered, is invariably and immediately accompanied with regeneration"? Although Nevin noted the ambiguity of the phrase "baptismal regeneration," he made it clear that he rejected the idea of a "regeneration" as **necessarily** flowing from baptism, but he also affirmed his full acceptance of the notion of an objective grace in the sacrament.   And he compared the baptismal act with the outward call of the disciples "which did not of itself convert them, as we see clearly from the case of Judas; though it certainly carried with it objectively a full real title to all that is comprehended in the Christian salvation, as this came to be actualized subsequently in all of them except Judas."[24]

That Nevin did not have in mind a mechanical *ex opere operato* conception of the sacrament as effective apart from the subjective disposition of the recipient is clear from his response to a second series of questions from the same inquirer. Question: "Is the grace which is communicated by baptism, **saving** grace or not?" Answer: "If this means grace that actually saves the subject, no; if the sense be that it is able through faith to save him, yes." Nevin reaffirmed that the sacrament has an objective force whose efficacy rests not upon the minister or the parents of the child baptized but upon Christ himself and least one think that this is a Romish doctrine only," he added, "as Calvin says."[25] On the other hand, for that objective grace to be truly effective, saving grace, it must be received in faith. Already in the *Anxious Bench* he criticized a mechanical, sacramental understanding and piety that take the place of a true Christocentric doctrine and devotion. In this regard he likened the use of the anxious bench to the Puseyite and Papist substitution of the baptismal font for Christ.[26]

Nevin's next expression of his views on baptism occurred in the March 1, 1849, issue of the *Weekly Messenger* in an article entitled, "A Romanizing Tendency." In this article he took delight in twitting his critic, Joseph F. Berg, minister of Race Street Church in Philadelphia and publisher of the *Protestant Banner*, for having been accused by the Baptist paper, *The New York Recorder*, of being a supporter of "the main pillar of the Papacy" with his strong advocacy of infant baptism. How ironic that Berg, who saw "a Romanizing tendency" in all that stands between his position and that of Rome, was here himself accused of the same error!

But Nevin thought that Berg should acknowledge the truth of the Baptist accusation. Berg did ally himself with the Roman Church to uphold one of the ancient bulwarks of the faith, just as much else is derived from this church, such as the Creed, Christian worship, sacraments, etc. On this subject, Dr. Berg should admit, according to Nevin, that "in defending infant baptism, he followed to a certain extent the authority of *tradition*, in its proper legitimate form, "for the Baptist paper was right that Dr. Berg did not draw his doctrine of infant baptism from the letter of Scripture, since "There is no direct, positive appointment of infant baptism in the whole Bible, and no clear and explicit example of its use."

He went on to argue what would be a major theme in his writings on the subject, that infant baptism makes no sense except as it is closely connected with the idea of the Church as the body of Christ and the "real bearer of a supernatural life." Infant baptism presupposes an objective force in the sacrament itself and this in turn "implies the presence of a divine and life-bearing constitution in the Church itself," to be sure, a cardinal doctrine of the Roman Catholic Church, but also of the Catholic Church in general, including reformation Protestantism, which, like the Roman Church, adheres to the creedal article "holy, catholic Church."

In contrast with Dr. Berg and other defenders of pedobaptism, Nevin chose not to argue with the Baptists on their own ground, namely the letter of Scripture, the interpretation of Greek verbs and prepositions. He determined rather to argue from the life of Christianity itself, "grace and truth made human first in Christ himself, and then perpetually in the Church." Without naming him, Nevin then drew on an argument of Irenaeus against the Gnostics that Christ showed by his having gone through all the stages of human life that he sanctified all ages and "recapitulated" or "summed up" all of humanity.[27] Nevin argued that, since Christ went through the stages of human development from the womb to the grave, it is necessary and proper that the process of salvation in the Church should include infancy and childhood as well as adulthood. To exclude a large portion of our universal humanity from baptism and participation in the process of Christianity "because incapable of any real comprehension in the kingdom of God, or the new life of Christ in the Church, is in truth to turn the fact of Christ himself into a Gnostic phantom, and to make his whole salvation unearthly and unreal." It's no wonder that the Church from the beginning took a different view and brought "her children into covenant with God by holy baptism."[28]

Further reflections on this "chief" argument for infant baptism and on the origins of infant baptism in the Church are found in his first extensive engagement with the Baptist position, a lengthy review of an *Essay on Christian Baptism* by the English Baptist W. Noel, printed in the *Mercersburg Review*, May 1850. The controversy with the Baptist, Nevin contended, hangs on two questions, the first, concerning the mode of baptism, and the second, concerning its proper recipients.

Regarding the first issue he conceded that the Baptists have a strong case. "Baptize" did have "immerse" as its original meaning and immersion seems to have been the regular practice of the early Church according to the New Testament. Though he criticized the literalness of the Baptist understanding and thought that the later Western freedom concerning the mode of baptism harmonized fully with "the true idea of Christianity," he insisted that the present practice of only a few drops on the head of the infant carries that freedom too far. Such a practice suggests an unsacramental feeling not far removed from Quaker spiritualism.

Before taking up the second far more important issue, Nevin considered two methodological questions: concerning biblical hermeneutics and concerning the nature of a sacrament. He took issue with Noel for pretending to come to Scripture as an empty vase with no theological presuppositions or tradition. It is blindness on his part not to recognize his own prejudices and impudence to give to his private judgment a universal value. For Nevin the proper interpretation begins not with one's own particularistic viewpoint but with an understanding of and feeling for "the general fact of Christianity as a living comprehension in its true Catholic mystery as it has stood from the beginning."[29]

Fundamental to the general fact of Christianity and "its true Catholic mystery" is the use of the sacraments, and the question of their use rests "on the true idea of their nature." A sacrament in the old Church sense is no mere outward rite or ordinance as Baptists like Noel think; it is both "a viable terrene sign and an invisible celestial grace; not related simply as corresponding facts, brought together by human thought; but the one actually bound to the other in the way of most real mystical or sacramental union, causing the last to be objectively at hand in one and the same transaction with the first." To Nevin a sacrament conveying no objective grace is a contradiction in terms. Baptism is no mere sign of a subjective state of the believer; it is a divine act. "It is the washing of regeneration; it saves us; it is for the remission of sins." But then he qualified these strong statements that might suggest a mechanical *ex opere operato* interpretation by adding: "The mere ceremony of course is not this *per se*; but it goes actually to complete the work of our salvation, as the mystical exhibition in real form of that divine grace, without which all our subjective exercises...amount to nothing."[30]

With this view of the sacrament, the idea of the Church is closely linked. The Church is not simply a union of all who embrace the gospel, but it is the mystical body of Christ in which "the power of redemption is truly and really present." Indissolubly connected with the Church, therefore, is Christ as the new creation embracing humanity in an organic whole.

Thus, Nevin reached what he now called "the grand argument for infant baptism." Just as in the article concerning Berg's Romanizing, he argued: "It lies not in the letter of Scripture, but in the life of Christianity itself, the true idea of the Church, the mystery of Christ as the Second Adam, in whom redemption and salvation are brought to pass for the race." As Christ is the mediator representing in himself all humanity, having himself sanctified, as Irenaeus said, all the stages of human life, so his salvation is available to all human beings, including infants.[31] Such a view of Christ and his work shaped the life of the early Church and "found its natural, we might say almost necessary expression, in infant baptism." Nevin went so far as to argue that:

> If it could be clearly made out that the household baptisms of the New Testament included no infants; nay, if it were certain that the Church had no apostolical rule whatever in the case, but had gradually settled here into her own rule; we should hold this still to be of truly divine authority, and the baptism of infants of necessary Christian obligation, as the only proper sense and meaning of the New Testament institution, interpreted thus to its full depth by the Christian life itself.[32]

In the section on "The Apostolical Origin of Infant Baptism" in his *History of the Christian Church* published in the *Mercersburg Review* in 1852, Schaff had likewise called the argument suggested by Irenaeus the strongest one in favor of infant baptism, but in contrast to Nevin, Schaff pointed to specific biblical passages to support the view of a redemption of all persons and ages in Christ, for example the Great Commission in Matthew 28 in which Christ instructed his followers to make disciples of all nations, by baptizing in the name of the triune God, and by teaching them. Schaff asked "...do none but adults belong to a nation, and not youth and children and infants"?[33] The arguments here of both Schaff and Nevin were probably based on the famous German church historian Neander, who, though skeptical about the foundation of infant baptism in the New Testament, thought infant baptism grew out of "the deepest conception of the very nature of Christianity," and Neander likewise referred to the thought of Irenaeus.[34]

Nevin buttressed this principal argument by referring also to the traditionally most important argument of the Reformed tradition, the analogy of the Jewish covenant community which included both adults and children. But it is remarkable how small a role that argument with its analogy of baptism to circumcision played in his thinking. Without laying great stress upon it, Nevin added the argument, also traditionally a favorite one, in support of infant baptism, the doctrine of original sin. Corresponding to the law of sin which applies to infants as well as adults is the universal law of life in Christ.

On the basis of this theological rationale perceived by the Church in the beginning, she incorporated "infants into her communion by the initiatory seal of holy baptism." Thus, Nevin moved from general considerations of hermeneutics, doctrine of sacraments, ecclesiology, Christology, and soteriology, all of which are closely bound up with one another, to a consideration of the specific issue of baptism. Here he argued from its theological to its historical necessity. More important to him is establishing infant baptism's theological ground than its explicit practice in the early Church. He seemed to be bothered less than Schaff by Neander's claim that infant baptism was not introduced into general practice until the early third century. Even if that were true, the Baptist's case is by no means established, for the question then arises, "How came such baptism **then** into quite general use? Was it in full antagonism to the genius of Christianity as it stood before; or did it spring spontaneously out of this, in the way of natural and necessary derivation"?[35] If the unchurchly, the unsacramental, spiritualistic, rationalistic theory of the Baptists had been held by the primitive Church, how could infant baptism have emerged in so short a time? But Mr. Noel argued that the Church adopted also infant communion before, after centuries of practice, it came universally to be recognized as an abuse. Nevin countered that again on the Baptist sacramental theory one cannot account for how this practice could possibly have come about. One can more easily explain how infant communion, like infant baptism, issued from the genius of Christianity as understood by Nevin than how both could emerge out of the Baptist understanding.

In the light of the current debate on infant communion, it is interesting to observe that Nevin regarded infant communion, like transubstantiation, as an excess but preferred it to the exclusion altogether of infants from the life of the church just as he no doubt, like Luther, would prefer transubstantiation to a rejection of the real mystical presence of Christ in the Eucharist. I think he would scarcely deny the link in logic between infant baptism and infant communion. The same ecclesiological and sacramental understanding that undergirded his views of infant baptism should move him also to favor infant communion. He was probably held in check here only by the Reformed tradition.

Though Nevin was not as concerned as Schaff to prove the historical argument, he agreed with his colleague against Neander that there probably was infant baptism prior to the third century and he referred to the testimonies of Origen, Tertullian, and Cyprian. He argued that since the advocates of infant baptism have the clear testimony of the Fathers in the first half of the third century on their side, the burden of proof lies with the proponents of the Baptist position to show that infant baptism was not practiced before that time especially since Origen, for one, assumed that it was handed down from Apostolic times.

But lest one think that with his stress upon the objective power of the sacrament he has overlooked its subjective appropriation in faith, Nevin emphasized near the conclusion of his review that infant baptism is only the beginning of the process of salvation; it assumes catechetical instruction under the hand of the Church and requires confirmation "to bring to its true and full sense." This demand for a personal response on the part of the recipient of baptism should not be regarded as an independent transaction but rather as "the natural and

suitable close of the baptismal act itself."[36]   Here Nevin
showed himself aware of the early Church's theology and
practice which made the closest connection between baptism
and confirmation, a fact which has come to be better
understood and appreciated in studies on the subject since
World War II.

Schaff likewise insisted upon catechetical instruction and
confirmation in which the believer confirms the baptismal vows
and makes free and full surrender to God. Thus, he considered
that the baptism of the children of unbelievers, even of
professing Christians when there is no likelihood of religious
training, is a travesty and a profanation of the sacrament. He
objected, however, to the Baptist limitation of faith "to a
particular stage of human consciousness" and to their making
the dispensation of grace dependent upon it. Like Nevin he
argued that the true ground of salvation is not the subjective
mind of the creature but the divine compassion. However, he
supplemented Nevin's view by arguing like Luther and in
anticipation of faith development theory that faith itself has
"different grades, from the first bud, to the ripe fruit" and that
we should therefore think of a level of faith as present already
in children.[37]

Nevin concluded his long review article by admitting that
there are "great difficulties" associated with the subject of
baptismal grace. He did not even tell us exactly what these
are, much less did he pretend to solve them. Presumably, he
had in mind the lack of a faith response in infants and a
magical, mechanical view of the sacrament expressed in that
well-worn phrase about "having the baby done." Nevin did not
at all suggest the view of Luther, adopted, as we noticed, by
Schaff, that there is a hidden faith even in infants. In fact, he
stated that he has stayed clear of the question as to what
specifically constitutes the power of baptism in the case of
infants. He simply confessed to the belief that grace is
objectively present in the sacrament "under some form." That
conviction, in his view, is consonant with the view of Christian
antiquity and the Reformation. From that persuasion not only
the Baptist viewpoint, but crypto-baptist thinking of much of
American Protestantism must be distinguished.   While
acknowledging problems connected with baptismal grace in the

case of infants, he thought the alternative to the assertion of baptismal grace in some sense even in infants is rationalism.[38]

In the article "The Anglican Crisis" Nevin strongly affirmed the doctrine of baptismal grace without admitting any difficulties concerning it.[39]   The occasion for the article was the crisis for the Church of England which was set in motion by the famous Gorham case of March 1850.   The Privy Council had ruled in favor of Gorham, a priest, against his bishop, Phillpotts, on the subject of baptismal regeneration.   The priest, an evangelical, rejected the Tractarian position favored by the bishop that the ancient doctrine of baptismal regeneration of infants must be maintained.[40]   Nevin emphasized the seriousness of the crisis not only for the Anglican Church but for all of Protestantism.   The crisis centered not just on the issue of baptismal grace, however important that issue was, but also on the issue of the doctrine of the Church—whether or not it is a divine, sacramental institution in the old catholic sense.   The notion of the efficacy of sacramental grace depends upon the ancient idea of the Church as a supernatural, grace-bearing institution.   In Nevin's view the issue for Anglicanism as well as for Protestantism was whether the Church in the mid-nineteenth century could understand itself as truly standing in continuity with the ancient Church.   As I have discussed elsewhere, this issue posed also a theological crisis for Nevin himself as he seriously questioned the legitimacy of the claim of sectarian American Protestantism to be called the Church in light of the vast difference in outlook and practice between it and the ancient Church.[41]

As applied to baptism, the issue was "whether baptism is to remain a sacrament at all for Protestantism, in the old universal church sense." That sense included "the idea that the holy sacraments are divine acts, that they carry in them a mystical force for their own ends, that they are the media of operations working towards salvation which have their efficacy and value, not from the mind of the worshipper, but from the transaction or thing done itself...." Baptism, in the ancient view, according to Nevin, is identified with the forgiveness of sins and regeneration. The practice of infant baptism was from the beginning predicated altogether upon the assumption of such an "objective force in the ordinance...." Nevin thought

that this ancient view of baptismal grace was still held by the
Reformers, Luther and Calvin, though he admitted that Calvin
was more guarded in his espousal of it. But the question for
Nevin as he wrote this article was whether Protestantism was
a "sacramental system at all" and whether it had any sense of
sacramental grace as it had been recognized in the Church all
the way back "to the days of Ignatius, Polycarp, and the
Apostles." Though he could understand the Baptists' desire for
the destruction of the old sacramental system, he wondered
how the Lutherans, the Reformed, the Presbyterians, and even
the Methodists and Congregationalists could be swept along by
the Baptist "unchurchly humor" and themselves "not be struck
with some feeling of anxiety and dread at the thought of
making Protestantism by its own voice and vote constitutionally
baptistic and unsacramental..."?[42]

Though the church question continued to dominate Nevin's
concern in his essays on Cyprian in 1852, the subject of
baptismal grace is also an important theme.[43] He did not,
however, touch on the question of its precise meaning in
infants except to affirm that Cyprian's view was that baptism
is needed by infants who have entered into life with the
contagion of the old death from Adam. Repeatedly, Nevin
stressed that for Cyprian baptism is the sacrament of
regeneration, "the real ground and foundation of spiritual life.
It is a real translation from the sphere of nature, the fallen life
of Adam over into the sphere of truth and grace, the full
possibility of righteousness and eternal life, which is revealed
in Christ."[44] One should note that Nevin wrote here, "the full
possibility of righteousness and eternal life." His language was
no doubt carefully chosen to guard against the magical view
that the fruits of baptism are automatic, that baptism
guarantees salvation. He recognized that human response in
faith and obedience is necessary. But if baptism and faith are
so indissolubly linked that, unless the baptismal grace is
eventually appropriated by faith, it remains ineffectual; it is also
correct that there is no true faith which does not yield itself to
baptism in the Church. Making use of the Aristotelian four-fold
theory of causes, Nevin held that in Cyprian's view, "the
efficient cause of justification is the mercy of God, the
meritorious cause, the righteousness of Christ, the instrumental

cause, the sacrament of baptism, while what has been called the formal cause is the actual appropriation of this objective grace on the part of the sinner himself."[45]

But as in "The Anglican Crisis" Nevin argued that what was central in the Cyprianic doctrine was not the viewpoint of baptismal regeneration or of the episcopacy separately considered but rather the universal idea of the Church as "a divine constitution built on the foundation of the apostles and prophets, Jesus Christ himself being the chief cornerstone."[46] This Church though existing in historical form carries in itself actual heavenly and supernatural powers which are dispensed through the sacraments.   The notion of the sacrament of baptism as conveying an objective grace is a natural consequence of this theory of the Church, just as those who think of the Church as a human corporation only will necessarily think of baptism as a mere sign.

On the other hand, it's possible to have a view of baptism that is not far off the mark, and yet not have the correct doctrine of the Church.   He acknowledged that Alexander Campbell had a view of baptismal regeneration which recognized "the notion of an objective power" in the sacrament.[47]   Nevin was then correctly aware that Campbell, in contrast with the Baptists, with whom Campbell was for a while associated, regarded baptism as more than a mere sign of a regeneration already experienced. Although Campbell was an ardent advocate of believer's baptism, he concurred with Nevin that baptism is a means of grace which is ordained for the remission of sins. In his treatise on *Christian Baptism* he argued that baptism acts not as an efficient or meritorious but as an instrumental cause "in which faith and repentance are developed and made fruitful and effectual."[48]   However, to Nevin, Campbell's view, though deserving more respect than the views of some of his critics, was nevertheless defective because it sundered the sacrament of baptism from the living constitution of the Church with which it was originally intimately connected.[49]

This general view of baptism and of its intimate conjunction with the doctrine of the Church Nevin continued to espouse in articles written in the *Mercersburg Review* after his retirement from the Seminary and the College and his removal to

Lancaster. In the essay "Thoughts on the Church" in the *Mercersburg Review* (April 1858), he stated that it is of no use for the Baptist to argue for the obligation of the sacraments against the Quakers, or for the Congregationalist to defend the baptism of infants against the Baptists "without any faith, on either side, in the old doctrine of sacramental grace." Nor can the affirmation of infant baptism or of baptismal grace or of the mystical Presence in the Lord's Supper or of the three orders of ministry make any sense except "in union with the central life of the system to which they belong."[50]

He once more set forth with vigor the "Old Christian Doctrine of Baptism" in the *Mercersburg Review* (April 1860). His comments are a reflection on an extract from Chrysostom's Twelfth Homily on the Gospel of Matthew. He stressed that for Chrysostom Christian baptism, in contrast to the baptism of John, which was in figure and sign only, was a sacrament which brought about remission of sins, regeneration, and adoption for its subjects. The objective presence of grace in the sacraments which effected these benefits is not negated by the continuing presence of sin in those baptized. He pointed out that for Chrysostom the reality of the heavenly gift of new life conferred by baptism is not overturned by the fact that in thousands of Christians it does not bear fruit. Chrysostom's paranetic discourse does not give the impression that he was at all troubled by a seeming contradiction here. The objective presence of grace in the sacraments belongs to the sphere of faith; it is not to be measured by experimental tests of any kind.

As earlier in his articles on the Anglican Crisis and Cyprian, Nevin concluded his essay by comparing "The Old Doctrine of Baptism" with the modern view which rejects the notion that "any external rite...should take away sin, or carry with it the power of regeneration." This modern understanding considers religion to be "an inward spiritual transaction between God and the soul" that may be accompanied by outward forms of worship but is not affected by them in any fundamental way.[51] In Nevin's view this modern, "self-styled evangelical system" leads logically and ultimately to Quakerism and even to Rationalism, though it generally stops short of those extremes. It is prominently exhibited among the Baptists who stress individualistic conversion of which baptism is the mere profession and outward sign. He did not add what he had said earlier and what he perhaps implied with the publication of this essay, that the movement toward the Baptist persuasion can only be resisted with an adherence to the ancient doctrine of baptism. Nevin confessed at the end that there were difficulties also with his doctrine, but he did not explain what these are, whereas he does not hesitate to point out the perils of the modern evangelical view.[52]

His final word on the subject, as far as I can judge, is contained in his vindication of the new 1866 liturgy of baptism. Against objections raised at the Synod of Dayton (1866) to the baptismal liturgy for teaching that little children are in the grip of original sin and the devil and for affirming a doctrine of baptismal regeneration, Nevin set forth a spirited defense. He answered the first objection by referring to Scriptural texts as teaching that human beings are by nature under the power of sin and the devil and require a rebirth by water and the spirit (John 3:5-6) or a deliverance from the power of darkness and translation "into the kingdom of God's dear Son" (Col 1:13), and by quoting from the *Heidelberg Catechism* concerning the depravity of infants and the need for a new birth by the Spirit. He responded to the second objection by first stressing that the liturgy avoids the expression "baptismal regeneration" because of its ambiguity. He then reaffirmed his position that, though baptism does not save people by magic or make their salvation certain, it does convey an objective, special grace, and on this matter, the liturgy is correct.[53] While opposing a magical *ex opere operato* view of the sacrament, Nevin continued to be more concerned to reject what he regarded as a spiritualistic, rationalistic conception.

Conclusion

1. As in *The Mystical Presence*, Nevin made use of his knowledge of history to establish his position, in this case his knowledge of the Fathers, especially Irenaeus, Cyprian, Augustine, and Chrysostom. In contrast, however, with *The Mystical Presence*, he made little use of Calvin and the Reformed Confessions. Why? Perhaps, because he found Calvin's doctrine of baptism and that of some of the Confessions defective. Nevin knew better than his Reformed detractors, Charles Hodge and Joseph Berg particularly, that Calvin did not regard the inward grace and the outward sign as so indissolubly united that where there is the one, there is necessarily the other. According to Calvin, God transcends the instruments of which he makes use. He has not so bound himself to the sacrament that he cannot bestow grace without it. Calvin had in mind the case of infants who die before they can be brought to the baptismal font. Nor are all those necessarily saved who are baptized, since salvation is dependent on election. There is an unresolved tension in Calvin's thought between his doctrine of sacramental grace and his doctrine of election.[54] Nevin did not refer to the issue of infants who die before being baptized nor did he refer to the matter of election, a Calvinistic doctrine towards which he was quite cool, but he seemed to advocate a closer union between sign and thing signified than Calvin would allow. Likewise, Nevin made relatively little use of Calvin's chief argument for infant baptism, namely the inclusion of all persons in the convenantal community, with baptism replacing circumcision as the seal of divine grace and the sign of belonging to that community.

2. Even though he was a champion of infant baptism, Nevin was as critical, if not more so, of the pedobaptist wing of evangelical Protestantism as he was of the Baptist wing. They both exhibited the same anti-sacramental tendencies. The one position was the theological outcome of the other. On the other hand, he showed himself surprisingly sympathetic to Alexander Campbell's doctrine of baptism even though he was an advocate of believer's baptism because his was a

sacramental view. Of course, Nevin was sharply critical of Campbell and the Campbellites for what he regarded as their sectarian spirit, a disregard for the Creed, and a privatized reading of Scripture.

3. Nevin's writings on the subject emerge for the most part out of a polemical setting. He did not set forth a systematic, fully rounded treatment of baptism. He was interested almost exclusively in opposing a spiritualistic, unsacramental, and Pelagian view. He stressed the one side of baptism, the divine gift; he gave much less attention to the other side, the human appropriation of that gift in faith and obedience. Nevertheless, he gave some indication that he recognized the importance of this aspect. Toward the end of his article "Noel on Baptism" he referred to confirmation, but he did not elaborate on it very much.   While he pointed to the perils of an unsacramental understanding of baptism, he also acknowledged that there were difficulties connected with the sacramental view, but he did not clearly state what these are.

4. In advance of his contemporary champions of infant baptism, Nevin recognized what is now clearly a majority view of scholars, that a sure case for infant baptism cannot be made out of the witness of the New Testament. If a case is to be made for infant baptism, it must arise out of the theology of the New Testament and the early Church which did not clearly settle into the practice of infant baptism until about 200 A.D. Though less concerned than Schaff to prove the historical argument, he was inclined to agree with his colleague against Neander that infant baptism goes back to apostolic times. But he seemed to put little stock in the argument. His position is not far removed from that of Kurt Aland, the contemporary Lutheran scholar, who, while denying that there was infant baptism before about 200 A.D., nevertheless thinks that a strong theological case can be made for it.[55]

As I have already indicated, one might have thought that the same sacramental and ecclesiological considerations which upheld for him the validity of infant baptism would also support infant or child communion as is being proposed in many circles today.

Finally, as on the Eucharist, so on baptism, John W. Nevin contributed a needed perspective in his time, one which can still stimulate our thinking today as we in the Reformed family engage in discussion on the subject with one another and with our ecumenical partners in the light of the Lima statement, *Baptism, Eucharist, and Ministry.*

ENDNOTES

1. John W. Nevin, *The Mystical Presence: A Vindication of the Reformed or Calvinistic Doctrine of the Holy Eucharist* (Philadelphia: 1846); reprint in *The Mystical Presence and Other Writings on the Eucharist*, ed. Bard Thompson and George H. Bricker, Lancaster Series on the Mercersburg Theology 4 (Philadelphia: United Church Press, 1966), 92-93.

2. Charles Hodge, "Neglect of Infant Baptism," *Biblical Repertory and Princeton Review* 29 (January 1857):91f (hereafter cited as *BRPR*).

3. Ibid., 91.

4. Ibid., 92-97.

5. Nevin, *The Mystical Presence*, 92.

6. Ibid., 143.

7. C.C. Goen, *Revivalism and Separatism in New England, 1740-1800* (New Haven: Yale University Press, 1961).

8. Brooks Holifield, *The Covenant Sealed: The Development of Puritan Sacramental Theology in Old and New England, 1570-1720* (New Haven: Yale University Press, 1974), 229-30.

9. John W. Nevin, *The Weekly Messenger of the German Reformed Church*, 23, 30 June 1847, 7, 14 July 1847 (hereafter cited as *WM*). James Hastings Nichols has an illuminating discussion of Nevin's exchange with Bushnell in "Baptismal Grace," *Romanticism in American Theology* (Chicago: The University of Chicago Press, 1961), 239f.

10. Nevin, *WM*, 12:41 (23 June 1847), 2450.

11. John W. Nevin, *The Anxious Bench* (Chambersburg, PA: Publication Office of the German Ref. Church, 1844).

12. Horace Bushnell, "Discourses on Christian Nurture," in *Views of Christian Nurture and of Subjects Adjacent Thereto*, 2d ed. (Hartford: Edwin Hunt, 1848), 25; *WM*, 12:42 (30 June 1847), 2450.

13. Bushnell, *Discourses on Christian Nurture*, 31; *WM,* 12:42 (30 June 1847), 2450.

14. Bushnell, *Discourses on Christian Nurture*, 37.

15. Nevin, *WM*, 12:43 (7 July 1847), 2458.

16. Nevin, *WM*, 12:44 (14 July 1847), 2461.

17. Horace Bushnell, "Argument for Discourses on Human Nature," in *Views of Christian Nurture and of Subjects Adjacent Thereto*, 2d ed. (Hartford: Edwin Hunt, 1848), 103, 108.

18. Bushnell, *Argument for Discourses on Human Nature*, 101-103.

19. Nevin, *WM*, 12:5 (1 September 1847), 2490.

20. Charles Hodge, "Bushnell on Christian Nurture," *BRPR*, 19 (October 1847): 524.

21. Ibid., 507.

22. Nevin, *WM*, 12:44 (14 July 1847), 2461.

23. Hodge, "Bushnell on Christian Nurture," *BRPR*, 538.

24. Nevin, *WM*, 12:48 (11 August 1847), 2478.

25. Nevin, *WM*, 12:51 (1 September 1847), 2490.

26. John W. Nevin, *The Anxious Bench*, 2d ed. (Chambersburg, PA: Publication Office of the German Reformed Church, 1844); reprint in *Catholic and Reformed Selected Theological Writings of John Williamson Nevin, Pittsburgh Original Texts and Translations Series*, No. 3, eds. Charles Yrigoyen, Jr., and George H. Bricker (Pittsburgh: The Pickwick Press, 1978), 67.

27. Irenaeus, *Against Heresies* 11.22; 1.21-23.

28. Nevin, *WM*, 13:25 (1 March 1848), 2594.

29. John W. Nevin, "Noel on Baptism," *Mercersburg Review* 2 (1850): 242 (hereafter cited as *MR*).

30. Ibid., 243-45.

31. Irenaeus, *Against Heresies* 11.22.

32. Ibid., 249-50.

33. Philip Schaff, "The Apostolic Origin of Infant Baptism," *MR* 4 (1852): 390. See also Philip Schaff, *History of the Apostolic Church* (New York: Charles Scribner, 1853), 571-81.

34. Augustus Neander, *General History of the Christian Religion and Church* (Boston: Crocker and Brewster, 1854), 1:312; cited and quoted from the German edition in Schaff, *History of the Apostolic Church*, 573. See also his discussion of Tertullian's "On Baptism" in which he reiterates his rejection of an apostolic origin of infant baptism since in this first stage of development "baptism necessarily marked a distinct era in life when a person passed over from a different religious standpoint to Christianity, when the regeneration sealed by baptism presented itself as a principle of moral transformation, in opposition to the earlier development." But Neander goes on to argue that infant baptism developed naturally out of a very different context, "when from the midst of an already existing church-life and of a Christian family-life, the individual life was to be formed in communion with Christ." The time of Tertullian (c. 200 A.D.) marks a period of transition when both types of baptism, believers and infant, were vying with one another as is indicated by Tertullian's polemic against infant baptism. See *History of the Planting and Training of the Christian Church* (London: George Bell, 1880), 11:336-37.

35. Nevin, "Noel on Baptism," 252.

36. Ibid., 263.

37. Schaff, "Apostolic Origin of Infant Baptism," 392-93.

38. Nevin, "Noel on Baptism," 265.

39. John W. Nevin, "The Anglican Crisis," *MR* 3 (July 1851): 358-59.

40. Owen Chadwick, *The Victorian Church* (New York: Oxford University Press, 1966), 1:250-71.

41. John B. Payne, "Schaff and Nevin, Colleagues at Mercersburg: The Church Question," *Church History* 61 (June 1992): 169-90.

42. Nevin, "The Anglican Crisis," 369-72, 378-79.

43. John W. Nevin, "Cyprian," *MR* 4 (May, July, September, and November 1852): 259-77, 335-87, 417-52, 513-63.

44. Nevin, "Cyprian," *MR* 4 (1852): 376-377. On baptismal regeneration, see also 420, 423, 429, 438, 447.

45. Ibid., 550.

46. Ibid., 420.

47. Ibid., 418.

48. Alexander Campbell, *Christian Baptism; With its Antecedents and Consequents* (Bethany, VA; Printed and published by Alexander Campbell, 1843), 256.

49. Nevin, "Cyprian," *MR*, 418, 449.

50. John W. Nevin, "Thoughts on the Church," *MR* 10 (1858): 181, 191-95.

51. John W. Nevin, "The Old Doctrine of Christian Baptism," *MR* 12 (1860): 211.

52. Ibid., 213-15.

53. "Theology of the New Liturgy," *MR* 14 (January 1867), 57-63. Published as a separate tract under the title *Vindication of the Revised Liturgy, Historical and Theological* (Philadelphia, 1867).

54. For Calvin's view see *Institutes of the Christian Religion* 4:14-16, 20, 26; R. S. Wallace, *Calvin's Doctrine of the Word and Sacraments* (Edinburgh: Oliver and Boyd, 1953), 161f., 175 f.; and Egil Grisis, "Calvin's Doctrine of Baptism, " *Church History* 31 (1962): 46-65.

55. Kurt Aland, *Did the Early Church Baptize Infants?* (Philadelphia: The Westminster Press, 1963).

Nevin on Regeneration

Glenn Hewitt

When John Nevin arrived at Mercersburg in 1840 to assume his duties as Professor of Theology, he was already suspicious of American revivalism, as were most other old school Presbyterians. Nevin had experienced a "religious conversion" under the restrained preaching of Asahel Nettleton, but recalled the event with some displeasure in later years. The more sensational style of Charles Finney was even less appealing. By 1840, Finney had migrated west to Oberlin, but his followers and imitators were still in great demand in Pennsylvania and New York.

Nevin was concerned that Finney's style of revivalism was making inroads even in the established Lutheran and Reformed churches, and his fear was confirmed when the college church at Mercersburg began searching for a new pastor in 1842.[1] Late in that year a prospective pastor concluded his sermon at the church by bringing out the anxious bench. Nevin was appalled, but many students at the time were attracted to revivalism so the church called the evangelist as pastor. Nevin wrote the revivalist, informing him that if he should accept the call he could not expect Nevin's support. The revivalist wisely refused the call of the church. After this near-disaster, Nevin prepared a tract outlining the evils of "new measures" revivalism, published as *The Anxious Bench* in 1843. The following year a greatly expanded second edition was published that included Nevin's first detailed statements of the system he advocated against revivalism.

Concerned that the German Reformed Church and American Protestantism generally were moving away from the insights of the early church and the Reformation, Nevin opened his attack by noting that the system of new measures revivalism held nothing in common with the Reformers:

> The system of New Measures has no affinity whatever with the life of the Reformation, as embodied in the *Augsburg Confession* and the *Heidelberg Catechism*. It could not have found any favor in the eyes of Zwingli or Calvin. Luther would have denounced it in the most unmerciful terms. His soul was too large, too deep, too free, to hold communion with a style of religion so mechanical and shallow.[2]

Nevin asserted that American revivalism was more akin to Wesleyan Methodism than Reformed thought.[3]

In order to contrast new measures revivalism with his own preferred system of religious conversion, Nevin focused on the anxious bench as a symbol of the whole approach. He was careful to state that his opposition was not merely to this one "measure" but to the whole system of which it was representative. The anxious bench, Nevin declared, "opens the way naturally to other forms of aberration in the same direction and may be regarded in this view as the threshold of all that is found to follow, quite out to the extreme verge of fanaticism and rant. The measure belongs to the system, not in the name simply, but in its life and spirit."[4]

Nevin was not opposed to true revivals of religion, but argued that new measures revivalism was superficial and often false. There were dangers in creating false religious excitement. False views of religion would be taught, people would be deceived with a false hope of salvation, emotional extravagance would be mistaken for the power of God, and obstacles would be placed in the way of true holiness.[5]

The advocates of revivalism often pointed to the great results they produced, but Nevin dismissed this argument for the proof of their veracity. He noted that spurious revivals and false conversions were common, appearing most frequently when the most excitement and immediate effects were achieved. True converts should experience the "peace of religion" and be able to give evidence that they have been regenerated. The Church should be strengthened. Instead,

Nevin claimed, the converts of revivalism often lose interest in religion, resort to worldliness, and give no signs of life. The Church, instead of growing, actually loses ground. Nevin concluded that the anxious bench and its attending system were almost designed to produce spurious conversions.[6]

While criticizing the anxious bench for unduly promoting excitement, Nevin also suggested that the decision of repentance is one that demands reflection and sober judgment. The users of the anxious bench appealed to the imagination and to feelings of fear, sympathy, and excitement. This, in Nevin's view, distracted the judgment of a person from the proper consideration of the truth. The decision to repent and receive the gospel, he held, should not be made on the basis of impulse, but on the considered reflection of the truth of the gospel. What was required was a conviction of "inward force," and not simply an external show of commitment.[7]

True religion involved both an inward, living force, and external forms. The outward forms received their power from the inward force. Nevin admitted that old forms could lose their significance in an empty ritualism. This, however, did not necessarily mean that the old forms themselves were at fault. The revivalists, he charged, had dismissed the old forms as useless while advocating new measures. Nevin further admitted that God could use any form—even the anxious bench—to save sinners. The real problem with American revivalism was that it made the forms more important than the inner life force. The inward should be the bearer of the outward, but the anxious bench had reversed this order. Consequently, the forms were made all-important and true religion suffered.[8]

Nevin noted the Pelagianism inherent in the system of the anxious bench system, just as Finney's earlier critics had done.

> The fact of sin is acknowledged, but not in its true extent. The idea of a new spiritual creation is admitted, but not in its proper radical and comprehensive form. The ground of the sinner's salvation is made to live at last in his own separate person.[9]

Nevin insisted that flesh could not be stimulated to produce a spiritual nature by the exclusive action of the human will, as "Finneyism" falsely imagined. A man could fulfill a temperance pledge by his own will and strength, Nevin said, but he could not secure conversion by his own will and strength. That could only be accomplished by the Spirit.[10]

Nevin's criticism of the Pelagianism in Finney and other revivalists takes a different attack than that assumed by Charles Hodge, however. Hodge was critical of Finney for placing the initiative in the regenerative process with the human rather than with God. Nevin's point of attack is Finney's extreme individualism, which entailed a false view of the Church. Whether described as a new purpose to serve God or as a new feeling, regeneration in Finney's theology is "the result of a spiritual process which begins and ends with the sinner himself."[11] Such a view, according to Nevin, makes regeneration completely subjective, and therefore false:

> The life of the soul must stand in something beyond itself. Religion involves the will; but not as self-will, affecting to be its own ground and centre. Religion involves feeling; but it is not comprehended in this as its principle. Religion is subjective also, fill and rules the individual in whom it appears; but it is not created in any sense by its own subject and from its subject. The life of the branch is in the trunk.[12]

The organic metaphor is significant here. According to Nevin, the Church is the body of Christ, a living organism, that conveyed spiritual life to its individual members. Finneyism, he charged, perverts the true understanding of the Church by positing the individual as prior to the universal. In such a distorted view, the Church was simply a voluntary human association, and thus no different in nature from a temperance society or a political party.[13]

In opposition to revivalism and the anxious bench, Nevin proposes the more churchly "catechesis":

> It is a different system altogether that is required to build up the interests of Christianity in a firm and sure

way. A ministry apt to teach; sermons full of unction
and light; faithful, systematic instruction; zeal for the
interests of holiness; pastoral visitation; catechetical
training; due attention to order and discipline; patient
perseverance in the details of the ministerial work;
these are the agencies by which alone the kingdom of
God may be expected to go steadily forward among
any people.[14]

Just as the anxious bench is the representative type of
revivalism, the catechesis becomes Nevin's representative type
of churchly religion, a "vastly more deep and comprehensive,
and of course vastly more earnest" theory of religion.[15]   In
contrast to the shallow and fleeting experience offered by the
anxious bench, the catechesis promotes education, cultivation
of personal holiness, and a deep and abiding faith.

Under Nevin's catechetical system, the Church plays a far
greater role in instructing, examining, and admitting new
members. Nevin proposed a return to the "old forms" as a
means of converting sinners and training Christians; the
catechetical class, the sacraments, sermons, services of the
sanctuary, and family visitation were specifically advocated.[16]
These methods were most appropriate precisely because they
reflected Nevin's understanding of the relation of the Church to
the individual in the process of Christian conversion. For Nevin,
regeneration was the mystical union of the believer with Christ,
taking place through the medium of the Church.

Nevin placed his doctrine of regeneration in direct
opposition to Finney's individualism. For Nevin, "the true
theory of religion carries us continually beyond the individual to
the view of a far deeper and more general form of existence in
which his particular life is represented to stand."[17] Thus, sin
is not the individual act of an individual will, but "a wrong habit
of humanity...rooted in the race," which cannot be overcome
by any force less deep and general. So, while the human
individual is the subject of salvation, the human can in no sense
be the author of salvation. In order for the restoration to be
real, it must go beyond the individual. Just as humanity is
fallen in Adam organically, it must be restored through organic

relation to Christ.[18] Nevin described this "organic" conception
of regeneration as follows:

> The sinner is saved then by an inward living union with
> Christ as real as the bond by which he has been joined
> in the first instance to Adam. This union is reached and
> maintained through the medium of the Church by the
> power of the Holy Ghost. It constitutes a new life, the
> ground of which is not in the particular subject of it at
> all, but in Christ, the organic root of the Church. The
> particular subject lives, not properly speaking in the
> acts of his own will separately considered, but in the
> power of a vast generic life that lies wholly beyond his
> will, and has now begun to manifest itself through him
> as the law and type of his will itself as well as of his
> whole being. As born of the Spirit in contradistinction
> from the flesh he is himself spiritual, and capable of
> true righteousness. Thus his salvation begins, and thus
> it is carried forward till it becomes complete in the
> resurrection of the great day. From first to last it is a
> power which he does not so much apprehend as he is
> apprehended by it, and comprehended in it, and carried
> along with it as something infinitely more deep and vast
> than himself.[19]

Insisting that the general must precede the particular, Nevin
argued that the "spiritual constitution" established by God for
the purpose of human salvation is found in the Church. The life
of a particular Christian is discovered not in isolation but
through the medium of the Church, and is inaugurated and
strengthened through the established institutions and agencies
of the Church.[20] The members do not give life to the Church,
but the Church as mother gives life to her children. This
individual Christianity is the product, "always and entirely," of
the previously existing Church. Drawing again upon the Adam-
Christ analogy, Nevin states: "Christ lives in the Church, and
through the Church in its particular members; just as Adam
lives in the human race generically considered, and through the
race in every individual man."[21]

Nevin's understanding of salvation as accomplished through the normal ministrations of the Church widened the pool of potential converts. Finney and other revivalists addressed their preaching to adults, believing that conversion involved a self-conscious, rational decision that only adults could make. Nevin, however, insisted that infants and children were also proper subjects for salvation:

> Infants born in the Church are regarded and treated as members of it from the beginning, and this privilege is felt to be something more than an empty shadow. The idea of infant conversion is held in practical honor; and it is counted not only possible, but altogether natural that children growing up in the bosom of the Church under the faithful application of the means of grace should be quickened unto spiritual life in a comparatively quiet way, and spring up numerously "as willows by the water-courses" to adorn the Christian profession, without being able at all to trace the process by which the glorious change has been effected.[22]

Thus, the normal expectation in the system of the catechesis was that children should be baptized, nurtured in the family,[23] trained by catechetical instruction, visited by the minister, and strengthened by preaching and the sacraments. Through these various ministries, the Church should seek not only the salvation of children (and adults), but their continual spiritual growth. Conversion and sanctification were viewed by Nevin as a continuing process extending from the cradle to the grace, and not as an isolated experience of emotional frenzy in an individual with no prior relationship to the Church.[24] Thus, the Church should grow, not so much from external additions as from the expansion of its interior life. The dead flesh of humanity should be assimilated and given spiritual life.[25]

Having thus presented the system of the catechism for comparison with that of the anxious bench, Nevin defended it briefly against the arguments of its critics. He noted that the catechism need not degenerate into dead formalism, but that in the hands of a spiritual minister, it would become lively and vigorous. Nevin observed that the catechetical system was not opposed to true revivals of religion, but that true revivals would spring from it. Finally, Nevin reminded his German Reformed readers that Luther, Calvin, and Zwingli had used the catechetical system, leaving religious agitation and excitement to the Anabaptists.[26]

The Anxious Bench was a clear repudiation of Finney's revivalistic doctrine of conversion. By building his case against Finney around the doctrine of the Church, instead of the doctrine of divine decrees, Nevin also demonstrated his departure from Hodge. In one respect, however, Nevin agreed with both of them, for he maintained steadfastly that regeneration was strictly supernatural. He also indicated, in a footnote, that he favored the distinction (with Hodge and against Finney) between regeneration and conversion. Regeneration, he said, was instantaneous and might occur at any time: in the womb, in infancy, in childhood, or in advanced age. Regeneration was mysterious, like the wind, and could only be known by its effects. The effects belonged to conversion, the change of life flowing from regeneration. Conversions could occur suddenly, but they normally extended over longer periods of time, as, for instance, in the gradual conversions of children who were nurtured through the ministries of the Church.[27] In *The Anxious Bench*, as in his other writings, Nevin said relatively little about the instantaneous event called regeneration. His focus was consistently on the gradual conversion that takes place as the believer is united to Christ through the Church.

After publishing the second edition of *The Anxious Bench* in 1844, Nevin turned his attention to other matters. Still, the numerous essays, sermons, articles, and short books which were published in rapid succession yield additional information concerning Nevin's views of conversion in the context of the Church. In his sermon "Catholic Unity," delivered before the Triennial Convention of the German and Dutch Reformed Churches, Nevin developed the idea of the Church as an organic body. Christ is viewed as the head of the Church, filling it with his life. Individual members find union with Christ only through the Church, his body. Again, the life of the general must precede the salvation of the particular.[28]

In his "Introduction" to Philip Schaff's *The Principle of Protestantism* (1845), Nevin mentions that salvation is not merely a transaction between God and the individual; the individual spiritual life must also be dependent on the general life of the Church.[29] Two years later Nevin reasserted the claims of the catechetical system for bringing children to faith in his *History and Genius of the Heidelberg Catechism* (1847).[30] Nevin produced a witty and sharp critique of popular American religion in *The Sect System* (1848), including charges of rampant individualism, lack of belief in the Church or creed, and a denial of the supernatural.[31] While writing on "Early Christianity" (1851), Nevin noted that Augustine viewed his conversion as "absolute and unconditional submission to the supernatural authority of the **Church**, in a form that would be considered anything but evangelical with the Pietistic or Methodistic tendency of the present time."[32]

These writings help complete the picture of regeneration as it functions in Nevin's theology. Regeneration, or the "new birth," is the mystical union of the believer with Christ in which the incarnate and glorified life of Christ is introduced into the believer, creating a new personality. This union takes place only in the context of the Church and its sacraments. Finally, while faith on the believer's part is essential, regeneration is a supernatural act beyond the power of the human to initiate.

In describing the mystical union, Nevin insisted that it was the **life** of Christ to which believers are joined. The believer does not simply apprehend the image of Christ or assent to a doctrine about Christ; rather, the life of Christ enters "actually" into believers as the fountain of a new creation.[33] This life is different from that which the believer possessed previously, for it is a spiritual life which comes from Christ:

> The Christian has his life from Christ. He is not only placed in a new relation to the law, by the imputation of the Savior's righteousness to him in an outward forensic way; but a new nature is imparted to him also, by an actual communication of the Savior's life over into his person. In his regeneration, he is inwardly united to Christ, by the power of the Holy Ghost, and thus brought within the sphere of that "law of the spirit

of life," by which in the end the "law of sin and death" is overpowered and destroyed in all them [sic] that believe. A divine seed is implanted in him, the germ of a new existence, which is destined gradually to grow and gather strength, till the whole man shall be at last fully transformed into its image. The new nature thus introduced is the nature of Christ, and it continues to be his nature through the whole course of its development, onward to the last day.[34]

Nevin rejected the idea that Christ simply subsumes the human personality. The believer continues to have a separate existence, but this existence is grounded in the life of Christ. Still, the Christian does not simply follow the example of Christ, as a person might admire Moses or Abraham. Instead "the very life of the Lord Jesus is found reaching over" into the Christian. The old nature is not immediately destroyed, but the new nature grows and eventually overcomes it entirely (in the resurrection). "Thus emphatically, Christ and the believer are one."[35] Just as each individual participates in the corrupt life of humanity through Adam, so the regenerate Christian participates in the life of the second Adam, Jesus Christ. "They are inserted into his life through faith, by the power of the Holy Ghost, and become thus incorporated with it, as fully as they were before with that corrupt life they had by their natural birth."[36] The emphasis on incorporation into the life of Christ in Nevin's theology indicates the profound change that he believed occurred at regeneration. Regeneration is not merely a reordering of natural powers, such as a commitment of will or assent of the understanding. The new birth is more than a reorientation of life; it is new life. This new life entered the world in the Incarnation and remained objectively present in the Church.

For Nevin, personality is not divided among various faculties. The new life issuing from Christ does not affect one or two functions of the mind, but the whole person. Deeper than thinking, feeling, or acting, the new life lodges itself in "the inmost core of our personality...the center of our being."[37] Furthermore, human life is a unity, undivided between body and soul. It is the "man," the "self," that is affected in its entirety by regeneration. The life of Christ in the human "works as a **human** life," becoming a law of regeneration for the body as well as the soul.[38]

The picture that emerges from Nevin's various writings[39] is that of an individual whose "personhood" is radically changed. The individual has by nature a personality, underlying and uniting body and soul. The personality, encompassing affections, understanding, and will, may grow and change as the individual matures, but the "person" remains essentially and unalterably sinful as organically related to Adam and all humanity. At the time of regeneration, a Christian receives a new personality, springing from the life of Christ, and the person is redeemed. The person is still related to Adam, but also organically related to Christ in a spiritual relationship. This new personality is also described as underlying and uniting body and soul. Again, affections, understanding, and will are all encompassed.

But what is the relationship between the old personality and the "new" personality in the life of a Christian? Does the new replace the old or exist alongside it? Nevin suggested that the two were united, with the new spiritual personality gradually replacing the old. As sanctification proceeds, the spiritual personality grows and comes to have dominance over the natural one. (The degree of dominance of one personality over the other obviously varies from Christian to Christian.) Finally, at the resurrection, the personality issuing from Christ emerges totally from the natural life and casts it off as a husk, as a butterfly emerging from its chrysalis.[40] Nevin's imagery and conceptual descriptions, however, like those of Paul in the seventh chapter of Romans, are ambiguous. There are two "laws" or "natures" or "personalities" striving in one person. The "personhood" of the individual remains singular, despite the internal fighting between the "old man" and the "new man." Despite the confusion of language, the central point remains clear: union with the life of Christ affects an individual radically, so that feelings, thoughts, actions, and even the body itself may be said to be completely new.

The introduction of divine life into the believer at the time of regeneration is not an isolated event in time or in space. It is but the beginning of the process of salvation; a process that

is not abrupt but gradual, as the divine life spreads its influence
from the center of the individual's life to its periphery. The
power of the new life grows stronger as the Christian attends
to the Word and partakes of the Lord's Supper. Nevin
continues to use organic metaphors in explaining the effects of
regeneration on the moral life. Regeneration is like the planting
of a seed in the core of an individual. Morality is like the
growth and blossoming of a plant. Again, regeneration is
incorporation into the body of Christ. Morality is the
"vivification of the members." The believer is **alive** in Christ
and **growing** in holiness. The believer is distinguished from
others not by a new purpose or new knowledge but new **life**.
At the time of regeneration the individual is incorporated in the
Church. The individual's salvation is not a solitary passage, for
it is accomplished only as the whole Church mores toward its
consummation. The individual believer is part of the vast Body
of Christ, joined to Christ in a mystical union.[41]

Thus clearly, John Nevin's response to Charles Finney's
revivalism was more than a passing polemical attack. Much
more was at stake. For the mystical union is the centerpiece of
Nevin's theology and the doctrine of regeneration is here shown
to be an integral part of his theological system.

ENDNOTES

1. The following account is based on Theodore Appel, *The Life
   and Work of John Williamson Nevin* (Philadelphia: The Reformed
   Church Publishing House, 1889, rpt ed., New York: Arno Press
   and the New York Times, 1969), 157-60.

2. John Williamson Nevin, *The Anxious Bench* (2nd ed.;
   Chambersburg, PA: Publication Office of the German Reformed
   Church, 1844). This edition has been reprinted in Charles
   Yrigoyen, Jr., and George H. Bricker, eds., *Catholic and
   Reformed: Selected Theological Writings of John Williamson
   Nevin*, Pittsburgh Original Texts and Translations Series, no. 3,
   gen. ed. Dikran Y. Hadidian (Pittsburgh: The Pickwick Press,
   1978). All citations follow the pagination of the Pickwick
   edition. The noted quotation is found on page 8.

3. Ibid.

4. Ibid., 18.

5. Ibid., 26-27.

6. Ibid., 36-37, 69-74.

7. Ibid., 41, 62-62, 78-80.

8. Ibid., 43-49.

9. Ibid., 98.

10. Ibid., 80, 98.

11. Ibid., 98.

12. Ibid., 99.

13. John Williamson Nevin, *The Church* (1847), reprinted in James Hastings Nichols, ed., *Mercersburg Theology* (New York: Oxford University Press, 1966), 60, 68. All citations are from the Nichols volume.

14. Nevin, *The Anxious Bench*, 100-101.

15. Ibid., 105.

16. Ibid., 49-50.

17. Ibid., 106.

18. Ibid., 106-107.

19. Ibid., 107-108.

20. Ibid. 110.

21. Ibid., 111.

22. Ibid.

23. Unlike Horace Bushnell, who was writing *Discourses on Christian Nurture* at the same time Nevin was completing *The Anxious Bench*, Nevin always placed the family's nurture of children in a subordinate role to the ministry of the Church.

24. *The Anxious Bench*, 112-15.

25. Ibid., 115-16.

26. Ibid., 116-21.

27. Ibid., 112, note.

28. John Williamson Nevin, "Catholic Unity," a sermon delivered at the opening of the Triennial Convention of the Reformed Protestant Dutch and German Reformed Churches, at Harrisburg, PA, August 8, 1844. This sermon was reprinted as an appendix in Philip Schaff, *The Principle of Protestantism as Related to the Present State of the Church* (Chambersburg, PA: Publication Office of the German Reformed Church, 1845). All citations are from this edition. See 119-201.

29. John Williamson Nevin, "Introduction," in Schaff, *The Principle of Protestantism*, 12-13; hereafter cited as "Introduction."

30. John Williamson Nevin, *History and Genius of the Heidelberg Catechism* (Chambersburg, PA: Publication Office of the German Reformed Church, 1847), 156-57.

31. John Williamson Nevin, "The Sect System," reprinted in Yrigoyen and Bricker, *Catholic and Reformed*. All citations are from this volume. "The Sect System" originally appeared as two articles in the *Mercersburg Review* in 1849.

32. John Williamson Nevin, "Early Christianity," reprinted in Yrigoyen and Bricker, *Catholic and Reformed*, 204. All citations are from this volume. "Early Christianity" appeared as three articles in the *Mercersburg Review* in 1851-1852.

33. John Williamson Nevin, "The New Creation in Christ," *Mercersburg Review* 2 (1850):1-11.

34. Nevin, "Catholic Unity," 195.

35. Ibid., 195-96.

36. Ibid., 197.

37. John Williamson Nevin, *The Mystical Presence: A Vindication of the Reformed or Calvinistic Doctrine of the Holy Eucharist* (Philadelphia: J. B. Lippincott and Co., 1846), reprinted in Thompson and Bricker, eds., *The Mystical Presence and Other Writings on the Eucharist*, 164-65. All citations are from the Thompson and Bricker edition.

38. Ibid., 170.

39. Each of these writings was undertaken for a different theological purpose; exposition of the doctrine of regeneration was not central in any of them. Though not as systematic as one might wish, Nevin's various comments on regeneration are basically consistent.

40. Nevin uses this image in "Catholic Unity," 170.

41. Nevin, *The Mystical Presence*, 175-76; Nevin, "Introduction," 25-26.

Nevin on the Pastoral Office

Sam Hamstra, Jr.

It took less than a year before my idealistic, though naive understanding of the Reformation doctrine of the office of the pastoral ministry conflicted with reality, that is, my congregation's perception of that same office. Two questions confronted me during my first pastorate. First, does the congregation need me? My predecessor had been released by the congregation. I sensed that the congregation viewed the pastor as a financial liability and a threat to the status quo. The pastoral office was not viewed as a necessary position in God's economy of redemption. Most believed they could experience God's grace in a sufficient manner outside of the regular ministry of the church. They did not need the pastoral office and its ministry. After all, they had the para-church.

Second, does the office of the ministry of the word and sacraments have a **unique** sphere of authority that can be exercised by the officeholder, i.e., pastor? Or is the authority of the office **common** to all Christians? My seminary training led me to believe the former. I was taught that the pastor was invested with authority to study, interpret, and proclaim the teachings within the Bible to the congregation. In addition, I learned that this proclamation was in some mysterious way the very word of God to His people. I never understood how that could be, but I quickly learned that it did not make any difference. My congregation did not grant such status to its pastor. It believed that the authority to study, interpret, and teach scripture was common to all Christians. In other words, it assumed the right of private judgment. This conviction was defended by generic references to the Reformation doctrine of the priesthood of all believers. In the end this meant that the sermon was a topic for opinionated discussion over a cup of coffee immediately after a service. It was something over which Christians could debate and even disagree.

The issues of pastoral function, pastoral authority, and private judgment have been debated since the Protestant Reformation when Martin Luther wrestled with the enthusiasts in Orlamünde. The debate, however, became especially intense in America during the years following the American Revolution. At that time the tenets of republicanism intersected with the theological traditions of European immigrants. Each tradition was forced to adapt to its new surroundings. The process, accented by the development and popularity of Finney-styled revivals, divided adherents into two groups: progressives, characterized by a willingness to adapt to the demands of a new world, and conservatives, who warned of compromising basic precepts of the tradition. The prevalent pattern of contemporary scholars is to designate the progressives as evangelicals and the conservatives as confessionalists.

At stake in the debate was the necessity of the pastoral office. The egalitarian principles of republicanism and the success of itinerant preachers caused the populace to reject the age-old distinction that set clergy apart as a separate order. Most rejected the notion that the office of the pastoral ministry was a necessary medium in the order of salvation. They denied that the properly installed pastor possessed unique authority as an officeholder to study, interpret, and proclaim the truths of the Bible. They believed, instead, that this authority was common to all Christians; each had the right of private judgment, a right which threatened the necessity of the pastoral office.

The debate took place in nearly every denomination in antebellum America, including the German Reformed Church where John Nevin led the confessionalist wing. He was spurred to action by the revivalistic antics of William Ramsey and others. Nevin, in prophetic fashion, called his denomination back to its theological roots, especially those of the Reformation and Patristic periods. On that foundation, he proposed a pastoral office as a necessary link in the process of redemption as the divinely ordained medium of saving grace. The properly installed pastor dispenses objective and spiritual realities that cannot be obtained elsewhere. Furthermore, the office is clothed with apostolic authority to administer the means of grace, interpret and proclaim the Scriptures, and discipline the wayward. The following summary was Nevin's personal contribution to the service of Ordination and Installation in the Provisional Liturgy of 1857.[1]

The office is of divine origin, and of truly supernatural character and force; flowing directly from the Lord Jesus Christ himself, as the fruit of his Resurrection and triumphant Ascension into heaven, and being designed by him to carry forward the purposes of his grace upon the earth, in the salvation of men by the Church, to the end of time.[2]

The purpose of this article is to present a concise summary of Nevin's theoretical view of the pastoral ministry. My exposition will be divided into three parts, following the pattern of Nevin's sermon the "Christian Ministry" in which he defines and describes the origin, nature, and design of the pastoral office.[3]

The Origin of the Ministry

Nevin taught that the pastoral office is an extension of the ministry of the apostles, the first ministers. Nevin built his theory upon two events from the life of Christ: the Great Commission and the Ascension. In the Great Commission Jesus appointed his apostles "to make disciples of all nations, baptizing them in the name of the Father and of the Son and of the Holy Spirit, and teaching them to obey everything" he commanded (Matthew 28:19-20 NIV). This was, in Nevin's view, a commissioning service whereby Christ authorized the apostles to administer both the word and sacraments. The apostles, then, were the first officeholders, the first pastors and teachers, "commissioned immediately by Jesus Christ himself." They held, furthermore, positions of authority in that only those they baptized entered "into the system of grace" consigned to them (Mark 16:16). They had the power of the keys to open the door and receive people into the body of Christ.

While the ministry was "appointed" in the Great Commission, it was not "inaugurated" until the Ascension, a two-fold event that in Nevin's scheme includes Pentecost as the final and inseparable half. The ministry appointed by Jesus in the Great Commission did not function until Pentecost when the apostles received the "Ascension Gift." There had to be a "real communication of supernatural power" because the apostles could not fulfill the commission on their own.[4] They were told to wait in Jerusalem for the "supernatural force" of the Holy Spirit before launching their work. So, while the apostles were appointed as ministers by the Great Commission, the office of the ministry did not become operative until the Ascension-Pentecost event. It was at Pentecost that Christ empowered some to be pastors and teachers through the gift of the Holy Spirit (Ephesians 4:7-11). It was then that the office of the ministry "received its baptism of fire."[5]

Pentecost and the "Ascension Gift" of the Holy Spirit are indispensable to Nevin's doctrine of the ministry. Nevin views the gift of the Holy Spirit at Pentecost as the completion of the Gospel. Jesus Christ conquered sin and death through the crucifixion and was raised from the dead for the justification of believers. But it was through the Ascension to the Father that he became the principle and fountain of a new order of life among people by which those who believe might be saved. He transcended this world and took possession of it under the form of a new and higher existence, one that is no longer natural but spiritual. Now the power of His glorified life is released with free effect in the world.

Nevin's understanding of the origin of the ministry is unique in nineteenth-century America. Nevin distinguished his own view from three popular alternatives: the natural, the mechanical, and the presbyterian. A natural theory of the origin of the ministry asserts that the ministry is like civil government. It is a natural development within the world as we know it.[6] Nevin believed that the natural theory was especially popular among those that ascribed to a "republican or democratic order in Christianity, by which the popular vote, or the will of any mass or majority of men, shall be regarded as sufficient to originate or bring to an end the sacred office wherever it may be thought proper."[7] Nevin's basic critique was that a natural theory of origin did not take into account the supernatural character of Christ's kingdom. It asserts no essential difference between the order of nature and the order of grace. It "drags the ministry down" to a natural level.

The mechanical theory of the origin of the ministry asserts that the ministry was appended to the world through direct intervention by God. The ministry does not come to concrete form through the general life of the church. It is not the "organic product and outbirth of the new creation."[8] Nevin believed that the Tractarian movement of John Henry Newman (1801-1890), the Calvinism of Charles Hodge, and the Roman Catholicism of Orestes Brownson espoused this view. Nevin's criticism of his perception of Brownson's view of the origin of the ministry is typical:

> The ministry is independent of the Church; it has a life of its own; it is a separate organization, through which the higher powers of Christianity are carried forward, by a wholly distinct channel, for the use of the world from age to age. These higher powers belong to (the church) in a mechanical, magical way, and not according to the ordinary law of truth and power among men.[9]

Nevin consistently attacked a mechanical understanding of the origin of the ministry that postulated a separate organization, independent of the Church, with a life of its own, through which the higher powers of Christianity are carried forward. In such a scheme the ministry is not a progressive actualization of the life of the Church in the form of authority. It is a supernatural constitution that must not conform to the order of nature; it is not organic or historical, but one long monotony of mere outward law and authority, superseding the natural order of the world, and contradicting it, age after age, to the end of time.

The presbyterian or congregational theory of the office of the ministry teaches that the office originates in the church either through the authority of the presbyters or that of the people. This theory represents a combination of the natural and mechanical theories. It involves a ministry created by the natural impulse of a local congregation that perceives the need for leadership, as in the natural theory. It also posits a separate ministry that grows from a divinely approved form of ecclesiastical government, as in the mechanical theory.[10] Nevin takes exception to any notion that the office of the ministry originates in and is empowered by the local congregation.

> There is no room then for the theory by which the Church at large, or any particular part of it, is taken to be the depository, in the first instance, of all the grace and force which belong to the ministerial office, just as in a political organization the body of people may be supposed to contain in themselves primarily the powers with which they choose to invest their own officers and magistrates. The order of dependence here is not ascending but descending. The law of derivation is downwards and not upwards, from the few to the many, and not from the many to the few.[11]

Nevin taught that the Church and ministry "spring from the same source and from the same time." They are "so joined together that they cannot be severed from one another." He was also convinced, based on his understanding of the Great Commission, that the Church began with the apostles and extends outward from them as people submit to their "embassy and proclamation." This means that, theoretically, the ministry came before the Church or, in Nevin's words, that the Church "is in truth constituted by the commission that creates" the ministry. The apostles stood between Christ and the world. They were "his witnesses, his legates, the representatives of his authority, the mediators of his grace among men." The Church was formed and held together by the apostles who were authorized and empowered to "carry into effect its conditions and terms." Nevin asserts that "the Church is said to be builded upon Peter, as the central representative of the college of the Apostles (Matthew 16:18)," and "upon the foundation of the apostles and the prophets, Jesus Christ himself being the chief cornerstone (Ephesians 2:20)."[12]

Nevin did not believe the pastoral ministry originated naturally, as if social group dynamics necessitated its creation. It did not drop out of heaven as a supernatural appendage to God's people, nor did it arise as the fruit of a divinely ordained form of ecclesiastical government, that is, by the will of presbyters. According to Nevin, the pastoral office originated with the apostles, the first ministers. Logically, then, the ministry preceded the Church and there would be no Church without it. It is clear that Nevin's understanding of the origin of the ministry involved some kind of apostolic succession. In Nevin's scheme succession was the method by which the ministry retained the supernatural force granted in the Ascension-Pentecost event. Succession is the conduit through which the power of Pentecost flows. The force of the ministry is maintained only as it remains in unity and perpetuity of its first appointment. Ministry outside of the succession is like a branch cut off the vine; it is powerless.

How is the conduit maintained? Jesus appointed the apostles as the first ministers. They, in turn, ordained others as pastors, and these set apart still others until the present.[13] There is only one ministry, that given to the apostles and passed on to those who followed them.[14] Nevin's line of succession, then, is in the office of the entire ministry. It is not maintained by the faithful transmission of the rule of faith; it is not a succession of doctrine or tradition, as if a deposit of faith is maintained by episcopacy. It is not a mechanical or physical succession transmitted by bishops through the laying on of hands. The line of succession is in the "office in unity with itself under a catholic form," the office that faithfully represents the "undivided and invisible Apostolic Commission."[15]

The office, of course, is always contained within the Church as an organic whole. The ministry is not the Church, but an indispensable characteristic of it.[16] For this reason Nevin will, on one occasion, refer to the apostolic office as the locus of succession, and, on another occasion, refer to the Church as the locus of succession.

The first ministers were the Apostles, who were called and commissioned immediately by Jesus Christ himself. They in turn ordained and set apart other suitable men, as pastors and teachers; and these in the same way appointed and sent forth others, carrying onward the true succession of this office; which, being regularly transmitted in this way from age to age in the Christian Church, has come down finally to our time.[17]

Nevin reiterated his point in his liturgy for ordination. The ordinand is asked, "Do you acknowledge the rightful authority of this Church, from which you are now to receive ordination, as being a true part in the succession of the Church Catholic; and do you promise all proper regard for its laws and ordinances, and all suitable obedience to its lawful government in the Lord? The ordinand answers - "So I confess, and so I promise."

The Nature of the Ministry

The second important ingredient in Nevin's understanding of the office of the ministry is its supernatural power. Nevin's pastoral office is a divine agency appointed by Christ and empowered by the Holy Spirit. It is, therefore, divine in nature and supernatural in force. It is not the product of humanity, a convenient appendage to a social and political group. It comes "from another economy or system, founded in a power which has actually surmounted the order of nature, and reigns above it in its own sphere."[18] As such, it is the most significant power in the world.

The genesis of this power is the incarnation. The Church, including its ministry, grows out of the mystery of the incarnation. It is the continuation of the life of Christ in the world and, as such, is a "repository of actual superhuman powers" that belong to no other constitution in society.[19] It is a permament source of life in the world springing "perpetually from Christ himself, as the vitality of the body descends into it from the head."[20]

The supernatural force of the pastoral office does not belong to the person who exercises it but to the "institution of the ministry." It is an official power. A minister's character may affect or prejudice its administration, but it is independent of these things. As long as the ministerial office holds to its legitimate form, it will be found true and equal to the purposes of its original institution. It is in this sense infallible. "Whatever may be said of single ministers in their private character, or in particular acts of their office, the institution as a whole, and taken in its corporate unity, must be held to be equal in full to the terms of this appointment."[21]

Nevin describes his view of the nature of the ministry in several articles. In his lengthy discourse on Cyprian, he writes that the ministry is a divine channel of a new order of life. "The office is not only to proclaim salvation, but with supernatural power to bring it actually to pass."[22] In his "Inaugural Address" at Mercersburg Seminary, Nevin contrasts the power of the pastoral office to the Senate chamber. In his estimation, the "agency of the pulpit" is "an institution whose operation will be found in the end to go deeper, and reach farther, than the policy and state machinery of cabinets can ever do."[23] In his defense of his liturgy for ordination he asks a rhetorical question:

Is the liturgy wrong in declaring the office of the ministry to be "of divine origin and of truly supernatural character and force, flowing directly from the Lord Jesus Christ Himself, as the fruit of His resurrection and triumphant Ascension into heaven?" Is not this precisely what St. Paul teaches us, in the notable fourth chapter of his Epistle to the Ephesians? May the office come to anyone, then, except from Christ, and through the order He has Himself established for handing it down in the Church?

A ministry of supernatural power is necessarily "exceedingly honorable." Nevin offers some of his most passionate thoughts concerning the dignity of the office is his 1842 sermon entitled "The Ambassador of God."[24] Those who hold office are "ambassadors of God" who represent among people the "august court of Heaven itself." "Where shall we find dignity like this?" Nevin asks. "There is no position or office in the world of greater significance. Monarchs, senators, scientists, princes, and kings all stand in less distinction." The "ministry of reconciliation" is of such honor and dignity that "there is not an angel before the Throne that would not rejoice to stoop this day from his dazzling height, to be invested with the same distinction." "It matters not, that the world has no power to discern this pre-eminence." The world saw no glory in the Son of God himself. The truth will not be obscured by the "errors of the blind."

Nevin's thought concerning the nature of the ministry is better understood by comparing it to a popular alternative. Many nineteenth-century Protestants believed that God created divine spheres of authority in the world, one of which was government while another was the Church. They would agree with Nevin that the pastoral ministry is divine in nature by virtue of its origin. But Nevin makes a distinction between the divine nature of civil government and the divine nature of the ministry, and in it his dependence upon idealism becomes clear. Civil government, he notes, is of the order of this world, while the office of the ministry "proceeds directly and altogether from a new and higher order of things brought to pass by the Spirit of Christ in consequence of his resurrection and Ascension."[25] While there are similarities, civil acts are not of the same order as ecclesiastical acts that "bind and loose, we are told, in heaven."[26] The office of the ministry is a constitution of grace on earth, differing from civil government of the constitution of nature. The one flows from the resurrection and Ascension of Christ, the other flows from nature. As we might say, the office of the ministry belongs to the order of redemption, while that of civil government belongs to the order of creation.

Nevin perceived that Calvinists, Catholics, and Anglicans also believed in a ministry that is divine in nature but not of this world. But, according to Nevin, these groups taught that the office of the ministry is an alien agency transplanted in the world, but not of it. The ministry in such a system is a divine provision of grace attached to the world in a mechanical manner to fulfill a preordained purpose. It is, then, hopelessly dualistic. The divine ministry is of another world and does not have any natural contact with this world. It does not flow from the Incarnation. The ministry is sundered from the world by an impassable gulph (sic).[27]

The result is an ultra spiritualistic, shadowing idea of redemption, in which no real union is allowed after all to have place between the powers of heaven and the necessities of earth; and in full correspondence with this, a complete dualism is brought into the conception of the Christian life also, regarded as the subjective or experimental appropriation, on the part of believers, of the grace thus objectively provided on their behalf.[28]

Nevin's theory of the nature of the ministry has a profound impact upon his view of ordination. It demands that ordination involve a real communication of supernatural power. In the New Testament the apostolic commission was followed by an inauguration that involved such a communication.[29] Since then a minister is a divinely appointed and supernaturally empowered in the rite of ordination. A candidate for ordination responds to the following question:

Are you truly persuaded in your heart, that you are called of God to the office of the holy ministry, and do you desire and expect to receive, through the laying on of our hands, the gift and grace of the Holy Ghost, which shall enable you to fulfill this heavenly commission and trust?[30]

Ordination, in Nevin's scheme, is the means by which supernatural force is transmitted to those holding the pastoral office. It is "the veritable channel through which is transmitted mystically, from age to age, the supernatural authority in which this succession consists."[31] It is a "tactual communication of heavenly powers." It is a sign and means of grace.

Ordination is not merely an impressive ceremony by which the right of such as are called to the ministry is owned and confessed by the Church; but it is the actual investiture with the very power of the office itself, the sacramental seal of a heavenly commission, and a symbolic assurance from God that their consecration to the service of Christ is accepted, and that the Holy Spirit will be with them in the faithful discharge of their official duties.[32]

The Design of the Ministry

The third essential ingredient in Nevin's understanding of the office of the ministry deals with its purpose and function. Nevin taught that God had designed the office of the ministry as **the** medium by which His grace is channeled to the world and his people so that individuals are elevated to true dignity and, thus the moral fiber of the community is enhanced.[33] Ministers are "ambassadors" of God's grace, transmitting the life-transforming power of God that will "build people in the faith and hope of the gospel unto everlasting life."[34] "Ministers of Christ," therefore, "are set in the world to be at once the representatives of His authority and the ambassadors of His grace."[35] As an extension of the work of the apostles, they continue the three-fold work of Jesus as prophet, priest, and king. Ministers fulfill the prophetic role as they proclaim the Gospel, the priestly role as they dispense the sacraments, and the kingly role as they administer Christian discipline.[36] Their work promotes growth in knowledge as well as individual moral improvement.[37]

Nevin's description of episcopal authority further illuminates his understanding of the design of the pastoral ministry. As episcopal, the office of the ministry possesses real pastoral jurisdiction, representing the authority of Jesus Christ.[38] Pastors are

shepherds under him who is the Chief Shepherd, clothed by delegation with his authority, and appointed to have charge of the flock in his name, with a power so real in its own sphere, and so absolutely irresponsible, at the same time, in any democratic or republican sense, that they are warned before Christ not to use it as lords over God's heritage.[39]

The office of the ministry in its broadest sense "involves the idea of real pastoral jurisdiction over the Church, representing in it immediately the authority of Jesus Christ, and deriving its force from the sovereignty of heaven and earth to which he has been advanced by his resurrection from the dead."[40] In particular, this authority involves "stewardship in the mysteries of God, the administration of the keys of the kingdom of heaven, and the negotiation of the terms of eternal life."[41]

This apostolic authority, however, was not given for each pastor to exercise in his own way and for his own pleasure. It belongs to the office as a "single institution, in harmony with all its parts." It is exercised in concert with a "college or corporation" of pastors similar to the historic episcopate.

> Just as among the Jews the priesthood was one, though the priests were many and of different orders, so in the Christian Church, however the ministers might be multiplied and the forms of their office varied, the office itself could be of force only as it retained always the character of a single body bound together, in union with itself. As there can be, by the very conception of Christianity, but one faith, one baptism, and one Church, so there can be also but one ministry.[42]

While Nevin did not identify his sources for this concept, he admitted that he was more Anglican on this point.[43] James Hastings Nichols concluded that Nevin was dependent on both Andreas Osiander (1498-1552) and the "Jus Divinum Ministerii Evangelici" of the London Provincial Assembly of 1654.[44]

How does the pastor of a local congregation fulfill his function as an ambassador of God's grace? **Not** by mimicking the revivalistic antics of Charles Finney and others. While Nevin did not oppose revival or spiritual commitment,[45] he did resist the system of the anxious bench developed by itinerant preachers and subsequently copied by resident pastors.[46] In Nevin's estimation, the system was superficial, deceptive, and susceptible to emotional extravagance. Nevin proposed that pastors fulfill their role by employment of the system of the catechism, by which he meant a return to the old forms of spiritual training.

It is a different system altogether that is required to build up the interests of Christianity in a firm and sure way. A ministry apt to teach; sermons full of unction and light; faithful, systematic instruction; zeal for the interests of holiness; pastoral visitation; catechetical training; due attention to order and discipline; patient perseverance in the details of the ministerial work; these are the agencies by which alone the kingdom of God may be expected to go steadily forward among any people.[47]

In his lectures on pastoral theology Nevin highlights three pastoral functions within the system of the catechism.[48] The primary area of work, in Nevin's estimation, is preaching. The minister is the authorized expounder of truth and duty.[49] It is interesting to note, and surprising to contemporary scholars, that Nevin exhausted more time in his pastoral theology class lecturing his students on the style of preaching than on its subject manner. He encouraged sincerity founded upon a consistent lifestyle that freed the speaker from hypocracy. He advocated simple, plain, practical, and experiential preaching in place of flourishing rhetoric. He emphasized passionate preaching that finds the balance between cold and heartless lecturing and angry condemnation. He summoned pastors to speak with authority and boldness as ambassadors of Christ, yet without dogmatism for pastors do not stand in the pulpit to dispute but to testify to God. He cautioned pastors to be sensitive to the diversity of the congregation; a sermon will be received by the converted, the unconverted, and by backsliders. Finally, we are not surprised that the hard working Nevin promoted diligence. Pastors should preach as often as strength and opportunity allows, but should not keep count of how many sermons have been preached since quality is more important than quantity.

The second major department of pastoral labor is catechetical instruction. The catechism is a powerful means whereby the pastor, and other qualified persons, provide systematic instruction for the children and young people of the congregation. The purpose of such instruction is to lead young people to profession of faith and participation in the sacrament of the Lord's Supper. In his lectures Nevin attempted to rescue catechetical instruction from "dead formalism." He encouraged his students to make the systematic instruction of children and young people a priority. In a strong series of statements, Nevin argued that young people have a special claim on the pastor and that he should make a distinct effort to develop a good relationship with them. In Nevin's opinion, if a child rebels and rejects the faith, the pastor must take some responsibility.

The third major part of pastoral labor is personal visitation. This form of ministry provides an opportunity for the pastor to bring the pulpit directly to the individual. Visitation is beneficial because it helps the pastor develop a closer relationship with members of the congregation who will, then, begin to view him as an advisor and friend who sympathizes with them. During his ministry the pastor will find opportunity to conduct several types of visits, including visitation of the sick, the poor, and the awakened.

The pastoral ministry, as so described by Nevin, fulfills a necessary role and indispensable function.[50] Nevin taught that as the apostles were a necessary ingredient in the life of the primitive church, so the office of the ministry is a "necessary medium" in the contemporary church. There is no salvation apart from the ordained ministry, he claimed. He challenged Americans to submit faithfully and obediently to the "economy of the gospel" if they hoped to experience redemption. People must understand that God's grace is dispensed through the visible organization, ordinances, and institutions of the Church:

> All the regular and proper organs and functions by which the life of the Church is carried forward among men for its own ends are divine organs and divine functions. They belong not to the sphere of mere nature, but to the sphere of supernatural grace. They include in themselves a value which transcends absolutely all powers that are lodged in our common human nature, under any other view. The ministry, for instance, is far more than any merely human institution could ever be possibly under the same form. The office is a necessary organ of the Body of Christ, and as such

it is the bearer of a divine supernatural power that may
never be measured safely by any common standard.[51]

Nevin lifted the pastoral office to a level unknown to most
nineteenth-century Americans who tended to deny its necessity
within the salvific process. Most Americans believed they
could attain salvation without the intervening medium of a
pastor. Hence, they opposed Nevin's design for the ministry.
While Nevin received criticism for his teaching concerning the
origin and nature of the ministry, opposition to his design for
the ministry was most intense. Attacks came from all wings of
American evangelical Protestantism, including the German
Reformed Church where Joseph Berg led the assault. Nevin's
opponents took exception to his insistence that the minister
function with authority as a prophet who interprets the Word
of God, as a king who rules the people of God, and as a priest
who intercedes on behalf of the people. They did not want an
office with such authority.   There were good reasons for
nineteenth-century Americans to oppose Nevin's design for the
ministry. The role of king ran face to face into the American
spirit of the sovereignty of the people. The role of priest ran
into a strong anti-Roman Catholic attitude. The role of prophet
ran into the popular principle of private judgment. The whole
design raised the issue of authority; it asserted a ministry of
authority to a people who were authorities unto themselves.

In summary, Nevin's idealism required a ministry that was
both necessary and authoritative. The true idea of authority
requires actualization.[52]   The ministry is the result of the
"progressive actualization of the life of the Church in the form
of authority."[53]   The office of the ministry is a necessary
organ of the Body of Christ, and as such, it is the bearer of a
divine supernatural power. Hence, the regular functions of the
pastor are divine functions.[54] If the ministry is without this
power and authority, it, as well as the Church, will fall.[55]

Conclusion

As Nevin surveyed the German Reformed Church that he
loved and served, he saw the office of the ministry modified by

the infiltration of both the Second Great Awakening and American republicanism. He saw ministers naively accepting new methods and measures to bring people to faith and spiritual maturity. He saw the catechism and sacraments slighted, and an inordinate amount of attention placed in tactics of persuasion. He found pastors without unique authority for ministry. In short, he saw the Americanization of the ministry.[56] In response, Nevin proposed a pastoral office that is a necessary link in the process of redemption and the divinely ordained medium of saving grace. He insisted that the properly installed pastor dispenses objective and spiritual realities that cannot be obtained elsewhere. Furthermore, he taught that the office is clothed with apostolic authority to administer the means of grace, interpret and proclaim the Scriptures, and discipline the wayward.

Nevin's proposal was a radical alternative to the predominant mode of thought found among most nineteenth-century evangelical Protestants. His alternative was simultaneously conservative, progressive, and evangelical. It was conservative by reason of its relationship to history, for Nevin's theory involved a retrieval of orthodox ideas from the Patristic and Reformation eras; he retrieved the past to inform the present. His alternative was progressive in that it was a drastic option for Protestants who advocated ecclesiatical republicanism. Nevin spoke of a ministry that originated in the apostles, that was given supernatural authority, that served as a necessary medium between God and His people, and that was given supernatural authority. It was evangelical in that it reflected a commitment to Scripture and to the necessity of spiritual transformation.

Nevin's alternative fell on deaf ears. Large numbers of Protestants found his writings anti-American, as most Americans would today. Now, his doctrine of the ministry is barely a memory, even among those who follow in his ecclesiastical tradition. Why, then, should it be resurrected?

Nevin's understanding of the ministerial office is relevant for several reasons. First, the pastoral ministry was the issue that moved Nevin as a theologian. His concern for the integrity of the pastoral office was the fire in the belly that fueled his prolific career as a writer and teacher. Yet, there is little

secondary research about Nevin's understanding of the theory
and work of the pastoral office. There has been a selective
retrieval of Nevin's thought in our generation. The liturgists
claim Nevin to defend their efforts for renewal. The ecumenists
claim Nevin as a spokesperson for their causes. The
sacramentalists, especially those of a Calvinistic persuasion,
love to talk of "Mystical Presence." But Nevin, as evidenced by
his first major work, *The Anxious Bench*, was deeply concerned
about the pastoral ministry. Any attempt to understand him
outside of that concern is flawed.

Second, it has been argued that Nevin clearly broke with his
Calvinist tradition on the doctrine of the ministry. Nichols, for
example, believes Nevin's theory is more consistent with that
of the German Reformer Osiander, propagated by the Lutheran
pastor and theologian Wilhelm Löhe who taught that the
powers of the clergy are not those common to all Christians but
those peculiar to Christ. There is, then, a basic dichotomy
between the congregation and the ministry.[57] But no
systematic presentation of Nevin's understanding of the
pastoral ministry exists that may be compared to Calvin's.

Third, Nevin's doctrine of the pastoral ministry is significant
for students of nineteenth-century Protestant thought in
America. His view represents an alternative Protestant and
evangelical model of pastoral ministry that stands on the
authority of Scripture, insists on the need for spiritual
transformation, and emphasizes evangelism.[58] Contemporary
evangelicals, however, fail to recognize Nevin as an alternative
stream of thought in their historical line. While mainline
Protestants look to him for confirmation of their liturgical and
sacramental renewal, evangelicals should look to him for a
unique doctrine of the pastoral ministry that integrates theory
with practice. Nevin insists that the function of the ministry
flow from a scriptural and historical stream and refuses to
divorce pastoral ministry from pastoral theology. Contemporary
evangelicals must realize that contemporary models of pastoral
ministry have been more greatly influenced by the founders of
republicanism than by the founders of the Christian faith. Nevin
challenges contempoary pastors and theologians to develop
theories of ministry so that its practice is rooted in Scripture
and theology rather than in fads of the day.

ENDNOTES

1. See Jack M. Maxwell's delineation of Nevin's sources in
   Worship and Reformed Theology (Pittsburgh: The Pickwick
   Press, 1976), 458-66.

2. John Williamson Nevin, "The Ordination of Ministers," *Order of
   Worship for the Reformed Church* (Philadelphia, 1866),
   reprinted in *The Mercersburg Theology*, edited by James
   Hastings Nichols (New York: Oxford University Press, 1966),
   346-47.

3. Nevin's doctrine of the pastoral ministry emerged in five
   documents. While from different periods in Nevin's career, they
   advance a consistent viewpoint with contrasting emphases.
   The earlier writings emphasize the personal qualities of the
   pastor as the "ambassador of God." They clearly reflect the
   pietistic influence of men like Richard Baxter. The later writings
   deal with pastoral office and function. In them Nevin stresses
   the importance of properly installed pastors providing Christian
   nurture through the sacraments and catechism.
   The first of the five documents is "Personal Holiness," a lecture
   delivered in June of 1837 at the opening of the summer term in
   the Western Theological Seminary. According to student notes,
   this lecture continued as part of his seminary course in pastoral
   theology at the Theological Seminary of the German Reformed
   Church in Mercersburg, hereafter called Mercersburg Seminary.
   The second document is "Inaugural Address," offered during his
   installation as professor of theology at Mercersburg Seminary
   on May 20, 1840. It affirms the "grandeur and solemnity of the
   work in which the Church has embarked" through the support
   of a theological seminary. In the third document, a sermon
   entitled "The Ambassador of God: or the True Spirit of the
   Christian Ministry as Represented in Jesus Christ," Nevin
   returned to the theme of personal fitness for the ministry. The
   sermon was delivered at the German Reformed Church in
   Chambersburg, Pennsylvania on July 10, 1842. The fourth is a
   sermon entitled "The Christian Ministry." This systematic
   portrait of the pastoral office was given in 1854 during the
   installation service of Bernard C. Wolff (1794-1870), Nevin's
   successor as professor of theology. The sermon delineates
   three essential propositions in Nevin's doctrine: the pastoral
   office is of divine origin, is of supernatural force, and functions
   as a conduit of the life-transforming power of God. The fifth

work is a liturgical form. As a member of the committee of the German Reformed Church that produced the Provisional Liturgy of 1857, Nevin developed the service of Ordination and Installation. His ordination service was included in the Provisional Liturgy and approved with minimal changes for inclusion in the *Order of Worship* of 1866, an official publication of the German Reformed Church. Much of the service comes from secondary sources, such as the Mayer Liturgy, the Book of Common Prayer, and the Catholic Apostolic Liturgy.

4. John Williamson Nevin, "Cyprian," *Mercersburg Review*, 4 (1852): 360.

5. Nevin, "The Christian Ministry," 350.

6. James Hoppin, professor of homiletic and pastoral theology at Yale College, provides a philosophical exposition of this theory in his *The Office and Work of the Christian Ministry* (New York: Sheldon and Company, 1869).

7. Nevin, "The Christian Ministry," 358.

8. John Williamson Nevin, "Brownson's Quarterly Review," *Mercersburg Review* 2 (1850):61.

9. Ibid.

10. An example of this viewpoint is "The Office of the Evangelical Ministry in its Relation to the Church." In B.S. Schneck, *Mercersburg Theology Inconsistent with Protestant and Reformed Doctrine* (Philadelphia: J.B. Lippincott & Co., 1874), 157-58. Schneck's criticism of Nevin focuses on the issue of justification by faith, but it includes an appendix that provides a list of theses concerning the origin of the ministry. While the list is not his own, Schneck commends it to his readers as valuable and worthy of study.

11. Nevin, "The Christian Ministry," 359.

12. Ibid., 354.

13. Nevin, "The Ordination of Ministers," 346-47.

14. Nevin made the traditional distinction between the extraordinary office of the apostle and the ordinary office of the pastor. The apostolic office, in his view, was a special office designed for a limited time, while the pastoral office is for the regular use of

the Church throughout all ages. This distinction, however, is of minimal significance in Nevin's scheme, since one is simply an extension of the other. The two offices are essentially the same in that they originate in the same biblical event and have been empowered by the same Spirit.

15. Nevin, "Cyprian," 386.

16. John Williamson Nevin, "Letter to William R. Whittingham" (August 2, 1845). In David Hein, "The Letters of John Williamson Nevin to William R. Whittingham," *Anglican Episcopal History* 60 (June 1991):197-211.

17. Nevin, "The Ordination of Ministers," 346-47.

18. Nevin, "The Christian Ministry," 357.

19. John Williamson Nevin, "Wilberforce on the Incarnation," *Mercersburg Review* 2 (1850): 186.

20. John Williamson Nevin, "The Church," in *The Mercersburg Theology*, edited by James Hastings Nichols (New York: Oxford University Press, 1966), 71.

21. Nevin. "The Christian Ministry," 362.

22. Nevin, "Cyprian," 376.

23. John Williamson Nevin, "Inaugural Address," *Addresses Delivered at the Inauguration of Rev. John Williamson Nevin, D.D., As Professor of Theology in the Theological Seminary of the German Reformed Church, May 20, 1840* (Chambersburg, PA: Publication Office of the German Reformed Church, 1840), 13.

24. John Williamson Nevin, *The Ambassador of God: or the True Spirit of the Christian Ministry as Represented in the Mind of Jesus Christ* (Chambersburg, PA: Publication Office of the German Reformed Church, 1842), 17.

25. Nevin, "The Christian Ministry," 356.

26. John Williamson Nevin, "Jesus and the Resurrection," *Mercersburg Review* 13 (1861):190.

27. Nevin, "Brownson's Quarterly Review," 63.

28. John Williamson Nevin, "Hodge on Ephesians," *Mercersburg Review* 9 (1857): 60-61.

29. Nevin, "Cyprian," 360.

30. Nevin, "The Ordination of Ministers," 347.

31. Nevin, "The Christian Ministry," 365.

32. Nevin, "The Ordination of Ministers," 347.

33. Nevin, "Inaugural Address," 15.

34. Nevin, "The Christian Ministry," 361.

35. John Williamson Nevin, "The Ordination Service," in *Worship and Reformed Theology: The Liturgical Lessons of Mercersburg,* ed., Jack M. Maxwell (Pittsburgh: The Pickwick Press, 1976), 461.

36. Nevin, "Brownson's Quarterly Review," 61.

37. Nevin, "Inaugural," 15.

38. Nevin, "The Christian Ministry," 359.

39. Ibid., 359.

40. Ibid., 360.

41. Ibid., 363.

42. Ibid., 360.

43. John Williamson Nevin, "Our Relations with Germany," *Mercersburg Review* 14 (1867): 632.

44. James Hastings Nichols, *Romanticism in American Theology: Nevin and Schaff at Mercersburg* (Chicago: The University of Chicago Press, 1961), 260-61.

45. Glenn A. Hewitt, *Regeneration and Morality: A Study of Charles Finney, Charles Hodge, John W. Nevin, and Horace Bushnell* (Brooklyn: Carlson Publishing, 1991), 93.

46. One of the most popular tools of revivalists was the anxious bench, a special seat for inquirers. Having heard the call of the gospel during a stirring message from a guest speaker, those whose hearts were warmed were invited to come forward to the anxious bench for more personal instruction. While such

was given, the rest of the congregation could pray that the inquirers would make a personal commitment of faith.

47. John Williamson Nevin, *The Anxious Bench* (2nd ed.; Chambersburg, PA: Publication Office of the German Reformed Church, 1844), 55.

48. Classroom notes of Nevin's *Lectures on Pastoral Theology* are available in the library of the Evangelical and Reformed Historical Society located on the campus of Lancaster Theological Seminary. Three volumes are available: notes by E. W. Reinecke (Winter 1845), George Wolff (May 1847), and E. W. Santee (July 1850).

49. Nevin, "Inaugural," 3.

50. S. R. Fischer, "Qualifications for Christian Ministry," *The Mercersburg Review* 8 (1854): 423.

51. Nevin, "The Church," 72-73.

52. Nevin, "Brownson's Quarterly Review," 61.

53. Ibid.

54. Nevin, "The Church," 72-73.

55. Ibid., 73.

56. See Sam Hamstra, Jr., "The Americanization of the Church and its Pastoral Ministry," *The New Mercerburg Review* 11 (Spring 1992):3-19.

57. Nichols, *Romanticism in American Theology*, 259.

58. See description of evangelicalism by Timothy L. Smith, *Revivalism and Social Reform* (Nashville, TN: Abingdon Press, 1957).

Nevin's Holistic Supernaturalism

David Wayne Layman

The use of Nevin's thought in contemporary theology has often been confined to the concerns of ecumenism, sacramentology, and liturgical practice. But these limitations have obscured the special genius of Nevin's insights and their continuing significance for contemporary theology. For Nevin, sacramental and liturgical theology is premised on a more fundamental doctrine of revelation that teaches that theology points toward and is grounded in the radically present **experience** of God's presence and activity.

For Nevin, revelation is the supernatural transformation of human experience and is therefore a living reality, taking place in the flow of human experience. Nevin's understanding of revelation as transcendent and transformative embodies a rejection of theological naturalism; his assertion of revelation as living and historical embodies a rejection of the dualistic supernaturalism that dominated the evangelical theology of his era. Revelation, according to Nevin, is not a supernatural message—whether in the Bible, in Jesus' earthly teachings, or in the church's tradition—that has to be verified by proofs or natural reason. Rather, revelation is the living experience of the spiritual power of Jesus Christ. Therefore, it is **holistic**: it rests in the whole person of the incarnate Christ.

Scholars tend to disregard this living, holistic quality of Nevin's theology largely because they overestimate his adaptation of German theology to the American context.[1] Research into Nevin's thought has been preoccupied with the search for the theological and philosophical sources of his Mercersburg Theology. The standard interpretation, classically articulated by James Hastings Nichols, argues that Nevin's theology emerged only after a radical "conversion" out of

Puritanistic evangelicalism.[2] But Nevin's adaptation of German thought was a spontaneous incorporation of certain elements specifically and to the degree to which they enabled him to integrate prior developments intrinsic to his native Presbyterian piety and education at Princeton. These include an emphasis on union with Christ through sacrament and religious experience; the affirmation that religion is to be transformative, not merely rote dogmatic profession, mundane practice of religious rituals, or external adherence to some moral code; and the category of the "organic" as descriptive of the unity of individual and communal experience. Nevin's eventual rejection of the evangelical dualism of the Princeton theology in favor of a holistic supernaturalism arose naturally out of his own life and efforts to bring coherence and meaning to his spirituality and theology.

Nevin, Bushnell, and Hodge on Christian Nurture: The Affinities

Nevin's attempt to balance religious naturalism and supernaturalist dualism is most clearly evident in his debates with Horace Bushnell and Charles Hodge on the subject of Christian nurture. Nevin's position can be identified by first examining the essential points on which the three men agreed: all rejected the solution of revivalism to the problem of Christian nurture and all agreed that religious nurture was in some sense dependent upon larger socio-psychological structures that "organically" enveloped individual choice and behavior.

According to all three, revivalism shatters the inherited modes of religious practice by bypassing the common religious life and tradition of the community in favor of grounding religious experience in the individual. Bushnell called such supernaturalism "ictic," for the supernatural was understood to break abruptly into nature.[3] Likewise, Hodge argued that revivalism's "sudden and violent paroxysms of exertion [are] out of analogy with all God's dealings with men."[4] Nevin agreed. Revivalism is a false view of religion when "regarded ...as a transient excitement to be renewed from time to time by suitable stimulants presented to the imagination."[5]

Moreover, their common critique of revivalism was rooted in the theme of the "organic." Bushnell held that "all our modern speculations" are susceptible to "an extreme individualism" that failed to take into account "organic laws."[6] For Bushnell, these "laws" are the structure of covenantal community familiar to every Puritan prior to the Great Awakening. Hodge readily concurred: Bushnell's theme of the organic "is as familiar to Presbyterians as household words" and give his work "very much of an 'old-school' cast."[7] By organic Hodge meant that "every church, nation and society has a common life, besides the life of its individual members.... No community can isolate itself."[8] So it is not surprising that in 1838 the Presbyterian Nevin criticized religion that is "grafted on...lives from without. It stands in no organic connection, as a development of life from within." Here, "organic" means living as opposed to artificial, the spontaneous externalization of "a supernatural change, wrought in the moral constitution of the soul by the Spirit."[9] Consequently, Bushnell, Nevin, and Hodge were agreed on two central points: the Church's salvific work on behalf of those included in her life and occurring through gradual education, not through spontaneous conversions; and the existential interconnection that grounded this salvific effectiveness as in some sense "organic."

Nevin and Bushnell: The Meaning of Supernaturalism

These agreements bring into higher relief the difference that soon emerged between them, differences that exemplify Nevin's holistic supernaturalism. While Nevin was almost effusive in his praise of Bushnell's organismic view, he nevertheless criticized what he perceived its naturalistic character. "...it bases its theory of educational piety on the constitution of nature, in the case of men, rather than upon the constitution of grace, as a strictly supernatural system." On one hand, Nevin and Bushnell agreed that there must be an organic unity of nature and supernature. The living power found in Christianity is manifested in and through the structures and processes of ordinary religious experience, not "magically" apart from them. But Nevin continued to insist that "Christianity can never resolve itself...into the constitution of the world's life, as found beyond its own sphere." If it is wrong to sunder Christian experience from its historical and spiritual continuity with mundane existence, it is equally wrong to "sink the conception of the supernatural in Christianity into the sphere of **mere** nature....[10] For Nevin, the supernatural is neither a separate reality magically breaking into nature from on high, nor simply continuous with nature. It is incarnate in nature, yet transformative of it.

Nevin found this improper emphasis exemplified in Bushnell's treatment of original sin and baptism. For Bushnell, Nevin believed, original sin is a "necessary accident merely to our moral probation," and redemption a purely immanent development of nature out of its own resources. Nevin ascribed this error to Bushnell's failure "to distinguish...between the idea of principle or ground, and the idea of mere occasion or condition."[11] According to Nevin, the incarnate life of Christ manifested in the Church is the **principle** of new life in a regenerate person. Supernatural transformation did not happen simply because a person was exposed to correct educational **conditions** such as orthodox instruction and nurture in piety. These conditions brought to life a power not naturally present, but present only in and through a transcendent power, a supernatural life. In other words, spiritual life requires the proper conditions, but those conditions bring forth spiritual fruit only out of a supernatural principle of life.

The second issue that exemplifies Bushnell's naturalistic organicism is that of baptism. Nevin read Bushnell as arguing that baptism creates "an organic relation between parents and their children in our common human constitution." Children are putatively Christian insofar as they were born into a putatively Christian home which would, presumably, inculcate Christian values—"the general law of educational, hereditary religion already established in the order of the world."[12] Baptism is merely a mechanical and external religious symbol of this given natural fact; the truth signified by baptism governs whether or not the ordinance takes place. Replied Nevin:

[Christianity] is the supernatural in human natural form. The higher life of the Church is the life of humanity

itself, exalted into its own proper sphere. The new
creation then carries out and completes the sense of
the old creation. It is the old organism still, with all its
original necessary laws; only lifted into a higher order
of existence. Such...results spring not from the flesh
as such, but from the presence of supernatural powers
and resources made permanent in the flesh by Jesus
Christ.[13]

Bushnell, it appeared to Nevin, understands the organic in its
literal and natural sense: children become Christian through the
natural processes of propagation, nurture, and cultural
influence. Individual choice is subsumed into the more
fundamental influences of parental and cultural stimuli.
However, according to Nevin, the organic structure of the
incarnation still adheres to the "form" of nature, while
transforming its substance. The laws of organic interconnection in supernatural reality are analogous to those of
natural organicism, but the ground of that reality is substantially
different. The principle of natural organicism is nature; the
principle of supernatural organicism is the revelation of the
incarnate Christ in his body, the Church. "We need...not an
organic law in the sin-disabled nature of our children
themselves, but the law of the spirit of life in Christ Jesus,
organically joined to our nature...in the Church."[14] So for
Nevin, the organic implies a supernaturally transforming power
that holistically enters into the structures of human experience.
Since human experience is by definition temporal and historical,
the incarnate Christ progressively becomes ever more closely
united with the structures of personal and communal existence.
But in no case is the "life" that makes true religion possible to
be identified with natural human existence or the power of "sin-
disabled" selfhood.

Nevin and Hodge: Holism Versus Dualism

Though Hodge agreed with Nevin's critique of Bushnell's
naturalistic organicism, Nevin found Hodge's supernaturalism
dualistic. Since the seminal work of Archibald Alexander, the

Princeton theology had always affirmed the central importance of a living, morally transforming religious experience. Yet the Princeton theologians distinguished themselves from revivalistic emotionalism by balancing subjective religious experience with the objectivity of Christ's work as revealed in Scripture. Although subjective religious experience was essential, it had to be grounded in the objectivity of God's revelation of Jesus Christ in Scripture. But for the Princeton theologians, this emphasis on the alleged objectivity of scripture quickly became an external authority that stood against the immediacy of the believer's experience of the transforming presence and power of Jesus Christ.[15]

Nevin's theology was rooted in the tension between religious experience and objective authority that the Princeton formulation represented. However, two of the central themes of the Mercersburg Theology through which Nevin would later overcome this dualism—the Church as the central locus of God's activity, and the content of this activity as discerned in the unfolding processes of time and history—were already embryonically present in his earliest writings. Therefore, his movement away from the Baconian tendency of the Princeton theology to view theology as a dogmatic system scientifically derived from Scripture was not entirely owing to his later reading of German theology and history, as many scholars have maintained.

For example, in *A Summary of Biblical Antiquities,* composed in the late 1820s, Nevin emphasizes the role of the Church and its historical development: "...although the Church has been substantially the same in all ages, its measures of spiritual advantage, and its outward constitution, have been greatly altered with the progress of time."[16] Moreover, Nevin's claim that the Christian covenant spiritually reinterprets the Hebrew covenant implicitly undercuts the structure of Reformed covenant theology which argues that the two covenants are essentially one, thus allowing the Princeton theologians to read Christian dogma back into the Hebrew scriptures. In other words, by arguing that the new covenant provides the true meaning of the old through the coming of the Holy Spirit, Nevin had introduced an incipient concept of development into his hermeneutic.[17]

These themes are also evident in a lecture on biblical interpretation that Nevin delivered in Pittsburgh in 1831. On one hand, he affirmed the standard notions of Princeton's Baconian hermeneutic that every student of theology must "labor to derive his views of truth from the direct and simple interpretation of the Bible."[18] Yet, simultaneously, he insists that the Bible presented an **existential** realm of spiritual activity: "...living realities of truth...exist[ing] in the general texture of the thought at large, and the spirit which pervades the whole."[19] Furthermore, one is only prepared to properly interpret the New Testament if one recognizes the transformations that had taken place in Hebrew-Jewish life and thought. For example, Second Temple Judaism is different from Hebrew religion under the monarchs, which in turn is different from still earlier forms.

Three years later, writing in *The Friend*, Nevin argued that Scripture is not "a **theory** of religion...in the world of the mind, [but] a transcript of the great truths of religion...as they are found historically active in the mind of God and the mind of the human sinner." Religion is not "a system of theology scientifically wrought into the abstract, [but] a representation of facts the development of which is going forward in the moral history of men."[20] Religious experience denotes a process of vital transformation and its "facts," whether of nature or Scripture, are phenomena in the realm of spiritual and moral experience. Just as Scripture sets forth the ongoing experience of men and women, it is not enough to intellectually analyze their experience as empirical data in a Baconian manner; a contemporary believer had to realize those spiritual "facts" in his own life. Consequently, for Nevin, religious experience is itself objective, consisting in its existentially present and historically developing spiritual power and reality: Christianity "had life in itself, and entered as a living history into the experience of the souls by which it was truly embraced."[21]

Thus, Nevin's earliest Presbyterian writings indicate an early historical and hermeneutical sophistication through which Nevin attempts to overcome the dualistic tendencies of Hodge's thought. Texts are not dead and finished constructs to be interpreted independently of the spiritual pilgrimage behind the texts; secondly, insofar as truth is only known by entering into the spiritual struggle of an individual and community, it is also historical. To properly integrate the content of that process into one's own spiritual journey, one has to recognize the real historical differences within the historical process.

Nevin's Later Critique of Dualism

In contrast to the tendency of the Princeton theology to polarize objective dogma and subjective experience—thereby creating a dichotomy between supposed Christian and mundane realities—Nevin articulated the holistic unity of nature and supernature as grounded in the incarnation of God in Jesus Christ. For Nevin, the incarnation is not primarily a doctrine, law, or even an event; it is an "historical enduring fact," **historical** because it enters into the flow of human experience, **enduring** because it continues to manifest itself in that flow, and **fact** because it is a "new order of life," a "concrete revelation of life."[22] The incarnation inserts a new realm of powers, a new spiritual reality, into the material. But the incarnation is not a mere event to be relegated to past empirical history, for the supernatural power revealed in the incarnate Christ has become integrated into the flow of history itself, and is now transforming it. In Christ the supernatural is "brought into real, organic, abiding union with the natural...filling it permanently...with powers it never possessed before."[23] The transformative powers of the incarnation are holistically united with the process of existence, yet never reducible to those processes in their natural flow.

Nevin also criticized popular evangelical piety for conceiving of salvation as "something wholly subjective; made to rest in some measure...upon the **thought** of something which is supped to have taken place also in the divine mind." According to Nevin, popular evangelical piety regards revelation as abstract theory rather than as objective, existential reality in the present. Popular evangelical piety is artificial because the believer is understood to require some artifice, or series of techniques, to bridge the gap between the supernatural and the natural, thus leaving the person "hopelessly in himself," unable to break out of the confines of unregenerate subjectivity.[24]

Rather, according to Nevin, the supernatural transformation of reality takes place in present historical experience; revelation consists of "divine powers objectively present through Jesus Christ in the Church." Since the powers are objectively present, the believer does not have to strive to create a set of feelings or state of conviction. Piety can "be at once profoundly earnest and profoundly calm." As existentially grasped by the revelation of Jesus Christ in the Church's life, the believer can be strongly moved, truly transformed and empowered, without surrendering to the momentary emotionalism of revivalism.

Nevin rejected the assumption that the believer has to bridge the chasm between doctrine and experience by means of the power of one's will. The supposed separation between the spiritual and material also implies a separation between experience and history, as if spirituality is the *de novo* realization of some esoteric truth apart from the historical concreteness of the Church's life. Nevin's holistic supernaturalism implies the opposite of each dualism. Doctrine is merely the expression of the supernatural experience of God's transforming power in contemporary experience. This power is the "incarnation" of the power revealed in the incarnate Christ. Thus, nature and supernature, body and spirit, are united in history; the incarnation is a transforming energy in mundane existence that can be recognized as such in faith. This unity is above all manifested in the Church, specifically in its sacramental and liturgical practice. The "mystical presence" manifests itself as a powerfully transforming reality, not through human subjectivity—in the mode of a thought, idea, or mood—but through its power to bring itself into reality, to realize itself in the liturgical community.

The Hermeneutics of Holistic Supernaturalism

According to Nevin, the experience of the revelation of the incarnate Christ in the Church's sacramental praxis does not deny the authority and power of Scripture. During the later part of his career, Nevin extended his holistic supernaturalism

202 John Williamson Nevin

to his doctrine of Scripture as the means or "condition" through which the incarnate Christ reveals himself, thus creating a fully integrated doctrine of revelation.

The first clear expression of his hermeneutic is found in the autobiographical essays of 1870. Here he begins to explicitly formulate his rejection of "grammatico-historical" hermeneutics with the argument that the proper object of faith must itself be "supernatural, and must be apprehended by the faith directly in its own supernatural objectivity."[25] Nevin argues that authentic "faith in the Bible" is not faith "in the outward credibility of the Bible as established by the usual proofs, but faith...in the objective supernatural substance" which is the "very soul and life" of the "outward revelation" as "its self-verifying presence."[26] Reminiscent of his earlier rejection of Hodge's dualism, Nevin now argues that the supernatural status of the Bible cannot be verified by quasi-empirical "proofs" that transformed Christian experience into the subjective "appropriation" of an allegedly objective content. Rather, the inscripturated *Logos* is the means in and through which the supernatural presence of the incarnate *Logos* immediately reveals itself: "...the self-witnessing power of the Lord's life actually lives in the Holy Scriptures, as their animating spirit and soul."[27] If the meaning of Scripture inheres in its spiritual life, the divine life of the ever-newly revealed word, then its meaning cannot be determined "by the same principles and laws that we apply to the interpretation of any other book written by men for the use of men."[28]

Consequently, Nevin criticized two different forms of rationalistic hermeneutics. Evangelicals claim that the Bible is a supernaturally revealed book, but dualistically maintain that this supernatural text can be interpreted by the same hermeneutical principles as any other book. Nevin insists that the supernaturalism of this evangelical hermeneutic is really illusory, since in the end Scripture is not interpreted by the self-interpreting power of revelation, but by "reason...posted at the gate of entrance to the Bible...**sitting** there as the impudent janitress of heaven."[29] This approach he calls "verbalism," the alleged alternative to "realism." This latter hermeneutic, says Nevin, originated among German scholars and holds that Scripture embodies merely "the form of common human though in common human speech," therefore denying the supernatural character of Scripture. While "verbalism" holds that the natural, mundane meaning of Scripture is supernaturally protected from error, "realism" denies such supernatural protection and thus affirms that errors exist in Scripture, just as in any other human production.[30]

Nevin was able to deny both sides of this apparent antinomy by asserting that Scripture as a supernatural revelation can only be truly comprehended as the believer participates in the supernatural life it expresses. It is not enough to obey Scripture in some external, legalistic, "mechanical" manner. At the same time it is insufficient to understand the gospel at some deeper "theoretic" level. "Outward obedience and inward knowledge" both must enter into the "very essential life of the Lord himself." A "vital mode" of religious experience is required where the transcendent, transforming power of the divine life enters into the existential core of the human subject and gives him the new power of being and acting. This is the "new birth," a "continuous ongoing of the life from above, determined by the sense of a new will, a new selfhood centering in God."[31]

After 1870 the conviction that the true meaning of Scripture is existential, not doctrinal or theoretical, undergirds Nevin's doctrines of inspiration and the testimony of the Holy Spirit. Indeed, the two doctrines are the same. Praising the Westminster Confession on the *testimonium* as "beautiful and grand...over against the reigning rationalistic tendency," he nevertheless criticizes its formulation because it makes the *testimonium* "external to the word, instead of by and in it there." Again, Nevin's holistic supernaturalism is evident. The testimony of the Spirit to the word is not a subjective confirmation of objective, doctrinal truth; it is itself the divine word. "The Spirit thus in the Word is no other than Christ himself. He...is the one universal sense of the Word, its inward life and soul.[32] Jesus Christ, as God incarnate, is both the form and content of revelation. Scripture is revelatory not simply because it tells us about Christ, but because **insofar** as it **is** revelatory, it **is** Christ as incarnate revelation, now inscripturated.

Likewise, the inspiration of Scripture does not refer primarily to "its mundane aspects—historical, pictorial, or simply scientific"—but to the ever renewed in-spira-tion, the "breathing into" of the Scriptures by the Spirit of the revelation of the incarnate Christ.[33] The "very idea of inspiration" has to do with "its inward spiritual sense universally, as distinguished from its outward literal and merely natural sense."[34] Consequently, the literal content of both Scripture's history and its doctrinal instruction have to be interpreted in and through the experienced presence of the revealed and revealing Christ. Moreover, Scripture can only be revealing when it is experienced within the Spirit of the incarnate Christ. The Spirit breaths the *Logos* into the mundane human words, making the spiritual power of Christ present and active—"self-attesting, self-interpreting, self-enforcing."[35]

Late in his career, Nevin elaborated his understanding of the power of the inscripurated *Logos* with respect to his long held affirmation of the mystical presence of Christ in the Lord's Supper. In an 1878 communion sermon, he affirmed that "it is the *word of God* divinely joined with the elements which makes the sacrament,...and this word, proceeding out of the mouth of the Lord, wherever it is found, hath that life in it by which only it is possible for men to live." This divine word is more than the outward words of Scripture or liturgical praxis; it is "a continuous going forth of life from the Lord," and is therefore "the living soul of the sacraments through all time."[36] Thus, the Word is neither a mundane text to be interpreted by the best efforts of human reason—whether or not reason takes the text to be supernaturally inspired—nor mundane religious actions to be carried out as a natural possibility of human culture. Rather, the *Logos* is found in both a supernatural text and a supernatural liturgical praxis in precisely the sense in which a supernatural **life** dwells in the text and in the praxis, which by its own power makes itself present and active. Perhaps reflecting upon the liturgical controversy he helped create in the German Reformed Church, Nevin observes:

In our past controversies with regard to baptism and the Lord's Supper, we may not have done justice always to what must be considered in this way the true and real pre-eminence of the Word above all sacraments, we may have failed to intone properly what the presence of the Lord in this Word means, without which there is no room to conceive of his presence among men in any other form.[37]

In sum, Nevin finally came to the conclusion that the Word of God is prior to Scripture, liturgy, and sacraments. Only insofar as the supernatural life of the *Logos* is present are both Scripture and sacrament truly spiritually alive, possessing the self-actuating power to bring life. This life is that of the mystical presence, the life of the incarnate Christ, experienced in the supernatural transformation of personal existence, history, cosmos, and human community.

Conclusion

Nevin's supernaturalism was always united with his affirmation that the powers of the incarnate Christ are manifest in and through mundane religious experience, community, and history. It is this unity that renders his supernaturalism "holistic." The structural form of this unity is ecclesial: the Church is the extension of the incarnate Christ. Moreover, the incarnate Christ is first and foremost the eschatological Christ. "Christianity...is a perpetual fact, that starts in the incarnation of the Son of God, and reaches forward as a continuous supernatural reality to the end of time."[38] As the natural cosmos ever increasingly comes under the new power of life in the incarnate Christ, it moves toward its proper consummation in him.

Consequently, Nevin emphasized the supernatural character of Christian experience. The participation of the believer in the sacramental life of the Church discloses a powerfully transforming presence. Therefore, Nevin's incarnationalism does not, as Alan P. F. Sell contends, "play down the novelty of the new [creation]," but emphasizes that the powers of the new creation have entered into this mundane, historical existence and given it a new ground of being, a new "germ" that unfolds its life in temporal, embodied reality. God's power is revealed in mundane reality; yet precisely as **power** it makes itself felt, for this incarnate, eschatological Christ is also the **crucified** Christ.[39] The cross is the path that Christ traveled, and therefore the Church and the individual believer must undergo the same journey in order to experience the unity of the incarnation.

This kenotic incarnationalism, as well as Nevin's theology as a whole, emerges first of all from Nevin's highly existential and personal native piety, not as the result of the influence of German historicism. Therefore, his thought can only be properly interpreted if one first comprehends his experience. Nevin's holistic supernaturalism is finally a reflection on the revelation of God's transforming power in his own life. It is the personal revelation of God's love and "mystical presence" in Jesus Christ, a presence that sustained Nevin throughout his own fragmented pilgrimage.

ENDNOTES

1. See, for example, Luther J. Binkley, *The Mercersburg Theology* (Manheim, PA: Sentinel Printing House, 1953), 23-28; and F. Russell Mitman, Jr., "The Implications for Christian Unity in the Theology of John Williamson Nevin," *The New Mercersburg Review* 9 (1991):21, 24-25.

2. James Hastings Nichols, *Romanticism in American Theology: Nevin and Schaff at Mercersburg* (Chicago: University of Chicago Press, 1961), 36-37.

3. Horace Bushnell, *View of Christian Nurture and of Subjects Adjacent Thereto* (Hartford: Edwin Hunt, 1848; New York: M. H. Newman & Co., 1848; Boston: Crocker & Brewster, 1848), 103, 107.

4. Charles Hodge, "Bushnell on Christian Nurture," *The Biblical Repertory and Princeton Review* 19 (October 1847):519-20.

5. John Williamson Nevin, *The Anxious Bench*, in *Catholic and Reformed: Selected Theological Writings of John Williamson Nevin*, Charles Yrigoyen, Jr., and George H. Bricker, eds. (Pittsburgh: The Pickwick Press, 1978), 58.

6. Bushnell, *Christian Nurture*, 23.

7. Hodge, "Christian Nurture," 502.

8. Ibid., 503.

9. John Williamson Nevin, *The Seal of the Spirit* (Pittsburgh: William Allinder, 1838), 8, 3.

10. John Williamson Nevin, "Educational Religion," *Weekly Messenger* 12 (7 July 1847):2458.

11. Ibid.

12. Nevin, "Educational Religion," *Weekly Messenger* (14 July 1847):2461.

13. Ibid.

14. Ibid.

15. See W. Andrew Hoffecker, *Piety and the Princeton Theologians: Archibald Alexander, Charles Hodge, and Benjamin Warfield* (Grand Rapids, MI: Baker Book House, 1981), 3, 63; and Lefferts A. Loetscher, *Facing the Enlightenment and Pietism: Archibald Alexander and the Founding of Princeton Theological Seminary* (Westport, CT: Greenwood Press, 1983), 170-73.

16. John Williamson Nevin, *A Summary of Biblical Antiquities* (Philadelphia: American Sunday School Unity, 1829-30; 2nd ed., 1849), 240.

17. Ibid., 251-52.

18. John Williamson Nevin, *The Claims of the Bible Urged upon the Attention of the Students of Theology* (Pittsburgh: D. & M. Maclean, 1831), 9.

19. Ibid., 11.

20. John Williamson Nevin, "Religion a Life," *The Friend* (25 December 1834):198.

21. Ibid., 230.

22. John Williamson Nevin, *Antichrist, or the Spirit of Sect and Schism* (New York: John S. Taylor, 1848), 21-23, 33-34.

23. Ibid., 23.

24. Ibid., 41, 48.

25. John Williamson Nevin, *My Own Life* (Lancaster, PA: Historical Society of the Evangelical and Reformed Church, 1874), 101-2.

26. Ibid., 113-14.

27. John Williamson Nevin, "The Spirit of Prophecy," *Mercersburg Review* 24 (April 1877):212.

28. John Williamson Nevin, "Sacred Hermeneutics," *Reformed Quarterly Review* 25 (January 1878):15.

29. Ibid., 18.

30. John Williamson Nevin, "Christ the Inspiration of His Own Word," *Reformed Quarterly Review* 29 (January 1882):38-42.

31. Ibid., 10-11,14.

32. Ibid., 39-40, 41.

33. Ibid., 41-42.

34. John Williamson Nevin, "The Inspiration of the Bible, or the Internal Sense of Holy Scripture," *Reformed Quarterly Review* 30 (January 1883):26-27.

35. Nevin, "Christ the Inspiration of His Own Word," 36.

36. John Williamson Nevin, "The Bread of Life," *Reformed Quarterly Review* 26 (January 1879):28-29.

37. Ibid., 29, note.

38. John Williamson Nevin, *The Church* (Chambersburg, PA: Publication Office of the German Reformed Church, 1847); reprinted in James Hastings Nichols, ed., *The Mercersburg Theology* (New York: Oxford University Press, 1966), 71.

39. Alan P. F. Sell, "J. H. A. Bomberger (1817-1890) Versus J.W. Nevin: A Centenary Reappraisal," *The New Mercersburg Review* 8 (1990):16.

Nevin and Methodism

Charles Yrigoyen, Jr.

John Williamson Nevin and Philip Schaff, faculty colleagues at the Theological Seminary of the German Reformed Church at Mercersburg and progenitors of the movement called the Mercersburg Theology, were deeply disturbed about the state of their denomination and American Protestantism. They were especially troubled by the New Measures revivalism of the time, its impact on the German Reformed Church, and the multiplication of "sects" which they believed characterized Protestantism in America in their day. Both of them pointed to the influence of John Wesley and his Methodism as a major source of revivalism and the "sect system."

Nevin correctly understood that New Measures revivalism was widely encouraged and employed by American Methodists in the early-nineteenth century. He also identified the close connection of Methodism to the three "sects" that had intruded into the life of German Christianity in America, namely the Church of the United Brethren in Christ, the Evangelical Association, and the Church of God. Methodism was a central factor in the development of each of them and, to that extent, promoted the "sect system" as Nevin defined it.

It is quite a different matter, however, to make John Wesley the principal culprit in the villainies which Nevin abhorred. Although Wesley was the founder of the Methodist movement, it is not correct to brand the New Measures as "Wesleyan" Methodism or to infer that he was a prime instigator of the American Protestant "sect system." Although Nevin claimed that Wesley was a "small man" compared to Melanchthon, it is difficult to determine on what basis he made his judgment. There appears to be little, if any, evidence that he was acquainted with any of Wesley's writings, though we have pointed out that many of them were available and circulated in America.

I

Nevin left little doubt concerning how he felt about the popular revivalistic techniques, known as the New Measures, employed by many American Protestants. His tract, *The Anxious Bench*, published in 1843, and revised and enlarged in 1844, represented his most vigorous and provocative assault on New Measures revivalism. Although the use of the anxious bench was at the center of his dispute, he saw it as the major symbol of the whole system of New Measures:

> New Measures, in the technical modern sense, form a particular system, involving a certain theory of religious action, and [are] characterized by a distinctive life, which is by no means difficult to understand. Of this system the Anxious Bench is a proper representative. It opens the way naturally to other forms of aberration in the same direction, and may be regarded in this view as the threshold of all that is found to follow, quite out to the extreme of fanaticism and rant.[1]

Nevin was aware that his criticism of the New Measures was risky. Even in his own church many claimed that the New Measures aided the cause of bringing people to faith; they were tools of the Holy Spirit. Others asserted that if the New Measures were not "positively helpful to the Spirit's work," they were not harmful or intolerable.[2] According to Nevin, that was not the case:

> The very design of the inquiry now proposed is to show that the Anxious Bench, and the system to which it belongs, have no claim to be considered either salutary or safe in the service of religion. It is believed that instead of promoting the cause of true vital godliness, they are adapted to hinder its progress. The whole system is considered to be full of peril for the most

> precious interests of the Church. And why then should
> there be any reserve in treating the subject with such
> freedom as it may seem to require.[3]

Notwithstanding, Nevin felt that there was a place for genuine,
legitimate revivals of religion:

> They are as old as the gospel itself. Special effusions
> of the Spirit the Church has a right to expect in every
> age, in proportion as she is found faithful to God's
> covenant; and where such effusions take place, an
> extraordinary use of the ordinary means of grace will
> appear, as a matter of course.[4]

Nevin was even willing to concede that certain "measures"
integral to the "system of the bench," his synonym for New
Measures, might be suited to advance "true vital godliness."
On occasion, protracted meetings might be required. Prayer
meetings might be beneficial. "Sermons and exhortations may
be expected to become more earnest and pungent. A greater
amount of feeling will prevail in meetings. It will become
necessary to have special conferences with the awakened."[5]
These valid revival "measures," however, were not to be
confused with the spurious New Measures.

> If...the anxious bench, revival machinery, solemn tricks
> for effect, decision displays at the bidding of the
> preacher, genuflections and prostrations in the aisle or
> around the altar, noise and disorder, extravagance and
> rant, mechanical conversions, justification by feeling
> rather than faith, and encouragement ministered to all
> fanatical impressions; if these things, and things in the
> same line indefinitely, have no connection in fact with
> true serious religion and the cause of revivals, but only
> tend to bring them into discredit, let the fact be openly
> proclaimed.[6]

While the popularity and apparent success of the "system
of the bench" were cited by its advocates as reasons for its

utilization, Nevin remained unconvinced about its ability to bring people to true Christian faith:

> Spurious revivals are common, and as the fruit of them, false conversions lamentably abound. An Anxious Bench may be crowded where no divine influence whatever is felt. A whole congregation may be moved with excitement, and yet be losing at the very time more than is gained in a religious point of view. Hundreds may be carried **through** the process of anxious bench conversion, and yet their last state may be worse than the first. It will not do to point us to immediate visible effects, to appearances on the spot, or to glowing reports struck off from some heated imagination immediately after. Piles of copper, fresh from the mint, are after all something very different from piles of gold.[7]

Nevin alleged that the "system of the bench" appealed to "persons in whom feelings prevail over judgment and who are swayed by impulse more than reflection."[8] He believed that, "In an enlightened, well-instructed congregation the anxious bench can never be generally popular."[9] As for the pastors who were deceived by the apparent success of the New Measures, Nevin noted:

> Let the power of religion be present in the soul of him who is called to serve at the altar, and no strange fire will be needed to kindle the sacrifice. He will require no new measures. His strength will appear rather in re-suscitating, and clothing with their ancient force the institutions and services already established for his use. The freshness of a divine life, always young and always new, will stand forth to view in all forms that before seemed sapless and dead. Attention will be engaged; interest excited; souls drawn to the sanctuary. Sinners will be awakened and born into the family of God. Christians will be builded up in faith, and made meet for the inheritance of the saints in light. Religion will grow

and prosper. This is the true idea of evangelical power.[10]

Nevin brought four specific charges against the use of the anxious bench. First, it produced "a false issue for the conscience." Instead of compelling the awakened sinner to concentrate on repenting and yielding to God, the sinner became preoccupied with the decision to go to the anxious bench.[11] Second, the anxious bench obstructed "the action of truth" for those who were serious about their salvation. The momentary excitement of coming to the bench overshadowed genuine desire for God's forgiving and renewing grace.[12] Third, by coming to the bench people were under the false impression that they had made "a real decision in favor of religion."[13] Simply coming to the bench did not make one a Christian. Fourth, the anxious bench caused "harm and loss" to [people's] souls. When the excitement it generated had subsided, people were left with feelings of delusion and despair. For some, coming to the bench would generate a destructive pride because they would believe that they had "gotten religion" when in reality there was virtually no spiritual depth to their experience.[14]

Nevin could not find any reason to justify the New Measures, the "system of the bench," because it was founded upon a "false theory of religion."[15] In the final analysis it was characteristically Pelagian with narrow views of the nature of sin, confused apprehensions of the difference between flesh and spirit, and involved in the end the gross and radical error that conversion is to be considered in one shape or another the product of the sinner's own will, not truly and strictly a new creation in Christ Jesus by the power of God. The man gets religion, and so stands over it and above it in his own fancy as the owner of property in any other case. From such monstrous perversion the worst consequences may be expected to flow. The system may generate action; but it will be morbid action, one-sided, spasmodic, ever leaning toward fanaticism.[16]

In contrast to the "system of the bench," Nevin described a more excellent way. He called it the "system of the catechism."[17] It included "sermons full of unction and light; faithful, systematic instruction; zeal for the interests of

holiness; pastoral visitation; catechetical training; due attention
to order and discipline; [and] patient perseverance in the details
of...ministerial work..."[18]   Nevin was convinced that the
"system of the catechism" was based on a "true theory of
religion" which in his words,

> carries us continually beyond the individual to the view
> of a far deeper and more general form of existence in
> which his life is represented to stand. Thus sin is not
> simply the offspring of a particular will, putting itself
> forth in the form of actual transgressions, but a wrong
> habit of humanity itself, a general and universal force
> which includes and rules the entire existence of the
> individual man from the very start. The disease is
> organic, rooted in the race, and not to be overcome in
> any case by a force less deep and general than itself...
> [With regard to salvation from sin, man] is the subject
> of it, but not the author of it in any sense. His nature
> is restorable,   but it can never restore itself.   The
> restoration to be real, must begin **beyond** the individual.
> ...Thus humanity fallen in Adam, is made to undergo a
> resurrection in Christ, and so restored flows over
> organically...to all in whom its life appears. The sinner
> is saved then by an inward living union with Christ as
> the bond of which he has been joined in the first
> instance to Adam.   This union is reached and
> maintained through the medium of the Church by the
> power of the Holy Ghost. It constitutes a new life, the
> ground of which is not in the particular subject of it at
> all, but in Christ, the organic root of the Church. The
> particular subject lives, not properly speaking in the
> acts of his own will separately considered, but in the
> power of a vast generic life that lies wholly beyond his
> will, and has now begun to manifest itself through him
> as the law and type of his will itself as well as of his
> whole being. As born of the Spirit in contradistinction
> from the flesh he is himself spiritual, and capable of
> true righteousness. Thus his salvation begins, and thus
> it is carried forward until it becomes complete in the
> resurrection of the great day. From first to last it is a

power which he does not so much apprehend as he is apprehended by it, and comprehended in it, and carried along with it as something infinitely more deep and vast than himself.[19]

Nevin was not reluctant to identify the source of the New Measures, the system of the bench. In the opening pages of *The Anxious Bench* he said, "The system in question is in its principle and soul neither Calvinism nor Lutheranism, but Wesleyan **Methodism**. Those who are urging it upon the old German churches are in fact doing as much as they can to turn them over into the arms of Methodism."[20] Nevin was obviously concerned about the influence of the Methodist New Measures on the churches of the German Reformation including his own denomination. And not only had Methodism's "system of the bench" introduced an inferior form of Christian faith into the Reformation churches, it was also responsible for the origin of certain religious sects, namely, Otterbein's United Brethren, Albright's Evangelical Association, and Winebrenner's Church of God. Undoubtedly, it was to those three churches that Nevin referred when he wrote, "Already the **life** of Methodism, in this country, is actively at work among other sects, which owe no fellowship with it in form."[21] Nevin continued:

But is not Methodism Christianity? And is it not better that the German Churches should rise in this form than not rise at all? Most certainly so, I reply, if that be the only alternative. But that is **not** the only alternative. Their resurrection may just as well take place, in the type of their own true, original glorious life, as it is still to be found enshrined in their symbolical books. And whatever there may be that is good in Methodism, this life of the Reformation I affirm to be immeasurably more excellent and sound. Wesley was a small man as compared to Melanchthon. Olshausen, with all his mysticism, is a commentator of the inmost sanctuary in comparison with Adam Clark. If the original, distinctive life of the Churches of the Reformation be not the object to be reached after, in the efforts that are made to build up the interests of German Christianity in this county, it were better to say so at once openly and plainly. If we **must** have Methodism, let us have it under its own proper title, and in its proper shape. Why keep up the walls of denominational partition in such a case, with no distinctive spiritual being to uphold or protect?[22]

Both Schaff and Nevin believed Methodism bore a major responsibility for the "sect system" in American Protestantism.[23] Nevin observed that the sects claimed no creed but the plain meaning of the Bible. But, he asked, if the Bible is so easily read and interpreted, why was there such a proliferation of sects with substantially different theologies and practices? Furthermore, although the sects declared the right of private judgment and theological freedom for each individual, each sect had its own system of doctrine and was quite inflexible in its expectation that its members would adhere to its body of beliefs.[24] The sects were "unhistorical." They had no appreciation for the historical development of the church, but understood themselves, "aboriginal, self-sprung from the Bible, or through the Bible from the skies."[25] "The idea of a historical continuity in the life of the Church, carries with it no weight whatever for the sect consciousness. It is felt to be as easy to start a new church, as it is to get up a new moral or political association under any other name."[26] The sects were "unchurchly." They had no real understanding of the church as the Body of Christ and no appreciation of its traditional faith. For example, they had no regard for the use of the Apostles' Creed. In fact, "wherever the sect spirit prevails the Creed falls into disuse."[27] The sects were also "unsacramental." "The forms of the sacraments may be retained, but the true inward meaning of them is more or less lost."[28] According to Nevin, sects were theologically unstable, captive to the whims of their leaders, and adverse to theology treated "as a science." In his treatment of the "sect system," Nevin frequently cited the churches founded by Otterbein, Albright, and Winebrenner as examples of the sects he so much despised. Schaff wrote:

The influence of Methodism on the Lutheran and German Reformed Church at the close of the last and the beginning of the present century, produced several new sects, in doctrine, government, and worship entirely conformed to the Methodist Episcopal model. Such are the United Brethren in Christ, founded about 1800, by William Otterbein, a pious Reformed Minister from Germany; [and the] Evangelical Communion (Evangelische Gemeinschaft), commonly called the Albrecht Brethren, founded somewhat later by Jacob Albrecht, a Lutheran layman of Pennsylvania....[29]

All three of these church leaders had significant ties to American Methodism. Schaff shared Nevin's understanding of the relationship between Methodism and the followers of Otterbein and Albright.

II

Clearly Nevin lodged some very severe accusations against John Wesley and Methodism. Some of them appear to have been formed on the basis of accurate information and impressions of American Methodist doctrine and practice. But others seem to be based on lack of information and misunderstanding. It would appear, for example, that Nevin's information about the relationship of American Methodism and the New Measures was correct as was his understanding of the relationship between the Methodists and the United Brethren, the Evangelical Association, and Winebrenner's Church of God as we shall see. However, Nevin's knowledge of John Wesley and his interpretation of Wesley's theology appears to be more problematic.

There is little doubt that Nevin correctly understood the situation among Methodists regarding their devotion to revivalism and camp meetings. There is hardly a survey of Methodist history that does not emphasize the popularity of revivals among American Methodists.[30] The diaries and journals of Methodist preachers and laypeople give numerous accounts of revival meetings and the religious excitement they generated.[31]   As Bernard A. Weisberger has observed, "From bishops to exhorters, the Methodists...were wide-ranging salesmen of the revival point of view..."[32] Richard Carwardine echoes Weisberger's view: "Methodism was wholeheartedly a revival movement; it had been born of a revival; its churches grew through revivals; its ministers preached revival; its success was talked of in terms of revival."[33]

While Charles G. Finney is usually given credit for popularizing the New Measures, it is generally agreed that Finney did not invent them. For example, while the Methodists did not make extensive use of the anxious (or mourners') bench, they did employ a similar technique in their services which they termed the "call to the altar." Instead of providing a pew or bench for the sinners who were anxious for their conversion, Methodist preachers invited them to come forward and kneel at the altar rail or at an open area in front of the congregation. This practice began in the early years of the nineteenth century. Carwardine states that, by the second decade of the century the call to the altar had become a standard feature of Methodist revivals. Indeed it sometimes happened that mourners would anticipate the minister's call and move to the altar before the invitation was given, so institutionalized had the procedure become.[34]

Not only was the "altar call" widely utilized by Methodists, but other practices associated with the New Measures, "the system of the bench," were also common among them. Direct, colloquial preaching, women praying publicly in mixed assemblies, and protracted meetings were common. Furthermore, Methodists were enthusiastic devotees of the camp meeting. Bishop Francis Asbury, considered by most the principal patriarch of American Methodism, registered his ecstasy about them. In 1809 he wrote: "Campmeetings, campmeetings, Oh Glory, Glory!"[35] While camp meetings and revivals were often the occasion for the emotional excesses that Nevin despised, it must be noted that many Methodist leaders had reservations about such practices as "the jerks," shouting, and other extremes.   Nathan Bangs, significant among the early Methodists, was annoyed by the emotionalism he observed at some revivals. He was critical of the "spirit of pride, presumption, and bigotry, impatience of scriptural restraint and moderation, clapping of hands, screaming, and even jumping, which marred and disgraced the work of God."[36]   It is Carwardine's contention that Finney was influenced by the revival practices of the Methodists. It is even possible that [Finney's] decision in Rochester in 1830 to adopt the anxious seat as a main feature of his revivals was Methodist-inspired. In the Methodist revival there in 1827-28, the call to the altar had proved "singularly beneficial" and had involved "some of our wealthy and respectable citizens." When Finney arrived in 1830 he was looking for "some measure that would bring sinners to a stand." He "had found, that with the higher classes especially, the greatest obstacle to be overcome was their fear of being known as anxious inquirers." He decided to use the anxious seat, and the response among "the highest classes of society" was good.[37]   But American Methodists did not derive their revivalistic techniques from Wesley. Neither did Wesley himself employ a system of "measures" to bring sinners to conversion, nor did he encourage American Methodists to do so.

Nevin's complaint about the "sect system" among American Protestants and the implication of Methodism's role in it must also be examined. Nevin was certainly right in his observation that three of the "sects" he most criticized, the Church of the United Brethren in Christ begun by Otterbein and Boehm, Albright's Evangelical Association, and Winebrenner's Church of God, had attachments to American Methodism.

Although Philip William Otterbein, ordained in the German Reformed Church, was nurtured in the tradition of Reformed Pietism in Germany, he was also well acquainted with American Methodism. His relationship with Francis Asbury, the famous American Methodist bishop, was especially cordial. Their close friendship is noted at several places in Asbury's journal.[38] Otterbein participated in Asbury's ordination to the Methodist episcopacy on December 26, 1784, at the time the Methodist Episcopal Church was formally organized in Baltimore, MD.[39]

The co-founder of the United Brethren, Martin Boehm, also enjoyed a genial relationship with Methodism. Boehm was excommunicated by the Mennonites sometime between 1775 and 1780 for certain doctrinal irregularities. In 1767 he and Otterbein began a close friendship which lasted until Boehm's

death in 1812. Boehm read Wesley's published sermons. In
1791 he gave the Methodists a piece of land for the
construction of a chapel and a cemetery. When the Methodist
building had been erected, Boehm's wife and children joined the
Methodists worshipping there.   Boehm did not join that
Methodist group, but he was often present, sometimes
preaching and leading celebrations of the Lord's Supper.[40]

It is plain that the United Brethren preached an evangelical
faith very similar to that of the Methodists. And while it is
difficult to trace the direct influence of Methodism's revival and
camp meeting techniques on Otterbein and Boehm, it is clear
that they adopted Methodism's discipline and polity. Nevin was
accurate in identifying American Methodism as an important
force in the creation of the United Brethren "sect."

Jacob Albright, another of the "sect" leaders subject to
Nevin's scorn, was the founder of the Evangelical Association.
While a young man, Albright, who was raised in a German-
speaking family, was affiliated with a Lutheran church in
Lancaster County, Pennsylvania. In 1791, one year after the
death of several of his children, Albright experienced conversion
and joined a Methodist class meeting. The Methodists granted
him an exhorter's license in 1796 which enabled him to be a
speaker in the class gatherings. However, he felt a call to
share his testimony more broadly and began preaching. In
1800 he gathered the people who had experienced new birth
under his preaching into three classes, organized along
Methodist lines. By 1807 his followers had grown to the point
that Albright was able to form a new church which later
became known as the Evangelical Association. The original
licenses issued to his preachers read, "the Newly-formed
Methodist Conference."[41]   Methodist influence in the
Evangelicals' doctrine and practices was evident from the
beginning.

The record of Nevin's disdain for John Winebrenner and the
Church of God is well documented. Richard Kern has described
the passionate controversy between the two men.[42]   Nevin
was especially incensed that Winebrenner, a fellow German
Reformed pastor, made use of the New Measures revivalism
and that he finally broke with his church in order to form a new
"sect," which he called the "Church of God."[43]   Was there

any apparent influence of Methodism in Winebrenner's theology and evangelistic techniques? A recent article by William A. Sloat, II, traces the role of Methodism and the Church of the United Brethren in Christ in the formation of Winebrenner's thought and the founding of the Church of God.[44] Sloat contends that, "it was Winebrenner's contact with the Methodists and United Brethren and participation in their camp meetings that transformed him from a respectable pietist to an unacceptable [from Nevin's perspective] New Measures revivalist."[45] There is also evidence that Winebrenner had contact with leaders of the Evangelical Association.[46] Kern also suggests that the Methodists were an important force in Winebrenner's ministry:

> ...on the basis of information available, it would seem that it was Winebrenner's whole-hearted adoption of "new measures," probably under the influence of the local Methodists, which led to his eventual separation from the German Reformed Church. After some experimentation, the [German Reformed] synod decided that it did not have room for such measures or John Winebrenner.[47]

There seems little question that Nevin was correct in citing American Methodism as the major force in the employment of the new measures, especially the anxious bench, or something like it, and in the formation of the "sect system," which Nevin so much despised. Methodism certainly played an important part in the formation of the Church of the United Brethren, the Evangelical Association, and the Church of God. But was he mistaken in calling this "Wesleyan," for American Methodism was hardly what Wesley envisioned and intended it to be?

The first issue we consider is whether John Wesley ever employed or promoted anything akin to the New Measures. Was the "system of the bench" really **Wesleyan** Methodism, as Nevin alleged? There is no doubt that John Wesley was committed to an evangelical message. It is also apparent that he was willing to utilize what some regarded as radical means in his preaching and organization. For example, he was willing to do some of his evangelical preaching in the open air. He began this on April 2, 1739, in Bristol with the urging of George Whitefield. Wesley wrote: "At four in the afternoon I submitted to 'be more vile,' and proclaimed in the highways the glad tidings of salvation, speaking from a little eminence in a ground adjoining the city, to about three thousand people."[48] Wesley's employment of lay preachers, his organization of societies and classes, the role he allowed women to play in the leadership of the Methodist movement, and his constant focus on bringing people to conversion were certainly unorthodox in the eyes of many church leaders in late-eighteenth-century England. However, it is very difficult to associate Wesley with the use of an anxious bench or an altar call, which American Methodists obviously used with some regularity at their revival meetings. Furthermore, the development of the camp meeting was an American invention unknown to Wesley. The "system of the bench" was certainly used extensively among American Methodists, but its origin could hardly be attributed to Wesley.

The second issue to be considered is Nevin's citation of Wesley and the Methodists as a chief, if not **the** chief, culprit in the formation of the "sect system" in American Protestantism. We have already acknowledged that American Methodism was a major influence in the shaping of three "sects" which Nevin often cited as specimens of the sects he so much disliked. But was John Wesley guilty of promulgating the "sect spirit" as Nevin defined it? In "The Sect System," Nevin claimed that "sects" were "unchurchly," "unhistorical," and "unsacramental." Each of these charges must be recalled and examined in light of Wesley's theology.

According to Nevin one of the chief evidences that the "sects" were unchurchly was their neglect of the Apostles' Creed. He wrote:

Sect Christianity is not the Christianity of the Creed, or at best it is this Christianity under a most mutilated form. Of this proof enough is found in the fact that wherever the sect spirit prevails the Creed falls into disuse. It may still be spoken of respectfully perhaps when spoken of at all; but what sect repeats it, or recognises [sic] in it the mirror of its own consciousness? The Creed has become almost universally a dead letter, in the religion of the sects. There are, no doubt, thousands of so called evangelical ministers in our country at this time, to say nothing of their congregations, who could not even repeat it correctly, were they called on suddenly to do so, as a test of their Christian knowledge.[49]

But this neglect of the Creed was not owing to Wesley, an Anglican priest who loved the *The Book of Common Prayer* and referred to the Apostles' Creed in one of his sermons as a "beautiful summary" of the essential truths of the Christian faith.[50] Perhaps the most important demonstration of Wesley's reverence for the Apostles' Creed was his inclusion of it in *The Sunday Service of the Methodists in North American: With Other Occasional Services*, a service book he sent to America with Thomas Coke, Richard Whatcoat, and Thomas Vasey in 1784. When Wesley determined that American Methodists should form a new church, he published this volume intending it to be the principal guide for the worship of his people in the United States and "the foundation stone for subsequent Methodist worship in this country."[51] In Wesley's order the Apostles' Creed was to be recited at both morning and evening worship "Every Lord's Day."[52] It should also be noted that *The Sunday Service* included a lectionary, litanies, orders for the celebration of the Lord's Supper, baptism, matrimony, communion of the sick, burial of the dead, the ordination of deacons, elders, and superintendents, and Articles of Religion. The basic pattern of the liturgies in it remained that of the Church of England. Wesley's *Sunday Service* was never popular with American Methodists and was quickly ignored in favor of a less formal liturgy in which the Apostles' Creed was not specified as a component.[53] Early American Methodists did not follow the use of the Creed prescribed by Wesley.

Nevin also charged that the "sect system" was unhistorical. The "sects" represented

...a real protest against the authority of all previous history, except so far as it may seem to agree with what is thus found to be true; in which case, of course, the only real measure of truth is taken to be, not this authority of history at all, but the mind, simply, of the particular sect itself. The idea of anything like a divine substance in the life of Christianity, through past ages, which may be expected of right to pass forward into the constitution of Christianity as it now stands, is one that finds no room whatever in this system.[54]

Several recent studies of Wesley's theology have shown the very high regard he had for the history of the church. Albert C. Outler was one of the first of the recent writers to call attention to the importance Wesley placed on the early theologians of the Christian church.[55] The most thorough analysis of Wesley's respect for the history of early Christianity is Ted A. Campbell's *John Wesley and Christian Antiquity*.[56] Campbell shows that Wesley not only studied the ancient Christian writers, but referred to them in the work of the Methodist movement. Among the early church theologians frequently cited by Wesley were Cyprian, Augustine, Clement of Rome, Justin Martyr, Clement of Alexandria, Ignatius of Antioch, and Marcarius of Egypt. Nevin himself was especially interested in the early church period as well.[57]

Wesley was not only interested in the early church, however. He was also a student of the medieval, Reformation, and later periods of church history. His *Christian Library*, a 50-volume set of "practical divinity" published between 1749 and 1755, included a variety of selections from early church writers, Catholics, Dissenters, and Latitudinarians, English, Scottish, and continental theologians. It may very well be true that American Methodism and the "sects" related to it did not manifest interest in, and appreciation for, the historical development of the Christian faith, but that accusation was much more difficult to sustain regarding the founder of Methodism.

The "sects" were also unsacramental in Nevin's estimation. He alleged that while they retained the form of the sacraments, they had lost the "inward meaning" of them.[58] As a result, the sacraments were signs or symbols, but were not the means for conveying divine grace.

Wesley certainly regarded baptism as more than a sign or symbol. He believed that baptism washes "away the guilt of original sin by the application of the merits of Christ's death."[59] He held that "...the merits of Christ's life and death ...are applied to us in baptism."[60] Baptism is "the ordinary instrument of our justification."[61] It is the initiatory sacrament by which "we enter into covenant with God."[62] By it "we are admitted into the Church and consequently made members of Christ its Head."[63] Receiving baptism, "we who were 'by nature children of wrath' are made the children of God" and hence, we become "heirs of the kingdom of God."[64] It is true that Wesley believed that baptismal grace was usually lost in a person, therefore requiring a subsequent experience of regeneration. Nevertheless, he was quite certain that the sacrament was a primary means for the mediation of saving grace.

American Methodists became increasingly doubtful of Wesley's doctrine of baptismal regeneration. In her recent study on the theology and practice of baptism, Gayle Carlton Felton provides an important historical account of development in American Methodism. She indicates that Methodists in America were embarrassed by Wesley:

> Some [Methodist] writers attempted to deny that Wesley had actually accepted baptismal regeneration, but this position proved difficult to sustain in the face of the explicit evidence in his writings. More commonly, American Methodists tried to argue that Wesley changed his views later in life and that the *Treatise** represented an early, transient phase of his thought. Perhaps it was this discomfiture with Wesley's position that motivated his American followers to deprecate so frequently what they saw as erroneous doctrine in Anglican and Episcopalian tradition.[65]

As in the matter of baptism, American Methodists did not precisely follow their founder's teaching of the sacrament of the Lord's Supper. The Lord's Supper for Wesley was no empty

---

*on Baptism

sign. Wesley wrote, "...it is the duty of every Christian to
receive the Lord's Supper as often as he can."[66] Why? First
of all, because the command of Christ obliged every Christian
to do it. Secondly,

> ...because the benefits of doing it are so great to all
> that do it in obedience to him—namely, the forgiveness
> of our past sins, the present strengthening and
> refreshing of our souls. In this world we are never free
> from temptations. Whatever way of life we are in,
> whatever our condition be, whether we are sick or well,
> in trouble or at ease, the enemies of our souls are
> watching to lead us into sin. And too often they prevail
> over us. Now, when we are convinced of having
> sinned against God, what surer way have we of
> procuring pardon from him than the "showing forth the
> Lord's death," and beseeching him, for the sake of his
> Son's sufferings, to blot out all our sins?[67]

Furthermore, Wesley wrote that God's grace given in the Lord's
Supper "confirms to us the pardon of our sins, and enables us
to leave them."[68] It is "the food of our souls" which

> gives strength to perform our duty and leads us on to
> perfection. If, therefore, we have any regard for the
> plain command of Christ, if we desire the pardon of our
> sins, if we wish for strength to believe, to love and
> obey God, then we should neglect no opportunity of
> receiving the Lord's Supper.[69]

It is obvious that Wesley's American brothers and sisters
strayed far from his intention of frequent communion. Although
he advised the ordained preachers in America "to administer the
Supper of the Lord on every Lord's Day,"[70] and included in the
Sunday Service which he sent to America in 1784 an "Order for
the Administration of the Lord's Supper," American Methodists
were celebrating the sacrament less frequently by the early-
nineteenth century.

Furthermore, as a number of scholars have pointed out,
Wesley did not intend that Methodists understand the Lord's

Supper as simply a memorial meal, even though it was a most important means for remembering the sacrifice of Christ. Paul S. Sanders writes: "Wesley held to a belief in the Real Presence of Christ in the Supper...Wesley's view of the Real Presence [was] essentially that of Calvin as transmitted through the seventeenth-century Anglican High Churchmen."[71] But in the early decades of the nineteenth century, Methodists began to emphasize the Lord's Supper simply as a memorial meal:

> The memorial aspect of the Eucharist, always a legitimate and important element, was probably now pushed to the fore. In common with Presbyterians, Baptists and Congregationalists, the Methodists in America somewhere lost the sense of the vital reality of Christ's presence there.[72]

Again, it appears that Nevin understood better the American Methodist theology and practice of the Lord's Supper than he did Wesley. Wesley's American followers did not follow his path regarding his practice and theology of the Lord's Supper.

If Nevin had been better acquainted with Wesley's views, he would have been able to understand the differences between what Wesley intended American Methodism to be and what it actually became. Furthermore, he would have been more cognizant of some of the ways in which he and Wesley shared similar interests and concerns. Some of these included a high regard for the history and tradition of the church, the sacraments as means of mediating grace, and the importance of education, nurture, and pastoral care. Perhaps Nevin even could have cited Wesley in his attacks on the New Measures and the "sect system." It is true that Wesley and Nevin were sometimes very different from each other in their understanding of the Christian faith, for example, salvation and sanctification, but each believed he drew his views from the Scriptures and classical Christian tradition.

ENDNOTES

1. John Williamson Nevin, *The Anxious Bench*, edited by Charles Yrigoyen, Jr., and George H. Bricker, in *Catholic and Reformed: Selected Theological Writings of John Williamson Nevin* (Pittsburgh: The Pickwick Press, 1978), 18.

2. Nevin, *The Anxious Bench*, 25.

3. Nevin, *The Anxious Bench*, 25.

4. Nevin, *The Anxious Bench*, 29.

5. Nevin, *The Anxious Bench*, 120. Cf., *The Anxious Bench*, 27, 119.

6. Nevin, *The Anxious Bench*, 30.

7. Nevin, *The Anxious Bench*, 36-37.

8. Nevin, *The Anxious Bench*, 41.

9. Nevin, *The Anxious Bench*, 41.

10. Nevin, *The Anxious Bench*, 49-50.

11. Nevin, *The Anxious Bench*, 59-60.

12. Nevin, *The Anxious Bench*, 62-64.

13. Nevin, *The Anxious Bench*, 64.

14. Nevin, *The Anxious Bench*, 68-71.

15. Nevin, *The Anxious Bench*, 100.

16. Nevin, *The Anxious Bench*, 105-106.

17. Nevin, *The Anxious Bench*, 101.

18. Nevin, *The Anxious Bench*, 101.

19. Nevin, *The Anxious Bench*, 106-108.

20. Nevin, *The Anxious Bench*, 12.

21. Nevin, *The Anxious Bench*, 13.

22. Nevin, *The Anxious Bench*, 13.

23. See Charles Yrigoyen, Jr., "Mercersburg's Quarrel with Methodism," *Methodist History* XXII (October 1983): 3-19.

24. John Williamson Nevin, "The Sect System," in Yrigoyen and Bricker, *Catholic and Reformed: Selected Theological Writings of John Williamson Nevin*, 135. See also *Antichrist, or the Spirit of Sect and Schism* (New York: John S. Taylor, 1848).

25. Nevin, "The Sect System," 145.

26. Nevin, "The Sect System," 146.

27. Nevin, "The Sect System," 148.

28. Nevin, "The Sect System," 148.

29. Philip Schaff, *America: A Sketch of the Political, Social, and Religious Character of the United States of North America* (New York: Scribner, 1855), 204.

30. See Frederick A. Norwood, *The Story of American Methodism* (Nashville: Abingdon Press, 1974), 156-58, and Emory Stevens Bucke, ed., *The History of American Methodism* (Nashville, TN: Abingdon Press, 1964), I, 245-46, 299-300, 398-99.

31. E.g., Peter Cartwright, *Autobiography* (Nashville: Abingdon Press, 1956) and James B. Finley, *Sketches of Western Methodism, Biographical, and Misellaneous, Illustrative of Pioneer Life* (New York: Ayer Co., 1969; reprint of 1854 edition).

32. Bernard A. Weisberger, *They Gathered at the River* (Chicago: Quadrangle Books, 1966), 46.

33. Richard Carwardine, *Transatlantic Revivalism: Popular Evangelism in Britian and America, 1790-1865* (Westport, CT: Greenwood Press, 1978), 10.

34. Carwardine, *Transatlantic Revivalism*, 13.

35. L. C. Rudolph, *Francis Asbury* (Nashville: Abingdon Press, 1966), 116-21.

36. Quoted in Carwardine, *Transatlantic Revivalism*, 12.

37. Carwardine, 16. Cf., Garth M. Rosell and Richard A. G. Dupuis, eds., *The Memoirs of Charles G. Finney* (Grand Rapids, MI: Zondervan Publishing House, 1989), 306-08.

38. See Elmer T. Clark, ed., *The Journal and Letters of Francis Asbury* (Nashville: Abingdon Press, 1958).

39. J. Bruce Behney and Paul H. Eller, *The History of the Evangelical United Brethren Church* (Nashville: Abingdon Press, 1979), 55.

40. Behney and Eller, 43-45.

41. Behney and Eller, 81-82.

42. Richard Kern, *John Winebrenner: 19th Century Reformer* (Harrisburg, PA: Central Publishing House, 1974), 55-92.

43. Kern, 81-92.

44. William A. Sloat, II, "The Role of the Methodists and the United Brethren in the Formation of the Church of God," *Evangelical Journal* X (Fall 1992), 55-64.

45. Sloat, 56.

46. Sloat, 63, n.12.

47. Kern, 40.

48. W. Reginald Ward and Richard P. Heitzenrater, eds., *The Works of John Wesley* (Nashville: Abingdon Press, 1990), Vol. 19, 46.

49. Nevin, "The Sect System," 147.

50. Albert C. Outler, ed., *The Works of John Wesley* (Nashville: Abingdon Press, 1985), Vol. 2, 592.

51. James F. White, ed., *John Wesley's Sunday Service of the Methodists in North America* (Nashville: United Methodist Publishing House, 1984), 7.

52. White, *The Sunday Service*, 12, 18.

53. See Kenneth Bedell, *Worship in the Methodist Tradition* (Madison, NJ: General Commission on Archives and History, 1987), 51-56.

54. Nevin, "The Sect System," 145.

55. Albert C. Outler, ed., *John Wesley* (New York: Oxford University Press, 1980), 9-10.

56. Ted A. Campbell, *John Wesley and Christian Antiquity* (Nashville: Kingswood Books, 1991).

57. E.g., John Williamson Nevin, "Early Christianity," in Charles Yrigoyen, Jr., and George H. Bricker, *Catholic and Reformed: Selected Theological Writings of John Williamson Nevin* (Pittsburgh: The Pickwick Press, 1978), 177-310, and Nevin's articles on Cyprian in the *Mercersburg Review*, 1851 and 1852.

58. Nevin, "The Sect System," 148.

59. Outler, *John Wesley*, 321.

60. Ibid.

61. Ibid.

62. Ibid., 322.

63. Ibid.

64. Outler, *John Wesley*, 322-23.

65. Gayle Carlton Felton, *This Gift of Water: The Practice and Theology of Baptism Among Methodists in America* (Nashville: Abingdon Press, 1992), 85-86. Cf., Ole E. Borgen, *John Wesley and the Sacraments* (Nashville: Abingdon Press, 1972), 121-82.

66. Outler, *John Wesley*, 335.

67. Ibid.

68. Ibid.

69. Ibid., 336.

70. Quoted in Bucke, I, 203.

71. Paul S. Sanders, "An Appraisal of Wesley's Sacramentalism in the Evolution of Early American Methodism" (Ph.D. diss., Union Theological Seminary, NY, 1954), 183.

72. Sanders, *Wesley's Sacramentalism*, 453-54.

Bibliography of the Writings of John Williamson Nevin 1803-1887

List of Abbreviations:

AR   *American Review*
EQR   *The Evangelical Quarterly Review*
ERHS Archives of the United Church of Christ and the Evangelical and Reformed Historical Society, Philip Schaff Library, Lancaster Theological Seminary, Lancaster, Pennsylvania
MR   *The Mercersburg Review*
NMR *The New Mercersburg Review*
RCM *Reformed Church Messenger*
RQR *Reformed Quarterly Review*
TF   *The Friend*
WM   *Weekly Messenger of the German Reformed Church*

A Summary of Biblical Antiquities. Philadelphia: American Sunday School Union, 1829-1830.

The Claims of the Bible Urged Upon the Attention of Students of Theology. Lecture delivered on November 6, 1831, at the opening of the winter session of Western Theological Seminary of the Presbyterian Church. Pittsburgh: D. & M. Maclean, 1831.

The Scourge of God. Sermon preached in the First Presbyterian Church of Pittsburgh, July 6, 1832. Pittsburgh: Johnston & Stockton, 1832.

"The Trinitarian and Unitarian Doctrines Concerning Jesus Christ," *Presbyterian Preacher*, 1833.

"Fancy Fairs," *TF*, May 30, 1833.

"Essay on the Interpretation of the Bible," *TF*, June 6, 1833; July 11, 1833.

"Election Not Contrary to a Free Gospel." Sermon preached on
    John 6:37-40 in the First Presbyterian Church. *Presbyterian*
    Preacher 2 (July 1833): 209-24.

"Is the Bible of God?" *TF*, January 23, 1834; March 13, 1834.

"The Psalms." *TF*, September 11, 1834.

"Religion a Life," *TF*, December 25, 1834; January 15, 22, 29,
    1835; February 5, 1835.

"The Grand Heresy," *TF*, February 5, 1835.

"The Idea of God," *TF*, February 5, 1835.

Ascension Day. Sermon preached in College Chapel, April 2, 1836.
    Copied from the original by a student. ERHS.

The Claims of the Christian Sabbath. Report, read and adopted at
    the meeting of the Presbytery of Ohio, April 21, 1836.
    Pittsburgh: William Allinder, 1836.

"The English Bible." Sermon preached on Deuteronomy 4:7-8 for a
    Bible Society of Pittsburgh on the last Sunday of November
    1835 in the First Presbyterian Church. *Presbyterian Preacher* 4
    (January 1836): 113-32.

"Our Synod and Our Paper," *Christian Herald*, January 15, 22,
    1836; February 5, 12, 1836; March 18, 1836.

"Separate Organization," *Christian Herald*, April 22, 29, 1836; May
    6, 1836; September 16, 1836.

Personal Holiness. Lecture delivered in June of 1837 at the opening
    of the summer term in Western Theological Seminary.
    Pittsburgh: William Allinder, 1837.

The Seal of the Spirit. Sermon preached in the Presbyterian Church
    in Uniontown, PA on January 21, 1838. Pittsburgh: William
    Allinder, 1838.

A Pastoral Letter. Letter on the subject of minister's salaries, addressed to the Presbytery of Ohio on January 18, 1840. Pittsburgh: William B. Stewart, 1840.

"Faith," *WM,* February 12, 19, 23, 1840; March 4, 11, 18, 1840.

"Inaugural Address," *Addresses Delivered at the Inauguration of Rev. J.W. Nevin, D.D., As Professor of Theology in the Theological Seminary of the German Reformed Church, May 20, 1840*. Chambersburg, PA: Publication Office of the German Reformed Church, 1840.

"Rauch's Psychology," *WM,* June 10, 1840.

"Worldly Mindedness," *WM,* June 24, 1840; July 1, 15, 22, 29, 1840; August 5, 1840.

"Party Spirit," *WM,* August 26, 1840.

The German Language. An address delivered before the Goethean Literary Society of Marshall College at its anniversary on August 29, 1842. Chambersburg, PA: Publication Office of the German Reformed Church, 1842.

The Ambassador of God: or the True Spirit of the Christian Ministry as Represented in the Mind of Jesus Christ. Chambersburg, PA: Publication Office of the German Reformed Church, 1842.

"The Heidelberg Catechism," *WM,* April 27, 1842; May 4, 11, 18, 25, 1842; June 1, 8, 1842; July 13, 1842; August 3, 10, 24, 1842.

"The Demand for Ministers," *WM,* September 7, 14, 28, 1842; October 5, 1842.

"Marshall College," *WM,* October 26, 1842.

The Anxious Bench. 2nd ed. Chambersburg, PA: Publication Office of the German Reformed Church, 1844.

"The 'Anxious Bench'," *WM,* January 24, 31, 1844; Feburary 14, 21, 28, 1844; March 6, 1844.

A Funeral Sermon with Reference to the Death of James Edgar Moore on June 23, 1844. Mercersburg, PA: Daignothian Literary Society, 1844.

Catholic Unity. Sermon delivered at the opening of the Triennial Convention of the Reformed Protestant Dutch and German Reformed Churches, at Harrisburg, PA, August 8, 1844. Also in *The Principle of Protestantism.* Philip Schaff. Chambersburg, PA: Publication Office of the German Reformed Church, 1845. Reprinted in *American Religious Thought of the 18th and 19th Centuries*, edited by Bruce Kuklick, 32 volumes, as Introduction to *The Principle of Protestantism.* New York: Garland Publishing, 1987.

A Baccalaureate Address to the Graduating Class of Marshall College. Chambersburg, PA: Publication Office of the German Reformed Church, 1845.

"Introduction," to Philip Schaff's *The Principle of Protestantism*, Chambersburg, PA: Publication Office of the German Reformed Church, 1845.

Lectures on Pastoral Theology. Classroom notes by three students from three sessions of the class. Notes by E. W. Reinecke (Winter Session of 1845), George Wolff (May 1847), and E. W. Santee (July 1850). ERHS.

"Pseudo-Protestantism," *WM*, August 13, 20, 27, 1845; September 3, 10, 1845.

"Schaf on Protestantism," *WM*, September 24, 1845.

"The Mystical Union," *WM*, October 8, 1845.

The Mystical Presence, a Vindication of the Reformed or Calvinistic Doctrine of the Holy Eucharist. Philadelphia, 1846. Reprinted, with an introduction by R. E. Wentz. Hamden, CT: Archon Books, 1963. Reprinted in *American Religious Thought of the 18th and 19th Centuries*, edited by Bruce Kuklick, 32 volumes. New York: Garland Publishing, 1987.

The Goethean Hall; or the Anniversary of Goethe's Birthday, August 28, 1846 in Mercersburg. Chambersburg, PA: Goethean Literary Society of Marshall College, 1846.

The Church. Sermon on Ephesians I.23, delivered October 15, 1846. Chambersburg, PA: Publication Office of the German Reformed Church, 1847.

A Baccalaureate Address to the Graduating Class of Marshall College. Chambersburg, PA: Publication Office of the German Reformed Church, 1846.

"Our Union with Christ," *WM*, January 14, 1846.

An Address - August 28, 1846 - at the Opening of the New Goethean Hall. Chambersburg, PA: Publication Office of the German Reformed Church, 1846.

History and Genius of the Heidelberg Catechism. Chambersburg, PA: Publication Office of the German Reformed Church, 1847.

"Educational Religion," *WM*, June 23, 30, 1847; July 7, 14, 1847.

"The Church Supernatural," *WM*, August 4, 1847.

"Dr. Berg on Justification," *WM*, August 11, 1847.

"Baptismal Grace," *WM*, August 11, 1847.

"Denominationalism," *WM*, August 18, 1847.

"Dr. Bushnell and Puritanism," *WM*, September 1, 1847.

"Holy Baptism," *WM*, September 1, 1847.

Antichrist or the Spirit of Sect and Schism. New York: John S. Taylor, 1848.

"A Plea for Philosophy," *AR* 1 (February 1848):143-55.

"Our Union With Christ," *WM* 13 (February 16, 1848).

"Human Freedom," *AR* 1 (April 1848): 406-18.

"Dr. Hodge on the 'Mystical Presence'," *WM*, May 24, 1848;
    August 9, 1848.

"Woman's Rights," *AR* 2 (October 1848): 367-81.

"Preliminary Statement," *MR* 1 (1849): 1-10.

"The Year 1848," *MR* 1 (1849): 10-44.

"True and False Protestantism," *MR* 1 (1849): 83-104.

"The Apostles' Creed," *MR* 1 (1849): 105-27; 201-21; 313-47.

"Sartorius on the Person and Work of Christ," *MR* 1 (1849): 146-
    69.

"False Protestantism," *MR* 1 (1849): 194-97.

"Kirwan's Letters," *MR* 1 (1849): 229-63.

"Zwingli No Radical," *MR* 1 (1849): 263-72.

"God in Christ," *MR* 1 (1849): 309-12.

"The Classis of Mercersburg," *MR* 1 (1849): 379-88.

"Morell's Philosophy of Religion," *MR* 1 (1849): 400-06.

"The Lutheran Confession," *MR* 1 (1849): 468-77.

"The Sect System," *MR* 1 (1849): 482-507; 521-38.

"Historical Development," *MR* 1 (1849): 512-14.

"Puritanism and the Creed," *MR* 1 (1849): 585-607.

"The Liturgical Movement," *MR* 1 (1849): 608-12.

"Sacramental Religion," *Protestant Quarterly Review* 6 (1849): 129-
    40.

Human Freedom and a Plea for Philosophy: Two Essays.
    Mercersburg: P.A., "Journal Office," 1850.

History of Philosophy Lectures. Transcribed by George B. Russel [1850]. AMsS [photocopy]. ERHS.

"The New Creation in Christ," *MR* 2 (1850): 1-12.

"Brownson's Quarterly Review," *MR* 2 (1850): 33-80.

"Faith, Reverence and Freedom," *MR* 2 (1850): 97-116.

"Wilberforce on the Incarnation," *MR* 2 (1850): 164-96.

"Noel on Baptism," *MR* 2 (1850): 231-65.

"Brownson's Quarterly Review Again," *MR* 2 (1850): 307-24.

"Bible Christianity," *MR* 2 (1850): 353-68.

"Doctrine of the Reformed Church on the Lord's Supper," *MR* 2 (1850): 421-548.

"The Moral Order of Sex," *MR* 2 (1850): 549-73.

"The New Testament Miracles," *MR* 2 (1850): 573-85.

"Trench's Lectures," *MR* 2 (1850): 604-19.

"Catholicism," *MR* 3 (1851): 1-26.

"Liebner's Christology," *MR* 3 (1851): 55-73.

"Modern Civilization," *MR* 3 (1851): 165-208.

"Cur Deus Homo," *MR* 3 (1851): 220-38.

"Adams' Christian Science," *MR* 3 (1851): 285-95.

"Schaff's Church History," *MR* 3 (1851): 296-304.

"The Anglican Crisis," *MR* 3 (1851): 359-98.

"Early Christianity," *MR* 3 (1851): 461-90; 513-62; 4 (1852): 1-54.

"Zacharius Ursinus," *MR* 3 (1851): 490-512.

"Fairbain's Typology," *MR* 4 (1852): 76-80.

"The Heidelberg Catechism," *MR* 4 (1852): 155-86.

"A Word of Explanation," *MR* 4 (1852): 202-205.

"Cyprian," *MR* 4 (1852): 259-77; 335-87; 417-52; 513-63.

"Dr. Berg's Last Words," *MR* 4 (1852): 283-304.

"Evangelical Radicalism," *MR* 4 (1852): 509-512.

"The Anti-Creed Heresy," *MR* 4 (1852): 606-620.

"Closing Notice," *MR* 4 (1852): 620.

"Franklin and Marshall College," *MR* 5 (1853): 395ff.

"Man's True Destiny," *MR* 5 (1853): 492-520.

"The Dutch Crusade," *MR* 6 (1854): 67-117.

"Wilberforce on the Eucharist," *MR* 6 (1854): 161-87.

"Inaugural Exercises: 'The Christian Ministry'," *MR* 7 (1855): 68-
    115. Reprinted as *The Christian Ministry*. Chambersburg, PA:
    M. Kiefer & Co., 1855.

"The Church Year," *MR* 8 (1856): 456-78.

"Christian Hymnology," *MR* 8 (1856): 549-86.

"Hodge on the Ephesians," *MR* 9 (1857): 46-83; 192-245.

"Thoughts on the Church," *MR* 10 (1858): 169-98; 399-426.

The Life and Character of Frederick Augustus Rauch. Sermon
    delivered on occasion of the re-interment of Rauch's remains in
    Lancaster, PA on March 7, 1859. Chambersburg, PA: M.
    Kieffer and Co., 1859.

"The Idea of a Liturgy," *WM*, June 15, 1859.

"Natural and Supernatural," *MR* 11 (1859): 176-210.

"The Wonderful Nature of Man," *MR* 11 (1859): 317-37.

"Eulogy on the Rev. Dr. Rauch," *MR* 11 (1859): 442-66.

"The Old Doctrine of Christian Baptism," *MR* 12 (1860): 190-215.

Moral Philosophy. Lectures transcribed by J. Conrad Hauler, 1861. AMsS [photocopy]. ERHS.

"Jesus and the Resurrection," *MR* 13 (1861): 169-90.

The Liturgical Question. Philadelphia, 1862.

"Undying Life in Christ," in *Tercentenary Monument of the Heidelberg Catechism*. Chambersburg, PA: Publication Office of the German Reformed Church, 1863.

Christ, and Him Crucified. Sermon at the opening of the First General Synod of the German Reformed Church in America at Grace Church, Pittsburgh, November 18, 1863. Pittsburgh: J. McMillin, 1863.

"Introduction," *The Heidelberg Catechism in German, Latin and English*. Tercentenary Edition. (New York: 1863).

"The German Language," *EQR* XV (Oct. 1864): 515-34.

"The Nation's Second Birth," *RCM* 30 (July 26, 1865):1.

A Vindication of the Revised Liturgy, Historical and Theological. Philadelphia, 1867.

"Theology of the New Liturgy," *MR* 14 (1867): 23-66.

"Arianism," *MR* 14 (1867): 426-44.

"Athanasius," *MR* 14 (1867): 445-57.

"Commencement Address," *MR* 14 (1867): 485-508.

"Athanasian Creed," *MR* 14 (1867): 624-27.

"Our Relations to Germany," *MR* 14 (1867): 627-33.

Moral Philosophy. Lectures transcribed by E. K. Eshback, 1868.
    AMsS [photocopy]. ERHS.

"Presbyterian Union Convention," *MR* 15 (1868): 73-109.

"Dorner's History of Protestant Theology," *MR* 15 (1868): 260-90;
    325-66.

"Answer to Professor Dorner," *MR* 15 (1868): 532-646.

"The Origin and Structure of the Apostles' Creed," *MR* 16 (1869):
    148-56.

"The Unity of the Apostles' Creed," *MR* 16 (1869).

Lectures of Aesthetics. Transcribed by George D. Gurley, 1870-
    1871. AMsS [photocopy]. Archives of Franklin and Marshall
    College. Uncatalogued.

Lectures of Aesthetics. Transcribed by John H. Seckler, 1870.
    AMsS [photocopy]. ERHS.

"My Own Life: My Childhood and Early Youth," *WM*, March 2,
    1870; March 16, 1870; April 6, 27, 1870.

"Once for All," *MR* 17 (1870): 100-24.

"Objective Preaching," *RCM*, July 20, 1870.

"Education," *MR* 18 (1871): 1-19.

"The Revelation of God in Christ," *MR* 18 (1871): 325-42.

"Revelation and Redemption," *RCM*, February 15, 1871.

"The Creed in Switzerland," *RCM*, September 13, 1871.

"Krauth's Conservative Reformation," *RCM*, October 4, 11, 1871;
    December 6, 13, 20, 27, 1871; January 3, 10, 17, 24, 31,
    1872; February 21, 1872; March 13, 20, 1872.

"Christ and His Spirit," *MR* 19 (1872): 353-93.

"Nature and Grace," *MR* 19 (1872): 485-509.

"The Old Catholic Movement," *MR* 20 (1873): 240.

"Christianity and Humanity," *MR* 20 (1873): 469. Also in *History, Essays, Orations, and Other Documents of the Sixth General Conference of the Evangelical Alliance*, edited by Philip Schaff and S. Irenaeus Prime (New York: Harper and Brother Publishers, 1874): 302-308.

"Baccalaureate Sermon," *RCM*, July 9, 1873.

"Decline of Protestantism," *RCM*, August 13, 1973.

Ethics. Lectures transcribed by J. A. Huber, 1873-1874. AMsS [photocopy]. ERHS.

"Apollos: or the Way of God," *MR* 21 (1874): 5.

My Own Life. Lancaster, PA: Historical Society of the Evangelical and Reformed Church, reprinted 1874. Originally published in *WM*, March 2, 16, 1870; April 6, 27, 1870.

"Krauth's Berkeley," *RCM,* January 21, 1874.

"Life-Pictures of the Prodigal Son," *RCM*, June 17, 1874.

"The Spiritual World," *RQR* 23 (1876): 501-27.

"Wisdom's Voice," *RCM*, January 5, 1876.

"The Testimony of Jesus," *RQR* 24 (1877): 5-33.

"The Spirit of Prophecy," *RQR* 24 (1877): 181-212.

"Biblical Anthropology," *RQR* (1877): 330-65.

"Sacred Hermeneutics," *RQR* 25 (1878): 5-38.

"The Supreme Epiphany; God's Voice Out of the Cloud," *RQR* 25 (1878): 211-57.

"The Bread of Life, a Communion Sermon. *RQR* 26 (1879): 14-47.

"The Pope's Encylical," *RQR* 27 (1880): 5-50.

"Christ the Inspiration of His Own Word," *RQR* 29 (January 1882):
   5-46.

"The Inspiration of the Bible, or the Internal Sense of Holy
   Scripture," *RQR* 30 (January 1883): 5-39.

College Chapel Sermons. Ed. Henry M. Kieffer. Philadelphia: 1891.

Selected Bibliography of Secondary Sources

Ahlstrom, Sydney E. "The Romantic Religious Revolution and the Dilemmas of Religious History." *Church History* 46 (1977): 149-70.

Appel, Theodore. *The Life and Work of John Williamson Nevin.* Philadelphia: The Reformed Church Publishing House, 1889.

Barker, Verlyn Lloyd. "John W. Nevin: His Place in American Intellectual Thought." Ph.D. dissertation, St. Louis University, 1970.

Bassett, Joseph. "Eucharist/Liturgical Renewal or John Williamson Nevin on BEM #15." *NMR* 1 (Autumn 1985): 20-30.

Berg, Joseph F. "Mercersburg Theology." *The Protestant Quarterly Review* 3 (1846): 75-87.

Binkley, Luther J. *The Mercersburg Theology.* Manheim, PA: Sentinel Printing House, 1953.

Bomberger, J. H. A. "Dr. Nevin and His Antagonists." *MR* 5 (1953): 89-123.

Bratt, James D. "Nevin's Life and Work in Political-Cultural Context." *NMR* 2 (Autumn 1986): 17-29.

Brenner, Scott F. "Nevin and the Mercersburg Theology." *Theology Today* 12 (April 1955): 43-56.

Brownson, Orestes A. "The Mercerburg Theology." *Brownson's Quarterly Review* 7 (1850): 353-78.

_____. "The Mercersburg Hypothesis." *Brownson's Quarterly Review* 11 (1854): 253.

Carlough, Williams Leslie. "A Historical Comparison of the Theology of John Williamson Nevin and Contemporary Protestant Sacramentalism." Ph.D. dissertation, New York University, 1961.

Clemens, Deborah R. "Towards a Common Expression of the Apostolic Faith: Nevin's Recognition." *NMR* 1 (Autumn 1985): 40-46.

_____. "Principles of Antagonism or the Mystical Nuisance." *NMR* 9 (Spring 1991): 33-53.

_____. "Towards a Common Expression of the Apostolic Faith: Nevin's Recognition." *NMR* 1 (Autumn 1985): 40-46.

_____. "With All The Saints: Ecumenical Liturgics and Mercersburg Theology." *NMR* 10 (Autumn 1991): 23-38.

Clemer, Robert, "Historical Trascendentalism in Pennsylvania," *Journal of the History of Ideas* 30 (October 1969): 582-89.

Cochran, Alice C. "Sin and Salvation in American Thought." *Perkins Journal* 30 (Fall 1976): 1-14.

Conser, Walter H., Jr. *Church and Confession: Conservative Theologians in Germany, England, and America, 1815-1866.* Macon, GA: Mercer University Press, 1984.

Cordoue, John Thomas. "The Ecclesiology of John Williamson Nevin: A Catholic Appraisal." Ph.D. dissertation, The Catholic University of America, 1969.

Cox, Martin, Jr. "To Be the Church: Nevin's Critique of Sectarianism." *NMR* 3 (Spring 1987): 23-31.

DeBie, Linden. "German Idealism in Protestant Orthodoxy: The Mercersburg Movement, 1840-1860." Ph.D. dissertation, McGill University, 1987.

DiPuccio, William. "The Dynamic Realism of Mercersburg Theology: The Romantic Pursuit of The Ideal in The Acual." Ph.D. dissertation, Marquette University, 1994.

_____. "The Foundations of Christian Theology: A Structural Study of the Philosophy and Prolegomena of the Mercersburg Theology." M.A. thesis, Wheaton College, 1988.

Dorner, J. A. *The Liturgical Conflict in the Reformed Church in North America, with Special Reference to Fundamental Evangelical Doctrines.* Translated by J. H. A. Bomberger. Philadelphia: LOAG, 1868.

Ebert, Clarence William. "The Liturgical Controversy in the German Reformed Church." Ph.D. dissertation, Temple University, 1959.

Erb, William H., ed. *Dr. Nevin's Theology, Based on Manuscript Class Room Lectures*. Reading, PA: I. M. Beaver, 1913.

Faber, Williams F. "John Williamson Nevin." *The Andover Review* (July 1891): 11-30.

Fackre, Gabriel. "Mutual Conversation, Consolation, and Correction." *Dialog* 29 (Spring 1990): 88-91.

Gerhart, Emanuel. An address delivered at the memorial service for Dr. John W. Nevin. ERHS. Reprinted in *NMR* 15 (Spring 1994): 51-54.

_____. "John Williamson Nevin: His Godliness." *RQR* 34 (1887): 5-19.

_____. *Institutes of the Christian Religion*. New York: Funk & Wagnalls, Co., 1894.

Gerrish, B.A. *Tradition and the Modern World: Reformed Theology in the Nineteenth Century*. Chicago: The University of Chicago Press, 1978.

Gilpin, W. Clark. "The Doctrine of the Church in the Thought of Alexander Campbell and John W. Nevin." *Mid-Stream* 19 (October 1980): 417-27.

Good, James Isaac. *The History of the Reformed Church in the United States in the Nineteenth Century*. New York: Reformed Church in America Board of Publications, 1911.

Goodman, Russell B. *American Philosophy and the Romantic Tradition*. Cambridge: Cambridge University Press, 1990.

Hageman, Howard G. "Back to Mercersburg." *Reformed Journal* 35 (August 1985): 5-6.

_____. "The Lessons of Mercersburg." *Reformed Journal* 33 (September 1983): 4.

Hamstra, Sam, Jr. "The Americanization of the Church and its Pastoral Ministry." *NMR* 11 (Spring 1992): 3-19.

_____. "John Williamson Nevin: The Christian Ministry." Ph.D. dissertation, Marquette University, 1990.

Hatch, Nathan O. *The Democratization of American Christianity*. New Haven: Yale University Press, 1989.

Hein, David. "The Letters of John Williamson Nevin to William R. Whittingham." *Anglican Episcopal History* 60 (June 1991): 197-211.

Hewitt, Glenn A. *Regeneration and Morality: A Study of Charles Finney, Charles Hodge, John W. Nevin, and Horace Bushnell*. Brooklyn: Carlson Publishing, 1991.

Hodge, Charles. "Doctrine of the Reformed Church on the Lord's Supper," *The Biblical Repertory and Princeton Review* 20 (1848): 227-78.

Holifield, E. Brooks. "Mercersburg, Princeton, and the South: The Sacramental Controversy in the Nineteenth Century." *Currents in Theology and Mission* 3 (1976): 239-44.

Jones, Charles A., III. "Mercersburg: A Reformed Alternative for the 20th Century." *Scholarship, Sacraments, and Service*, edited by Daniel Clendenin and W. David Buschart (Lewiston: E. Mellen Press, 1990), 159-77.

Josselyn, Lynne. "The Comparative Eucharistic Views of John Wesley and John Nevin." *NMR* 4 (Autumn 1988): 18-35.

Layman, David Wayne. "Revelation in the Praxis of the Liturgical Community: A Jewish-Christian Dialogue, With Special Reference to the Work of John Williamson Nevin and Franz Rosenzweig." Ph.D. dissertation, Temple University, 1994.

_____. "The Inner Ground of Christian Theology: Church, Faith, and Sectarianism." *Journal of Ecumenical Studies* 27 (1990): 480-503.

_____. "Evangelical Catholicity and Baptist Ecumenicity: A response to 'Christian Identity in Ecumenical Perspective'." *Journal of Ecumenical Studies* 27 (1990): 561-80.

L[ewis], T[aylor]. "The Mercersburg School of Theology and Philosophy." *The Literary World* 7,14 April 1849.

Marty, Martin. "Living with Establishment and Disestablishment in Nineteenth-Century Anglo-America." *Journal of Church and State* 18 (Winter 1980): 61-77.

Maxwell, Jack M. *Worship and Reformed Theology: The Liturgical Lessons of Mercersburg.* Pittsburgh: The Pickwick Press, 1976.

Miller, Samuel. *A Treatise on Mercersburg Theology; or Mercersburg and Modern Theology Compared.* Philadelphia: S.R. Fisher, 1866.

Mitchell, Nathan D. "Church Eucharist and Liturgical Reform at Mercersburg: 1843-1857." Ph.D. dissertation, University of Notre Dame, 1978.

Mitman, F. Russell, Jr. "The Implications for Christian Unity in the Theology of John Williamson Nevin." *NMR* 9 (Spring 1991): 13-31.

Myer, John Charles. "Philip Schaff's Concept of Organic Historiography as Related to the Development of Doctrine: A Catholic Appraisal." Ph.D. dissertation, The Catholic University of America, 1968.

Neander, August. "Practical Exegesis." Translated by John Nevin. *MR* 3 (1851): 162.

Nichols, James Hastings. *Democracy and the Churches.* Philadelphia: Westminster Press, 1966.

_____. "John Williamson Nevin (1803-1886): Evangelical Catholicism." *Sons of the Prophets: Leaders in Protestantism from Princeton Seminary*, edited by Hugh T. Kerr (Princeton, NJ, 1963), 69-81.

_____. *The Mercersburg Theology.* New York: Oxford University Press, 1966.

_____. *Romanticism in American Theology: Nevin and Schaff at Mercersburg.* Chicago: The University of Chicago Press, 1961.

Order of Worship for the Reformed Church. Philadelphia, 1866.

Paine, R. Howard. "John Nevin: The Man." *NMR* 2 (Autumn 1986): 12-16.

Payne, John B. "John W. Nevin and the Mercersburg Theology," *Lutheran Forum* 26 (May 1992): 40-45.

_____. "Mercersburg and Ecumenical Theology: What's the Connection?" *NMR* 7 (Spring 1990): 3-13.

_____. "Nevin and the Sacrament of Baptism." *NMR* 2 (Autumn 1986): 30-45.

_____. "Schaff and Nevin, Colleagues at Mercersburg: The Church Question." *Church History* 61 (June 1992): 169-90.

Plummer, Kenneth Moses. "The Theology of John Williamson Nevin in the Mercersburg Period." Ph.D. dissertation, The University of Chicago, 1958.

Reily, William M. "John Williamson Nevin, D.D., LL.D." *Magazine of Christian Literature* (September 1890): 324-27.

_____. "Schleiermacher and the Theology of the Mercersburg Review." *MR* 18 (1871): 165-82.

Richards, George Warren. *History of the Theological Seminary of the Evangelical and Reformed Church at Lancaster, Pennsylvania.* Lancaster: Rudisill & Co., 1952.

_____. "The Mercersburg Theology Historically Considered." Papers of the American Society of Church History. Second Series. Volume 3, 1912.

_____. "The Mercersburg Theology: Its Purpose and Principles." *Church History* 20 (1951): 42-55.

Ryan, Francis Patrick. "John Williamson Nevin: The Concept of Church Authority." Ph.D. dissertation, Marquette University, 1968.

Schaff, Philip. *America: A Sketch of the Political, Social, and Religious Character of the United States of North America.* New York, 1855; reprint ed., edited by Perry Miller. Cambridge, MA: The Belknap Press of Harvard University Press, 1961.

_____. *Church and State in the United States or The American Idea of Religious Liberty and Its Practical Effects.* New York: Charles Scribner's Sons, 1888.

_____. *The Creeds of Christendom with a History and Critical Notes.* New York: Harper and Bros., 1877.

_____. *The Principle of Protestantism.* Bard Thompson and George H. Bricker, ed., Lancaster Series on the Mercersburg Theology. Philadelphia: United Church Press, 1964.

_____. *What is Church History? A Vindication of the Idea of Historical Development.* Philadelphia: J. B. Lippincott and Co., 1846.

Schneck, B.S. *Mercersburg Theology Inconsistent With Protestant and Reformed Doctrine.* Philadelphia: J. B. Lippincott and Co., 1874.

Schneider, Robert A. "Mercersburg and Old First." *NMR* 10 (Spring 1991): 39-50.

Sell, Alan P. F. "J. H. A. Bomberger (1817-1890) versus J. W. Nevin: A Centenary Reappraisal," *NMR* 8 (Autumn 1990): 3-24.

Shetler, John. "The Influence of Mercersburg on the United Church of Christ." *NMR* 3 (Spring 1987): 3-16.

_____. "Reformed Church Theological Tradition." *Theology and Identity*, edited by Daniel Johnson and Charles Hambrick Stowe (New York: Pilgrim Press, 1990), 17-23.

Shriver, George H. "Passages in Friendship: John W. Nevin to Charles Hodge, 1872." *Journal of Presbyterian History* 58 (Summer 1980): 116-22.

_____. *Philip Schaff: Christian Scholar and Ecumenical Prophet.* Macon, GA: Mercer University Press, 1987.

Shriver, George H., ed. *American Religious Heretics.* Nashville: Abingdon Press, 1966.

Swander, John I. *The Mercersburg Theology.* Philadelphia: Reformed Church Publication Board, 1909.

Thompson, Bard. "Catechism and the Mercersburg Theology." *Essays on the Heidelberg Catechism,* edited by Bard Thompson. Philadelphia: United Church Press, 1963.

Tredway, J. Thomas. "High Churchmen in a Hostile World." *The Immigration of Ideas*, edited by O. F. Ander, J. I. Dowie, and J. T. Tredway (Rock Island, IL: Augustana Historical Society, 1968), 29-41.

Trost, Frederick R. "The Place of Preaching in the Mercerburg Tradition." *NMR* 11 (Spring 1992): 52-62.

Trost, Theodore, Jr. "Apostolic Tradition and Ordination: A Mercersburg Tradition." *NMR* 11 (Spring 1992): 63-74.

Van Hoeven, James. "Mercersburg Underground in the Dutch Reformed Church." *NMR* 9 (Spring 1991): 2-12.

Weiler, John R. "Notes of Nevin's Family I," *NMR* 13 (Spring 1993): 39-45.

_____. "Notes on Nevin's Family II," *NMR* 15 (Spring 1994):43-49.

Wentz, Richard E. "The World of Mercersburg Theology." Introduction to *The Mystical Presence* by John W. Nevin. Hamden CT, 1963.

_____. "John Williamson Nevin as Public Theologian." *Journal of Presbyterian History* 69 (Winter 1991): 295-305.

_____. "John Williamson Nevin and American Nationalism." *Journal of the American Academy of Religion* 58 (Winter 1990): 617-32.

_____. "Theology Through the Looking Glass." *First Things* 10 (February 1991): 32-36.

Westermeyer, Paul. "German Reformed Hymnody in the United States." *The Hymn: A Journal of Congregational Song* 31 (April 1980): 89-94.

_____. "German Reformed Hymnody in the United States." *The Hymn: A Journal of Congregational Song* 31 (July 1980): 200-204.

Wolff, George D. "The Mercersburg Movement: An Attempt to Find Ground on Which Protestantism and Catholicity Might Unite." *The American Catholic Review* 3: 151-76.

Woolverton, John F. "John Williamson Nevin and the Episcopalians: The Debate on the 'Church Question', 1851-1874." *Historical Magazine* 49 (December 1980): 361-87.

Yoder, Don. "The Bench Versus the Catechism: Revivalism and Pennsylvania's Lutheran and Reformed Churches." *Pennsylvania Folklife* 10 (Fall 1959): 14-23.

Yrigoyen, Charles, Jr. "Emanuel V. Gerhart and the Mercersburg Theology." Ph.D. dissertation, Temple University, 1972.

_____. Yrigoyon, Charles, Jr. "Mercersburg's Quarrel with Methodism." *Methodist History* 22 (October 1983): 3-19.

_____. "John Williamson Nevin's *The Anxious Bench* and Evangelical Piety." *NMR* 1 (Autumn 1985): 3-19.

Yrigoyen, Charles, Jr.; and Bricker, George H., eds. *Reformed and Catholic: Selected Historical and Theological Writings of John Williamson Nevin*. Pittsburgh Original Texts and Translations Series #4. Pittsburgh, Pennsylvania: The Pickwick Press, 1978.

Index

About the Editors

ARIE J. GRIFFIOEN (B.A., Calvin College; M.A., University of Iowa; Ph.D., Marquette University) is Associate Professor of Religion and Theology at Calvin College in Grand Rapids, Michigan, specializing in American Historical Theology. He is the author of articles dealing with the thought of Orestes Brownson and Charles Porterfield Krauth.

SAM HAMSTRA, JR. (B.S., David Lipscomb College; M.A., Wheaton Graduate School; M.Div., McCormick Theological Seminary; Ph.D., Marquette University) is Vice President for Advancement at Trinity Christian College in Palos Heights, Illinois. An ordained minister in the Reformed Church in America, he served three congregations over a 15-year period. His dissertation is "John Williamson Nevin: The Christian Ministry."